Contributors:
Audry Bourne, M.S., M.A.
Ashley Lockman, M.A.
John Jensen, M.A.
Brenda Johns, M.A.
Don Kinsey, M.A.
Teresa Runge, M.A.
Sherry Simkins, M.A.
Mikki Stevens, M.S.
Tracy Struble, M.A.
Faith Valente, Ph.D.
Lewis Watkins
Lee Wallace, M.A.

Messages That Matter

Public Speaking for the Information Age

Author
Josh Misner, Ph.D.

North Idaho College
2019

hayden-mcneil
Macmillan Learning

Printed in the United States of America

10 9 8 7 6 5 4 3 2 1

ISBN 978-0-7380-9390-1

Macmillan Learning Curriculum Solutions
14903 Pilot Drive
Plymouth, MI 48170
www.macmillanlearning.com

Misner 9390-1 F19

Acknowledgements

The authors and contributors would like to thank the following individuals, whose insightful and thorough peer review proved invaluable and immensely helpful in the creation of this textbook:

Scott Behson, Ph.D.
Professor of Management, Fairleigh-Dickinson University

Craig Fischer, M.A.
Adjunct Instructor, Whitworth University

Lisa Power, Ph.D.
Associate Professor of Marketing, Saint Martin's University

S. Mitchell Walker, Ph.D.
Assistant Professor of Leadership, National University

Levy Zamora, M.A.
Communication Instructor, De Anza College

Table of Contents

Part II: Speaking to Persuade . . . 139

Chapter 1

What Is Communication?

"The problem with communication is the illusion that it has been accomplished."
—George Bernard Shaw, Irish author and playwright

When reading George Bernard Shaw's words above, most of us can easily identify with his sentiment. Undoubtedly, we have all experienced the pains and frustration inherent with instances of miscommunication before, which is likely the reason we so easily recognize the humor inherent in his statement. In fact, it may be easier for us to identify and define elements of *mis*communication than it is for us to identify and define this thing called communication. Whether we used the wrong word for the wrong audience, our tone failed to match our intentions, or we left out pertinent information in our conversation, we may find that it is often easier to *mis*communicate than it is to simply get our message across to our intended audience correctly and efficiently the first time.

Defining Communication

So, what is this thing we call communication? In explaining a potentially complex term, scholars often begin by examining the root or origin of the term, which, in this case, is the Latin word *communicare*, meaning "to share, divide out; communicate, impart, inform; join, unite, participate in" (Harper, 2015). Roots like this tell us more about the term's original intention, giving us clues as to the subtle nuances of the term, even beyond what most dictionaries or encyclopedias offer with their detailed definitions and explanations. In this case, we find something interesting, in that the original intent of the term was not to describe a novice who is learning about public speaking, but that to communicate refers to something much bigger and broader. To communicate is to share information via a process of joining others together. Communication, in this sense, is the means by which we make sense of our life experiences and it is the tool by which we relate those experiences with one another.

Why Study Communication?

The study of communication has vast benefits in both personal and professional contexts. For example, a study performed by the American Association of Colleges and Universities, released on January 20, 2015, surveyed 400 employers to determine what skills they valued most in recent college graduates, and their summary was as follows:

> The learning outcomes [employers] rate as most important includes written and oral communication skills, teamwork skills, ethical decision-making, critical thinking, and the ability to apply knowledge in real-world settings.

Regardless of industry or occupation, employers throughout the world still primarily value the ability to communicate effectively, which goes much further beyond public speaking. The ability to communicate includes interpersonal, small group, and mass communication, but also includes the ability to communicate interculturally (communication between people of vastly differing backgrounds, nationalities, ethnicities, etc.), nonverbally (skilled in reading body language, understanding environmental effects on communication, etc.), and the ability to wield persuasion and/or argumentation, which will be discussed at length later in this book.

Think about it: ten applicants apply for the same job, and all ten have similarly qualified backgrounds, training, and education, but one of them also provides evidence of proficiency in communication through a certificate program or award. Who among those candidates is more likely to be hired? According to surveys such as the one performed by the American Association of Colleges and Universities, the one with the background in communication is considerably more likely to land the job. Consider this as a potential employer, as the one doing the hiring. Which employee would you rather hire as an organizational leader: one who can effectively communicate with you as well as other employees, or one who needs constant coaching, fails to listen, and cannot get along well with others?

We also study communication because we recognize that revolutions in communication technology have changed the world. To date, there have been four major revolutions in the way humans communicate, all four of which have been predicated on a new form of communication technology: writing, the printing press, the Industrial Revolution, and the Information Age.

Writing

We don't often think of writing as a form of technology, but it is. Granted, it is the second-oldest form of communication technology, next to formal language, and we often take it for granted because we tend to learn it from an early age, but nonetheless, writing is a form of technology. Depending on where you look in the world, writing is thought to have originated between 3200 B.C.E. (Middle East), 1200 B.C.E. (Asia), and 600 B.C.E. (North America). These arbitrary (meaning, the symbols or letters used do not look like what they are being used to represent) systems of writing evolved from iconic, or pictorial depictions, of historical events recorded, such as the famed cave paintings of Lascaux, France, which are an estimated 17,300 years old.

Writing, as it exists today (perhaps you are taking notes with a pen or pencil on a piece of notebook paper as you read this), has not always looked this way. Paper was first invented in ancient China around 100 B.C.E., but in Western civilization (Europe and the near East), paper didn't come along until around the 10th century. This means that, for about 4,200 years, much of the Western world was taking notes and writing things down on media other than the paper we know and love to purchase during fall back-to-school sales today! Taking this a step further, we ask the question, what did they write on, if not paper? For four millennia, writing took place on media such as slate, leather, bark, and clay. Think of that the next time you are taking notes in class!

Writing, as a form of technology, was not always viewed in a positive light. Socrates (d. 399 B.C.E.), often credited as the founder of Western philosophy, had this to say about writing in his famous dialogue, *The Phaedrus*:

> ...this discovery of yours [writing] will create forgetfulness in the learners' souls, because they will not use their memories; they will trust to the external written characters and not remember of themselves. The specific which you have discovered is an aid not to memory, but to reminiscence, and you give your disciples not truth, but only the semblance of truth; they will be hearers of many things and will have learned nothing; they will appear to be omniscient and will generally know nothing; they will be tiresome company, having the show of wisdom without the reality.

In other words, Socrates' biggest complaint about the latest fad of writing was that it could potentially create a society of idiots who relied so heavily on technology that they could no longer function for themselves. Sound familiar? Brace yourself, because we are going to hear this argument against newer communication technology come up again and again.

The pros of writing, however, far outweighed any negative tradeoffs, much to Socrates' dismay, and in the end, we still use it to this day. Suddenly, we could store information more permanently without having to rely on someone with a great memory, we could transmit messages over greater distances, and we could record and analyze communications (politicians could no longer count on getting away with changing their stories so rapidly). With every rapid change in communication, there are winners and losers, benefits and drawbacks, and change will become permanent if the benefits outweigh what we need to give up to adopt the new technology. Watch for this pattern as we discuss the other three revolutions.

The Printing Press

Fast forward to the 15th century (more than 4,000 years later) to the next revolution in communication. During those millennia, improvements were made to writing, to language, and to the media societies used to write, but none of these changes amounted to a revolution, that is until Johannes Gutenberg came along. Gutenberg was interested in mass-producing writing, because at the time, the only way "commoners" (non-royals) could get their hands on a Bible was to purchase them from monasteries at an astronomical price. This was because these Bibles were produced by monks skilled in the art of calligraphy and often took months, if not years, to produce, depending on how ornate the copy was. As a result, very few people had access to religious texts, so they had to rely on priests to read to them when they attended religious services. Such imbalanced access to the governing religious text of the day presented the possibility for those in power to take advantage of the limited flow of information, and as a result, embellish or manipulate that information to suit their needs.

Gutenberg is credited with the invention of moveable type in Europe, which allowed him to print off about 180 copies of the Bible, but it is important to note that paper was still not the most commonly used medium of the time. For 135 copies, he used paper, but for the remaining 45, he used *vellum*, which is parchment made from calfskin. It took roughly 170 calfskins to produce just one Gutenberg Bible, which means that about

7,600 calves were slaughtered to produce the vellum first-edition Bibles! Think about that the next time you drop a dime on a college-ruled notebook.

Gutenberg's invention suddenly made the religious text of Europe available to considerably wider audiences, and shortly thereafter, Martin Luther published his 95 Theses to kick off the Protestant Reformation, which split the Christian church into fragments and began religious infighting that drastically changed Western civilization over the next three centuries.

Today, we still have artists around who are skilled in calligraphy, yet they do not hold a monopoly in the book-publishing world, showing us that again, there are winners and losers in each revolution.

Industrial/Electrochemical Revolution

While the printing press enjoyed its heyday with respect to transformation, another revolution was brewing on the side. By the late 1700s (a mere 200 years after the last revolution), the Industrial Revolution began changing the way humans communicate worldwide in a much more dramatic fashion. Take a look at the following table of communication inventions from this time period:

Invention	Date	Transformational Effect
Camera	1839	No longer had to sit for a painting to get a portrait; Photos were instant
Telegraph	1844	No longer had to wait for postal service to deliver messages; Communication took place in real time (though had to be able to translate Morse code)
Typewriter	1875	Printing press that formerly took up an entire room now fit on a table; Anyone could publish professional quality printing at home
Telephone	1876	No longer had to know Morse code; Could communicate using voice in real time
Phonograph	1877	Could record and store sound for the first time; Musicians began recording and selling music; No longer had to go to concerts to hear music; File sharing debate commences
Motion Picture	1891	Improvement upon the camera; Moving pictures could be recorded and played back again
Radio	1895	Mass communication transformed; Politicians could communicate using a one-way medium with their constituents, thus nearly eliminating the need for long travel and delivering speeches; Music transmitted to wider audiences
Television	1923	Combination of radio and motion pictures; Further development of one-way mass communication
Computer	1946	Early computers took up the size of a warehouse and cost millions of dollars to produce; Had the computing power of a modern-day basic wristwatch

Invention	Date	Transformational Effect
Satellite Comm.	1962	First development of wireless communication between continents; No longer needed expensive cables routed on the ocean floors
Transistor	1970	What used to require the space of a warehouse to build a computer now fit on a silicon chip the size of a postage stamp; Considered among the most important developments of the 20th century
Home Computer (Apple)	1976	Steve Jobs and Co. produce the first personal computer in a garage in California from plywood and spare parts
Home Computer (Microsoft)	1981	Bill Gates and Co. produce their version of the personal computer with a different operating system, and the Mac vs. PC debate is born
Cellular Phone	1983	Invented in 1973, the first commercially available cell phone hit the market 10 years later; Emitted enough radiation to give constant users tumors on the side of their head they used the phone most; Cost was around $3,000 for a phone the size and weight of a brick
Internet	1991	Invented in the early 1970s as DARPANet (Defense Advanced Research Projects Association), a defense computer linking system; The modern-day internet was handed over to the public in 1991; At the time, a personal computer costing around $3,000 had less computing power than the most basic pocket-sized video gaming system

As we can see, moving through the history of these first three revolutions, the amount of time between each major communication breakthrough reduces exponentially, from 4,600 years between the first two, to less than 400 years between the next two, and finally, a mere decade or so between the third revolution and the most current one. Of course, the time reduces so drastically because, with each new form of communication, the sharing and spread of information increases. With increased information comes increased innovation.

The Information Age

While the internet was originally created as a Defense Department project in the mid-1970s, the release of the internet to the general public in 1991 kicked off our most recent revolution, which has been called by some "The Information Age." It is characterized by the convergence of multiple forms of technology, but is most evident in the widespread availability of information, as well as the ease with which information is created and shared. It has often been said that seeking information via the internet is like trying to take a drink from a fire hose, and for good reason!

While perusing online media in an attempt to make sense out of the scope of information currently being created, the term *zettabyte* became a new part of our collective vocabulary, and this is a 1 followed by 21 zeroes (Blair, 2010)! A zettabyte was the amount of information projected for all of humanity to create during the year 2010. Compare this to the amount of information created by the culmination of humanity previously, calculated by an IBM supercomputer to be five *exabytes* (Rieland, 2012), which is a paltry 1/1000th of a zettabyte. While a statistical debate currently rages as to the accuracy of these numbers, a core truth remains evident. Thanks in part to the vast array and ever-growing repertoire of tools available for creating and sharing information, we, as a species, have entered the Information Age, which may be viewed by future societies as a turning point for the human race. With radical change, however, comes a natural human tendency toward anxiety. Communication technology continues to advance further with each passing year, presenting ever-approaching potential for rapid or radical change to occur, even for those who are born into the Information Age and know no other reality. When this natural fear of radical change is combined with feeling overwhelmed by the ever-present onslaught of information—some useful, but mostly not—one begins to see that the Information Age is not without its hazards. It might be tempting to subscribe to the notion that the proverbial sky is falling, so to speak, had such a scenario not been without historical precedent, as we have seen in our glance at the history of communication technology.

Wurman (1989) famously proposed that, "A weekday edition of *The New York Times* contains more information than the average person was likely to come across in a lifetime in seventeenth-century England" (p. 32). Furthermore, he suggested that, for one to be a successful member of modern society, one must "assimilate a body of knowledge that is expanding by the minute" (p. 32). Taking into account that this was written two full years before the release of the internet to the general public, this proposition becomes more salient now than ever.

As information becomes easier to create and share with others through an increasingly networked society, the dissemination characteristics of information have altered the behaviors of certain types of organizations. Industries such as journalism, book publishing, filmmaking, and music producing were once the prerogative of the well-networked or well-funded. In the past, to get a book published, an author had to write the tome, polish it to perfection, and spend months, if not years, querying agents and publishers in hopes that someone would find it worthy of elevation to the status of "published." Similarly, with music producing, artists would often play free shows with the hopes of being "discovered" by talent agents who may occasionally descend from their ivory towers to offer recording contracts. The Information Age, however, has turned these industries inside out and upside down. Anyone with a desire, a computer, and an internet connection can publish a book or an article, and produce and distribute music or film. As a result, the information marketplace has become flooded to the point of supersaturation with information in various media. New organizations, such as Netflix or Pandora, are arising to fill the role of information curators—organizations whose sole purpose is to sift through the tide of new production, extract the best of the moment, and present it for all to consume. The deluge of emerging information often sacrifices quality for timeliness in an attempt to be first, rather than best, evident in the changing nature of journalism and the 24-hour news cycle. As our technological infrastructure becomes more efficient at the creation and distribution of new information, this trend will likely continue.

Because of this growing trend, the Information Age has transformed the information marketplace from one that purports to sell media tailored to consumers' needs into one that simply competes for attention. The information marketplace has not made getting our drink from the fire hose easier; it has simply presented more fire hoses from which to choose. As a result, the information marketplace is now being run as an *attention economy* (Davenport & Beck, 2001). Herbert Simon (1971), writing from the early precursor years to the Information Age, stated the following:

> ...in an information-rich world, the wealth of information means a dearth of something else: a scarcity of whatever it is that information consumes. What information consumes is rather obvious: it consumes the attention of its recipients. Hence a wealth of information creates a poverty of attention and a need to allocate that attention efficiently among the overabundance of information sources that might consume it. (pp. 40–41)

As attention spans are taxed, becoming more fragile with each passing day, organizations operating within an attention economy will need to compete more ruthlessly for the attention of potential consumers, a complication of which is felt by us, the consumers, via additional unique anxieties as attention spans are pulled in several directions simultaneously.

The Future of Communication

Now, our question, as students and scholars of communication, is this: What will the future hold for communication studies, and what will the next big revolution be? That is a question yet to be answered, though there are many theories. Perhaps the next leap forward will be in the communication of emotion, as our limbic brain (the part of the brain responsible for the way we *feel*) has no capacity for language. Will future technology allow us to sense and translate emotions from human to human, allowing us to empathize with one another more efficiently? Perhaps the next big advance will be along the lines of telepathy, allowing us to transmit thought without the need for language. Today, however, verbal communication, whether vocally through the act of speaking or in writing, remains our primary means of sharing information, requiring us to seek mastery of this skill.

Regardless of what the future may hold, we are now living in an exciting time of flux and dynamic change. There are vast oceans of information at our fingertips, bringing with them myriad possibilities, but also potential for disaster. To navigate the seas of information overload, we must take a step back and observe such changes from a more mindful, objective perspective, rather than allowing ourselves to be caught up like rats in a psychology experiment (see B. F. Skinner), mindlessly clicking away on links generated by an algorithm that knows our deepest secrets. As with the alphabet, the printing press, and the Industrial Revolution, we will eventually grow accustomed to this change in due process, but only if we chart a careful, rational course. There are destined to be winners and losers emerging from the dust as it settles, so which side will you be on? This is the impetus for our study of the complexities of human communication.

Basic Communication Theory

This new understanding of the history and basic idea of communication provides us with a great jumping-off point from which to examine the actual process of communication more clearly. However, there may be nearly as many theories of communication as there are scholars studying in the field, as every communication expert likely has her or his individual opinion on exactly how the process works.

Activity

Go to www.google.com/images, type "communication model" into the search field, and then hit enter. Scroll through a few pages' worth of images and take note of the staggering number of diverse visual depictions of communication. Why are there so many ways of explaining the same "basic" concept?

Communication, diluted to its most basic form, includes four major components: a **message** being transmitted from a **sender** to a **receiver**, via some form of **medium**. It's as simple as that, right? Sadly, if communication was truly that simple, then we could close this book now and be done with it, but from experience, we know all too well that this is only the beginning.

The communication process becomes more complex starting with the **message**, as it must first be formed, which involves translating our brain's electrical signals into some form of language, which could be verbal, nonverbal, or a combination of both. This translation process often involves trying to transform emotional impulses into language, which can be an extraordinarily difficult process to achieve successfully. Our emotions reside in our limbic brain, which is the oldest portion of our central nervous system and the one most like our animal cousins in nature (i.e., our "lizard brain"). This portion of our brain has zero capacity for language, which explains why it can be so difficult for us to verbalize our emotions at times. This could explain why humans have been trying to define concepts such as "love" for millennia, and still, nobody has gotten it 100% right! Language processing takes place in our neocortex, which is the more evolved, developed portion of our brain that is responsible for rational thought, and that which separates us from the rest of the animal kingdom. Transferring an emotional impulse from our non-language limbic brain over to our language-processing neocortex, and then effectively and accurately translating that impulse into a message that can easily be understood, presents a gargantuan challenge in many cases!

Once the message has been formulated, it has to travel from sender to receiver, and in that journey, we see a plethora of all-new challenges, called **interference**, which comes in two forms: internal and external.

- **Internal interference** (also called *semantic interference*) arises from within in the form of mental distractions. For example, if I got into an argument with my spouse before arriving to teach a class, I might be thinking of great comebacks to say to her later on, or I might also be distracted by perhaps thinking of an appropriate apology. Another example could be a student who has a math exam later in the day and is consumed by worry over how difficult the test may be. The speaker might even generate this type of interference within listeners by using offensive, inappropriate, or confusing language that detracts from the message.
- **External interference** comes from outside and arrives via any of our five senses. A visual distraction might be a shirt with distracting text or a person with an unusual physical stance while speaking. An auditory distraction might be the noise coming from an air conditioner or horns honking outside the room. A tactile distraction might be the itchy tag on a brand-new shirt or the pain on the back of your heel

while breaking in new shoes. Taste can even be a distraction, such as when drinking orange juice too soon after brushing your teeth, and smell can be equally distracting if someone in the room decides to bring their fast-food lunch to class and not offer to share with everyone else!

The **channel** (or medium) through which these messages travel presents a wide variety of challenges as well. In the case of this textbook, the channel is writing. In a live speech, the channel is the human voice, and while watching a pre-recorded speech on YouTube, the channel is the internet. Each channel brings a unique set of challenges. For example:

- **Voice:** Speakers must project their voices loud enough to be heard evenly throughout the room; Speakers must speak a common language for the audience to understand; Speakers must speak slowly enough for the audience to keep up; Speakers must have a variety of inflection suitable enough to maintain the audience's attention; etc.
- **Internet:** Connection speed must be suitable enough to avoid lag or lengthy downloads; Data must be compatible with all operating systems and browsers; People tend to be more comfortable expressing themselves online, often resulting in more candid discussions that may often become heated; etc.
- **Writing:** Message must be in a language the reader can understand; Font face, type, and size must be legible and not strain the eyes; Colors must have enough contrast to be easily legible; Language used must match the level of the reader; etc.

Once the message arrives at the receiver, it must then be decoded in much the same way the original message was encoded by the sender. As before, the receiver must be able to understand the language that the sender used to encode the message (both verbally and nonverbally), but additionally, the receiver will run the message through various "filters." These filters might include preconceived notions, such as when a speaker wearing a UW Huskies shirt addresses a group of students at Washington State University. That speaker could proverbially be "preaching to the choir" and saying everything the group agrees with, but due to the visual distraction, their preconceived notions of what that speaker stands for may prove too difficult to overcome.

Cultural norms also provide us with filters. In many countries in the Middle East, a speaker who fails to stand close enough to be able to smell the other person's breath may be viewed as untrustworthy, while in the U.S. such a breach of personal space would create a high level of anxiety. That anxiety creates an internal distraction that acts as an almost impenetrable filter.

Lastly, a filter most of us use daily comes by way of a differential between verbal and nonverbal communication. Nonverbal communication is powerful and difficult, if not impossible, to ignore. We begin learning nonverbal communication before we are even born, via the pounding rhythm of our mothers' heartbeats, the warm touch of the womb, and external sounds transmitted through the amniotic fluid. Conservative estimates state that we send and receive over 80% of our messages nonverbally, which means that, if our verbal messages contradict our nonverbal behaviors, our audience will accept the nonverbal message as the more accurate one. Going back to our earlier example of getting into a heated argument with my spouse, if I show up at home later on and sheepishly peek in through the opening door, saying, "Hi honey, how was your day?" and she replies in an angry tone with her arms crossed, "Fine!" Are things fine? No, not a chance. I'm in trouble. Nonverbal communication almost always overrides verbal communication, should the two ever disagree with one another from the same speaker.

Once the message has penetrated through these filters, the receiver (hopefully) comprehends the message, and if communication has been successful, the receiver understands it as the sender originally intended. At that point, the receiver may opt to give the sender **feedback**. Feedback may be nonverbal, such as head nods, smiles, facial expressions conveying interest, or even "paralanguage" (sounds we make that have meaning but are not necessarily words), like "Hmm" or "Uh-huh." Feedback may also be verbal, such as asking follow-up questions or providing clarifying information to add on to the speaker's message.

Activity

Find a partner and sit down facing each other. For two minutes one of you will be the speaker. The speaker may talk about absolutely anything, but for this experiment to work, you *must* speak continuously. The other person who is not speaking must sit silently and give the speaker ***no*** feedback whatsoever. The listener must look the speaker in the eyes, but may not smile, nod, speak, or provide any nonverbal feedback. After two minutes have passed, switch roles. Do not speak during the switch; simply switch quickly such that the speaker becomes the listener and vice versa. Again, interact this way for two minutes, with the speaker speaking continuously and the receiver giving no nonverbal feedback with the one exception of steady eye contact. After you have completed the experiment, consider the following questions:

- What did you feel during this experiment?
- What were you thinking?
- Was it easy or hard? Why?
- Which was more difficult, being the listener or the speaker and why?
- What role does nonverbal feedback play in communication?

The last aspect of the communication model for us to examine is **context**, or the situation in which communication takes place. A conversation held via Skype between longtime friends, for example, is going to follow a completely different set of "rules" than a presentation before a board meeting, where you might be trying to sell a product proposal. Or, the same speech delivered in front of a live audience might read very differently when produced as a transcript for reading. To see this effect firsthand, try looking up the famous "I Have a Dream" speech by Martin Luther King, Jr., and instead of watching or listening to it, read it. While still remarkably beautiful, passionate, and well versed, the written version of one of the most famous speeches in history does not seem to have the same impact as hearing Dr. King speak! This is a phenomenon that communication theorist and researcher Marshall McLuhan referred to by saying, "The medium is the message," meaning that contextual cues will heavily influence how a message is perceived. Context must be taken into account with communication, from the composition stage all the way to delivery of that message.

Now that we know the basics of the communication cycle, you might be left with the impression that this cycle is a perfectly linear process, moving from message sent to message received, but we all know deep down inside that communication rarely (if ever) happens like this. Communication is messy. Remember those diagrams and models from the activity of looking up models via Google Images? The best models are those that look more like a plate of spaghetti than an ordered process because human dynamics are remarkably unpredictable.

Advanced Communication Theory

Now that we are primed to discuss the intricacies of communication, let's look at some of the more detailed theories. George Herbert Mead, a philosopher and sociologist from the early 20th century, developed a communication theory known as Symbolic Interaction. This theory states that meanings for things and experiences are derived from our social interaction and modified through interpretation, but furthermore, that we act toward those things and experiences based on the meanings we create.

Let's use an example to look at this further. Let's pretend for a moment that you have never seen a table before in your entire life, but you walk into your communication classroom, and it is filled with several large objects with broad, flat surfaces, and they are suspended a few feet above the floor by stick-looking things at each corner. To make sense out of these completely new objects, the first thing you will do is name the objects, and the name you choose to bookmark these objects in your mind will likely be based upon something similar that you have experienced before, so you come up with "four-legged monoshelf." Now that you have a name for it, you will seek out validation for your hypothesis by trying to share your newfound meaning with others, so you approach a classmate, who has just entered the room, and you suggest your newly minted moniker to your classmate, while simultaneously asking if that person has ever seen such an object before. As you talk about the object, the other person might look at you strangely and say, "It's a table," which starts up a conversation about what it is and its purpose. Through your mutual dialogue, you both derive meaning for the object, which has solidified your *sensemaking* of the new experience. Every time you see a "four-legged monoshelf" (or table) from that point forward, you will act toward that object partially or wholly based upon the interaction that helped you to understand it.

Types of Communication

Mead's theory is but one of practically hundreds of communication theories that may be studied. While Mead's theory deals more with the general concept of human interaction, other theories branch off into more specific areas within communication studies, so it becomes helpful for us to review various types of communication.

Intrapersonal Communication

Earlier, we explored the basics of the communication model (message, sender, receiver, channel or medium), but what if the sender and receiver are the same person? At its most absolute basic, we find **intrapersonal communication**, or communication within ourselves. Now, before you start thinking about whether or not it might be "crazy" to talk to yourself, relax—we all do it, and we call it thought, or communication where we are simultaneously sender and receiver. Intrapersonal communication is a communicator's internal use of language, but we might find that we use it in any or all of the following situations:

- Reading out loud to ourselves
- Internal monologues
- Formulating our thoughts as we write, whether by hand or typing (doodling and drawing also fall into this category)
- Making gestures while thinking (some of us do this while practicing speeches in our heads)
- Sensemaking, as in the previous Mead example, before the classmate walked in
- Interpreting others' nonverbal communication symbols
- Communication between parts of our bodies (i.e., "My legs are telling me that I should not go to the gym today.")

Healthy intrapersonal communication provides the foundation for all other forms of communication, for it is within intrapersonal interaction that our messages we send outward, to others, are formed. Dysfunctional (or nonexistent) intrapersonal communication behaviors often result in sending messages without thinking about them first, only to end up regretting having done so.

Intrapersonal communication precedes external communication in forms such as the conscious thought process of composing messages before delivering them and deliberate decisions we might make regarding how we send the message, such as accompanying nonverbal tone, inflection, or facial expressions. These choices affecting how messages are composed and delivered form our foundation for human interaction. Whether verbal or nonverbal in nature, external communication does not appear out of nowhere. Such messages originate from an internal cognitive process, which may be deliberately thought-out or unintentionally reactive, but regardless, intrapersonal communication requires careful monitoring and control to ensure effective interpersonal communication.

Interpersonal Communication

As we examine communication further and begin adding other people to the conversation, intrapersonal communication transforms into **interpersonal communication**. McCornack (2010) defined interpersonal communication as "a dynamic form of communication between two (or more) people in which the messages exchanged significantly influence their thoughts, emotions, behaviors, and relationships" (p. 13). While this definition provides a basic overview of interpersonal communication, it distinguishes it from intrapersonal communication by externalizing the receiver of the message as well as the channel or medium for transmission, all while creating an interaction in which meaning is mutually created through sharing. It is through this form of communication that meaning is constructed, as we saw earlier, in Mead's theory of Symbolic Interaction.

Small Group Communication

If more than two people are communicating simultaneously, we refer to this form of communication as **small group communication**. Small groups are becoming not only more commonplace within working environments, but are also becoming more integral to organizational success. Small group sizes generally range from three to 20 persons, and in most cases, are formed to accomplish a specific purpose, whether for short-term (ad hoc committees) or for longer-term use. Sometimes, a group might be informal, such as a group of friends that typically spend time together, or the group might have a more formal charge, such as a workgroup within a professional organization, but regardless, a small group consists of members seeking to use communication to achieve a commonly held goal.

Public Communication

As the audience for a speaker's message grows, the form of communication changes from being a small group discussion format, where each member has the opportunity to contribute, to more of a public speaking scenario, where the group becomes an audience focused on the speaker's sole message. What makes this form of communication unique is that the feedback loop is partially and temporarily cut off, causing information to flow one way, from speaker to receiver, with the speaker receiving only nonverbal feedback as the audience listens.

Mass Communication

Public communication transitions to mass communication as the audience continues to grow and the feedback loop is almost completely eliminated. Mass communication most often relies on technological mediation, meaning that, other than speeches to large crowds in arenas, mass communication is accomplished through radio, television, web, or telecommunication means. In most instances, the receiver has no direct access to the sender, allowing the sender complete control over the message. However, emerging media have challenged mass communication by providing more direct access from consumers of mass media (i.e., comment sections and discussion boards).

Types of Public Speaking

Certain types of communication will continue to be in high demand, one of those being the art of public speaking. Public speaking is more of a general term, applied to situations in which a message is communicated to a wider (most often, live) audience. More specifically, public speaking can be examined in even more specific forms, however: impromptu, manuscript, memorized, and extemporaneous.

Impromptu speaking is unplanned, unrehearsed, and unscripted. Sometimes, an impromptu speech might be a situation in which the speaker has no time to prepare and has to speak in a completely improvised manner, but in other situations, impromptu speaking may also involve characteristically short preparation times. Such times may only be a matter of a few minutes to consider what the speaker is going to say before taking the stage. Impromptu speeches are most often given without notes, and successful impromptu speakers are spontaneous, engaging, confident, and have a knack for thinking quickly, on a moment's notice. Impromptu speakers are faced with the challenge of staying on topic, but also with keeping the "flow" of their conversational style going to keep the audience's attention. Regardless of the varying needs of one's career or industry, impromptu speaking opportunities arise frequently, such as when one is called upon to explain a project, product, or process to members of management or constituent groups. Being able to respond in a timely manner and with control of the information goes a long way with establishing credibility.

Manuscript speaking is one of the most formal speaking styles, in that it uses an entirely pre-written script from which the speaker reads. Manuscript speeches can be found in large, formal settings, such as commencement ceremonies or political affairs, and may utilize teleprompters to allow the speaker to maintain eye contact with the audience, rather than being limited to reading off of a piece of paper. Herein lies the drawback of this type of speech. Instead of interacting with the audience, keeping the speech fresh and engaging, manuscript speeches can feel canned or inauthentic to the audience.

Memorized speeches are similar to the manuscript speech, in that they are entirely pre-written, but unlike the manuscript speech, which is entirely read to the audience, a memorized speech is exactly what its name implies. The speaker memorizes the speech as though it was lines from a Shakespeare play and recites them, verbatim, to the audience. Memorization has its pitfalls, however, as the speaker may forget a "line," and subsequently be forced to either stumble and stutter, or rely on improvisation techniques to fill in the gaps in memory.

Extemporaneous speaking differs from impromptu in that it allows for much more preparation and structure. Extemporaneous speaking utilizes outlines as a foundation for a persuasive or informational speech, where the outline provides a roadmap for the speaker to follow, but not a complete script of the speech. In addition, extemporaneous speeches are those in which research is utilized with a structure similar to the classic five-paragraph essay, with an introduction, main points, and a conclusion that reinforces a thesis or central idea. Speaking extemporaneously ultimately means speaking fluidly, yet with extensive preparation. For the vast majority of speeches, extemporaneous speaking is preferred, since it provides the best of all worlds: well-prepared information and structure, but with enough flexibility to remain conversational and fluid.

The Secret to Success in Public Speaking

In any public speaking scenario, there exists a triad of priority that must be remembered and revered, and it is in this triad that you will find the secret to public speaking success. At the top of this priority list, you will find the message, followed by the audience in second place, with yourself, as the speaker, taking last place.

Priority #1: The Message. In any given speech, you will have an impetus, or driving force, which is causing you to face your fears, stand in front of an audience, whether it be 10 people or 10,000 people, and speak. The core of that driving force is your *message*. All too often, speakers forget to prioritize their original central idea or core message, and as a result, allow their message to be distorted by either delusions of being an entertainer (i.e., seeking laughs as a priority instead of delivering information), or fear of how the message will be received, resulting in the message being watered down. Don't forget the reason you stood up to speak in the first place. Before you speak, remind yourself that you have one job to do: deliver your message. However, don't forget about the other two components rounding out this triad.

Priority #2: The Audience. Arguably, the audience could theoretically be on par with the message, as they are nearly equally important in order of priority, for without the audience, you might as well be speaking to yourself in the mirror. While the core of your message ultimately comes first, how you will present that message depends upon your audience. Your message must be wrapped up and delivered to your audience in such a way as to be memorably understood as you originally intended. How your audience members receive the core of your message is highly dependent upon how they filter your message through their lens of understanding, so you must get to know what to expect with your audience. What drives them? What are their feelings, attitudes, opinions, values, and beliefs? How much or little do they know about your topic? These questions and more are the types of questions an effective speaker considers before embarking on the composition of a speech, and they will be addressed later in the book, in Chapter 4.

Priority #3: The Speaker. Last in our list of public speaking priorities, you will find the person or people delivering such messages. Why place the speaker last in this order of importance? Frequently, most novice speakers spend more time and effort thinking about their self-image and how audiences will perceive them than they do on considering the strength of their message and/or how the audience is receiving that message. As a result, novice speakers begin noticing nervous symptoms (shaking hands, sweating profusely, dry mouth, etc.) and dwelling on them, fearful that the audience can see such symptoms, magnifying the natural fear of public speaking exponentially. By placing the speaker last in our order of priority, we return our focus to the message and how well the audience memorably understands that message as you originally intended. Instead of wasting mental energy on thinking about how we look or sound, we redirect our focus where it is needed, and that is where communication happens.

Chapter Summary

Communication, at its most simple, involves only the four most basic components of sender, receiver, message, and medium, and we now know that the sender and receiver can be the same person, but we cannot let this oversimplified definition lull us into the delusion that communication is a simple process. If it was truly that simple, then George Bernard Shaw's quote at the beginning of this chapter would have little relevance. Communication is messy. Communication is difficult. Communication often results in misunderstanding, hurt feelings, confusion, and damaged relationships, but we don't have to accept this as a fact of life. Communication can be learned, just like any other skill, such as a sport, playing a musical instrument, or singing, but to do so requires practice and preparation. Simply reading this book will not automatically transform you into an effective communicator. This book provides principles, theories, and suggestions to implement practice and preparation strategies into your life, so that you can work toward becoming more effective.

One thing we do know about communication is that it is what we use to make sense out of the world around us. As we share our naming processes for things, experiences, and phenomena, we effectively define the world around us, and this is the essence of communication. Whether we like it or not, communication affects each and every part of our daily lives at nearly every moment. Learning to communicate effectively is power. Public speaking may only be one form of communication for you to study, but in learning how to speak in public effectively and confidently, you are likely to find benefits in many other contexts in which communication can be wielded with precision.

Chapter 2

The Dread Behind the Podium

> *"According to most studies, people's number one fear is public speaking. Number two is death. Death is number two. Does that sound right? This means that, to the average person, if you go to a funeral, you're better off in the casket than doing the eulogy."*
>
> *—Jerry Seinfeld*

Seinfeld was certainly right about one thing: public speaking consistently tops just about any compiled list of fears. In fact, according to a 2015 study conducted by Chapman University, public speaking topped the list of personal phobias, narrowly beating out heights, bugs and snakes, and drowning.

Why is a crippling fear of public speaking, also known as **glossophobia**, so pervasive that it is seemingly a universal human trait? What is it about getting up in front of an audience and speaking that strikes terror in the hearts of so many? As we think about this response to public speaking, our rational minds come to a crossroads, confused as to why such a situation—the sharing of information with people who are likely interested in what we have to say—would cause so much anxiety in even the most confident of individuals. Coming up with a logical reason to explain the source of this fear can seem confusing, if not impossible, that is, until we know where to look, and that source for our exploration of this cause is in biology.

Relatively speaking (i.e., in comparison to the history of our species), humans have not been living in civilization for very long. The vast majority of us do not encounter wild animals as a part of our daily lives, nor do we come face to face with hostile tribes seeking to do us harm. However, we still have the biological mechanisms built into our brains to cope with such situations.

When we perceive a potential threat, our body's limbic system kicks into high gear, producing what we know as our "fight or flight" response. This supposed threat is acknowledged by the limbic system when we recognize prolonged eye contact from multiple sources, such as a room full of people waiting for us to speak. However, the limbic system views this situation as a room full of people who mean to do us harm, so a signal is wired to our adrenal glands, which sit atop our kidneys, and they begin pumping adrenaline and other hormones into the bloodstream.

As adrenaline hits our bloodstream, it acts like pure liquid energy, and rightly so. We've probably all heard stories of panicked mothers who single-handedly lifted cars off of their children to save their lives, because when we need an extra boost immediately, adrenaline is the stuff that gets the job done! The problem is, our logical neocortex (the thinking portion of our brain responsible for language and rational thought) is trying to calmly deliver an effective speech. Herein lies the problem.

The adrenaline immediately increases our heart rate, thereby also increasing our blood pressure. Next, the air passages to the lungs expand, the pupils enlarge, blood is redistributed to our muscles, and blood glucose is re-routed to the brain. As our senses go on high alert, the increase in blood pressure also increases the amount of heat our bodies produce, and as a result, we begin sweating to compensate. The differential between the amount of available energy from the adrenaline rush and the demand for energy we are placing on our bodies while trying to remain calm and collected results in seemingly uncontrollable trembling. The hands shake, knees wobble, and our voices begin to shake, all because our bodies' muscles are trying to expend this extra energy. Meanwhile, we try to stay still, so our muscles tremble involuntarily in protest. As the body's hydration is redirected to our muscles, the throat begins to dry up, followed by the mouth, as the salivary glands temporarily shut down, causing a "cottonmouth" effect. Our stomachs tighten up because the parasympathetic system that covers the "rest and digest" function of our bodies is put on hold while we deal with our anxiety. Suppression of this function is why the stomach feels like it's tied up in knots. As the blood sugar continues increasing in our brains, it feels similar to how a computer reacts when opening up too many programs at once, shutting down due to overload, and suddenly, in extreme cases, it feels like we are going to pass out!

The good news (perhaps the only good news) is that, if any or all of these symptoms sound familiar to you, based on previous public speaking experience, then you are completely 100% normal. This is a naturally instinctive biological response to such a scenario, but the even better news is that it can be effectively managed. Just because we are pre-wired to want to flee the room once our nerves kick in does not mean we have to allow ourselves to become slaves to such a response.

Acknowledging Fear

To better acknowledge our fears, let's take a look at exactly what most of us are afraid of:

- *Fear of eye contact.* Most of us have a natural desire to avoid being the center of attention within a crowd, and when that moment strikes, it can be very unnerving.
- *Fear of failure.* Similarly, making a fool of oneself presents an almost equally daunting phobia.
- *Traumatic public speaking experience.* Many students can recount stories from either high school speech class or earlier, from elementary school, where they had to stand in front of their peers and vividly recall botching their presentations, effectively creating a mental block, often leading to higher than average anxiety when faced with the prospect of public speaking.
- *Clinical anxiety.* Some rare individuals, due to a variety of reasons, whether social or biological, have cases of extreme anxiety in any social situation. For these individuals, public speaking presents not only a challenge, but often may seem insurmountable.

Most of us possess not merely one of these fears, but combinations of these fears (or perhaps, all of them). Regardless, the most important place to start in learning to cope with these fears (and later, use them to our advantage) is to recognize their onset and acknowledge their existence. One of the worst tactics a novice speaker can commit is to ignore these fears or pretend they are not going to affect our performance—because they most certainly will. Ignoring these fears can lead to a false sense of confidence, allowing them to creep up on us, striking at the worst possible moment and catching us off guard.

All too often, novice speakers make the mistake of thinking they need to conquer or overcome their fear, but that type of thinking can set a speaker up for failure. Fear is a necessary component of public speaking. If you ever find yourself standing up to speak to an audience, and you find an absence of fear, retire and never speak in public again. Fear is part of what makes us human. It keeps us alert, provides us with necessary energy, and above all, it makes us care about how well we perform. In public speaking, there is a saying: "Speakers who say they are as cool as a cucumber usually give speeches about as interesting as a cucumber." Overconfidence has probably flattened more potentially interesting and engaging speeches than nervousness ever has.

Instead of avoiding nervousness and hoping that the butterflies in our stomachs will simply fly away, never to bother us again, we need to practice strategies for coping with stressors, redirecting these energies to more useful outlets, and learning to use them to our advantage. The following sections detail various strategies and techniques for coping with anxiety, as well as preparing ourselves as a way to redirect this nervous energy into a more positive outcome.

Talk About What You Love

As we will learn later, one of the root causes for public speaking anxiety has to do with uncertainty, and one of the greatest potential sources for uncertainty has to do with content. Imagine having to deliver a presentation on a topic you know virtually nothing about; such a scenario probably ranks up there with giving a speech in our underwear for scary nightmare material! Selecting topics we either love, know something about, or are interested in knowing more about automatically reduces our nervousness, because it reframes the way we look at the presentation. By speaking about our passions, we no longer view the speech as a chore or a burden, but an *opportunity* to share what we care about with others. For topics about which we would like to learn more, the act of learning can often imbue us with even more excitement, providing us with fresh, unique, and innovative information to present to others.

Practice, Practice, Practice

Public speaking is a learned skill. Other learned skills include proficiency at various sports (shooting free throws, putting, ice skating, throwing a ball, etc.), learning and mastering a language, playing a musical instrument, and so on. As with any of these learned skills, one cannot simply read a book or manual on the skill and expect to master it, or for that matter, even hope to do remotely well their first time out. Learned skills require dedication, commitment, time, energy, and effort to master, and public speaking is no different in this regard.

One of the reasons practice makes perfect with respect to public speaking has to do with the concept of uncertainty. In approaching any given situation, we are likely to experience higher anxiety when we do not know clearly what to expect, but furthermore, if we can imagine a potentially disastrous outcome resulting from the situation, our anxiety further compounds exponentially. Public speaking, unfortunately for us, is rife with uncertainty. We worry about the possibilities of: forgetting what to say; saying something wrong or embarrassing; humiliation; failing to communicate effectively; and ridicule. Many of these pre-speech fears can be alleviated simply by eliminating sources of uncertainty. In other words, by practicing until we are confident that we know what to say in a number of different ways, we eliminate the uncertainty of forgetfulness and the anxiety of humiliation via saying the wrong thing or not knowing what to do. By getting to know our audience (which we will cover in much more depth later in the book, in Chapter 4), we eliminate the uncertainty of knowing whether or not the audience will connect with our message. In Chapter 8, we will also cover more detail regarding strategies for practice, as well as delivery tips for strengthening this newfound confidence.

Positive Visualization

Henry Ford once said, "Whether you think you can, or you think you can't, you're right." When you watch a top-level basketball player preparing to take a free-throw shot, what does that player do? She often goes through a routine, usually by dribbling a certain number of times, then assumes the shooting stance, and pauses. What goes through her mind, just before she takes the shot? Athletes like this, as well as successful professionals and public speakers employ a technique called **positive visualization** or **positive imagery**, which is taking a moment to imagine the best possible outcome before taking action. That basketball player, in the brief moment before taking her shot, is imagining to herself the ball releasing from her hands, arcing perfectly through the air, and swishing through the hoop, nothing but net. In real life, consider these examples:

- Muhammad Ali always stressed the importance of imagining himself victorious long before his actual fight.
- Michael Jordan would always take the last shot in his mind before he took that shot in reality.
- As a struggling young actor, Jim Carrey pictured himself being the greatest actor in the world.

The lingering question posed by these examples is this: why does this technique seem to work? Is there some mystical psychic power of which we are unaware? Again, turning to biology, we discover that there is nothing mystical going on with this practice technique. The human imagination is a powerful tool. CT scans of the human brain during exercises involving the imagination demonstrate that the very same areas of the brain that are active during a real-life activity are also active during the same activity being imagined (Schlegel, Kohler, Fogelson, Alexander, Konuthula, & Ulric Tse, 2013). What this means is that we can actually train our brains to perform by employing positive visualization and imagining ourselves as successful. When combined with practicing public speaking as close as possible to the desired end result, this technique works powerfully to reduce anxiety, eliminate uncertainties, and increase self-confidence.

Mindful Awareness and Authenticity

When most of us think of being mindful, we imagine being considerate of others and/or being aware and dwelling in the present moment, but there is more to being mindful than mere awareness. Mindfulness involves three main components:

- Being acutely aware of one's surroundings and senses within the present moment;
- Possessing a nonjudgmental acceptance of the way things are in that moment;
- Being intentional, or as Dr. Jon Kabat-Zinn states, "paying attention on purpose."

What does this have to do with public speaking though? The answer to that question is this—everything! Most of us, when placed into a public speaking scenario, have a sort of out-of-body experience. It may almost seem as though your conscious, rational, thinking self exits your body and is floating somewhere above you and off to the side, all the while pointing out a barrage of self-criticisms: *You're blowing it! Stop shaking so much! Talk louder! Why didn't you practice more?* This strange sensation often compounds and increases our natural biological anxiety response by shifting the focus away from where it should be, on the audience and how they are receiving our message, and instead, onto ourselves and subsequent nervous symptoms. As a result of this sensation, our communication style shifts into the antonym of mindfulness, *mindlessness*, or the act of going through the motions (i.e., on "autopilot"). Audiences can easily tell when a speaker has proverbially "checked out" and no longer seems "in tune" with the audience. Perceptions such as these are indicative of a speaker who is no longer fully in the present moment, and in such situations, the audience could likely stand up and walk out, while the speaker would not notice.

By incorporating techniques to facilitate more mindful behaviors, we, as public speakers, have the capability to reconnect that conscious self with our physical self. As we intentionally remain more focused on the present moment, we begin to develop the valuable communication skill of being able to consciously think about the words we are saying before they are spoken, allowing us to shape and choose our communication more carefully—more mindfully. Such a state is not easily achieved, however, for it also involves more than an intentional awareness.

The final facet of mindfulness involves nonjudgmental acceptance or acknowledgment. Nonjudgmental acceptance entails recognizing when we feel the peak of our biological anxiety response, usually within the first 60 seconds or so after your speech begins, and accepting those uncomfortable symptoms as a natural part of public speaking. Most of us find these symptoms rather unpleasant, so learning to accept them is an exercise in consciously altering our perceptions of them. To do this, think about the last time you were in line to ride a roller coaster that filled you with excitement and, simultaneously, dread. Your body and brain undergo an identical process prior to such a thrilling experience, and yet, you perceive the two situations all together differently. In one, the anxiety response might make you giddy, making the hairs on your arms stand on end and forcing an almost unstoppable smile. In the other, you might perceive pre-speech jitters as the worst punishment humankind has ever devised. Your brain, however, cannot tell the difference, biologically speaking, so it is up to your neocortex to redirect this energy and use it positively. How might you reframe the way you look at public speaking nerves? What if, instead of dreading the experience of speaking in front of an audience, you viewed it with anticipation by looking forward to an opportunity to share with others information that mattered to you a great deal? Combining this idea with positive visualization, we can see how beneficial reframing how we view public speaking anxiety could be, when viewed instead as anticipation.

As we adopt a more mindful approach to public speaking, our out-of-body experience dissipates, and we reconnect our "backstage self" with our "on-stage self," allowing us to interact more fully with our audience. We can then notice reactions from the audience, feel the "energy" of the room, and adapt in the moment to the changing nature of the presentation. This is ultimately what exudes authenticity to audience members, as it is the diametric opposite to speakers who "phone it in," speaking from a memorized script, regardless of the audience.

Plan Out Your Details

All too often, novice speakers find themselves derailed by seemingly insignificant mistakes not thought of beforehand:

- Technology details (i.e., extension cords available, software versions, DVD vs. Blu-Ray capability, etc.);
- Timing (i.e., when to advance the slide);
- Feeling of one's outfit during the speech (i.e., an itchy shirt tag or painful heels);
- How the room looks from the speaker's vantage point.

When anxiety levels are high, even the smallest overlooked detail can easily fluster a novice speaker, detracting attention from the message and/or the audience and instead, causing the speaker to focus on the self. The best speakers spend hours considering all of the details, imagining vividly how every moment of a successful presentation will go, and such speakers also incorporate all of these details into their practice sessions, again, eliminating all traces of uncertainty and subsequently, resulting anxiety.

Anxiety Peaks

In public speaking, students often describe two peak moments of anxiety: one at the beginning of the speech and another at the end. Anxiety generally begins from the moment we recognize the impending "doom" of having to deliver the speech, which may be different for all of us. Some might start experiencing this the night before a presentation, especially if social anxiety is already naturally high. Others might not feel this anxiety hit until the moment she turns to face her audience. On average, most of us begin to feel this major peak of anxiety about 60 seconds before the speech begins. This peak tops out around 60 seconds into delivery of the speech, where it quickly subsides. This two-minute window is consistent with other situations involving the body experiencing a sudden burst of adrenaline. As a result, speakers need to be able to know their introductions almost better than any point throughout the rest of the speech. That way, while we are coping with and redirecting nervous energy as its height, we are still able to communicate effectively with our audience. Taking this into account, devote extra practice to the introduction above all other parts of the speech, but avoid memorization. Learn the introduction so well that you can deliver it smoothly and conversationally.

The second peak of anxiety often feels considerably more positive in tone, and it occurs about 60 seconds before we leave the podium to return to our seat. This peak happens as soon as we recognize the end of our time in the spotlight being in sight, and feels more like anticipation than dread, as we are anticipating being done and out of the center of attention. This usually results in novice speakers rushing through their conclusions, forgetting elements of their conclusions, or both. To counteract this anxiety wave, bring attention to practicing your conclusions as well. Take your time and ensure that you are prepared to close your speech just as powerfully as it was opened in the introduction and supported throughout the body of the work.

Control Your Physical Activity

While adrenaline causes many involuntary responses as detailed earlier, such as profuse sweating, uncontrollable shaking, or forgetfulness, there are some physical responses we can enact that have a calming effect on us, no matter how hyped up the rush makes us feel:

- *Deep breathing.* Without hyperventilating, pause momentarily, just before you begin your speech, and take at least a couple of deep, cleansing breaths. Allow your diaphragm to fill your lungs completely, and then exhale slowly, releasing as much air as possible. Do this slowly and deliberately, as the calming power of slow, deep breathing cannot be reinforced often enough.
- *Use your body's muscles.* Adrenaline may be a powerful force in supplying the body with tons of extra energy, but it has a down side: it is burned off just as quickly as it sets in. As you move around the room, use your arms and hands to gesture. You will not need to do jumping jacks or pushups to burn off this excess energy; minimal effort and movement is all it takes. The last thing you want to do is stand still, gripping the podium for dear life. The more rigid your stance, the longer the adrenaline burst will last!

Nervous Symptoms Are Unseen

When our hands and knees tremble, our voice begins to squeak, our mouths go dry, and our hearts seem ready to leap out of our chests, we have a tendency to feel like a freak of nature and that everyone can see us! Of course, this is because all these symptoms are happening to us. However, in reality, the vast majority of nervous symptoms tend to go completely unseen. Unless someone from the audience is close enough to see these symptoms (as in, standing right next to us as we speak), then odds are, the audience is more focused on listening to the message. After all, few of us (if any), as audience members, attend speeches with the express purpose of seeing if we can detect nervous symptoms in a speaker.

Often, novice speakers will also apologize for their nerves, feeling as though the audience can see all and is distracted by the manifestation of such symptoms. However, apologizing only draws attention to symptoms that may have otherwise gone unnoticed. Additionally, apologizing for our nerves reinforces the internal narrative that we are more nervous than we should be, most likely compounding the anxiety and making it worse.

Managing Physical Symptoms

For dry mouth:

- Take no dairy products, soda, or alcoholic beverages, and don't smoke tobacco before speaking; all increase mucus production and the feeling of a lump in the throat.
- Gently bite the tip of your tongue (this helps you to salivate).
- Drink room-temperature or warm water (with lemon, if available).

For sweaty hands/body:

- Use talcum powder or corn starch on hands/body.
- Carry a handkerchief.

If you have red splotches on your face:

- Wear pink or red colors.
- Wear high necklines.
- Use humor to release endorphins.

If your voice trembles:

- Project your voice to the back row of the audience. Projection is felt in the diaphragm, as you push more air out when you speak.

If your hands are shaky:

- Gesture, but make small gestures; don't wave about wildly.

If your legs are shaky or your knees are knocking:

- Move around gently and easily, but don't pace.

If your heartbeat is rapid:

- Do some deep breathing.
- Avoid caffeine and nicotine.

Chapter Summary

Nerves go with public speaking like cookies and milk or fries and ketchup. Public speaking anxiety is a natural, biological reaction and an expected part of living. Instead of seeking to get rid of nerves and anxiety, speakers need to welcome this fear as a source of energy, reframing it as anticipation, rather than dread. This is most easily accomplished through redirecting the speaker's focus on the message and how the audience is receiving the message, as well as eliminating all sources of uncertainty through careful planning, preparation, and practice. Instead of allowing anxiety to control us, we rationally reclaim control, thereby redirecting our anxiety into useful energy, leading to a more mindful, authentic speech delivery, connecting with audiences on a deeper, more engaging level.

Chapter 3

Topic Selection and Purpose

> *"The newest computer can merely compound, at speed, the oldest problem in the relations between human beings, and in the end, the communicator will be confronted with the old problem of what to say and how to say it."*
>
> *—Edward R. Murrow*

Picture yourself, a student entering a college public speaking course for the first time (probably not terribly difficult if you are reading this book), faced with the prospect of having to deliver a speech to a classroom full of students like yourself. Immediately, the anxiety of the unknown starts to build, as we discussed in Chapter 2. It builds slowly at first, but eventually you are faced with the same problem as everyone else in your room, as well as anyone else in the history of a college speech course. What do you talk about in your speech? What points should you cover? Many, if not most, students lament this same question year after year, and as they should, because topic selection is often one of the single greatest predictors of success for novice speakers as they practice and refine their craft.

Imagine your anxiety levels if a speech topic was assigned to you, and you had absolutely zero interest in that topic whatsoever. For example, for a communication instructor, talking about public speaking anxiety, mass media studies, or interpersonal interaction between men and women might seem as though it comes naturally, partly because of high interest in the topic, but also due to a high level of training and experience. Ask the same communication instructor to discuss the ins and outs of health care administration or quantum physics, and the instructor is quickly reduced to quivering nerves in anticipatory anxiety. The same holds true for all of us.

Speaker interest automatically reduces our anxiety levels when speaking about topics we genuinely care about or have a passion for, primarily because it naturally shifts our focus toward our interests, rather than remaining on our nervous symptoms. For example, take a look at time spent on most social media. If we run across a scintillating story or fascinating article, our natural inclination is to share that piece with our entire social network, and many of us share without giving it a second thought. This is mostly because we naturally take pleasure from sharing with others information that fascinates, excites, and engages us. However, before we can settle in on a topic, we have to consider the purpose of our speech.

General Speaking Purpose

Typically, speeches can be divided among three main types or basic purposes: speeches to inform, speeches to persuade, and speeches to entertain and/or commemorate special occasions. All three have details that intricately determine how a topic must be approached to achieve that purpose, so it is critical that we look closer at each type:

- An informative speech provides an audience with new, unique, and/or innovative knowledge on a distinct topic. A speech to inform can: tell an engaging story with an intrinsic lesson; explain or clarify a difficult or complicated concept (often called the **definition speech**); and show an audience how to do something (often called the **demonstration speech** or **how-to speech**). An instructor giving a lecture is one example of a speech to inform, but we would also include typical student oral reports; skilled demonstrations such as cooking, woodworking, or welding; and biographical tribute speeches designed to honor a dignitary. Later, in Part I of this book (Chapters 4–10), we will discuss the details surrounding methods for effective informative speaking.
- A persuasive speech has most, if not all, of the elements of a speech to inform, but takes the information a step further and uses it to change audience attitudes, opinions, or behaviors. Examples of speeches to persuade might include advertisements, political speeches, religious services, donation/registration drives, negotiations of various types, or perhaps even our daily conversations. Some persuasive speeches seek to alter attitudes, some go further and seek action as a result, and others may seek to inspire others. In Part II of this book (Chapters 11 and 12), we will examine how persuasive speaking differs from speaking to inform, and you will learn strategies for effective persuasion and motivation.
- Finally, a speech designed to mark a special occasion or entertain audiences is simply that—speaking to amuse, commemorate, arouse interest, divert attention, or perhaps, in some cases, even "warm up" an audience for a larger event. Examples of speaking to entertain include stand-up comedy, storytelling (which differs from a speech to inform when there is no explicit lesson or moral to be learned), or even a toast for a colleague or friend. For the purpose of this book, we will only focus on the first two purposes (inform and persuade).

While these three general purposes all have their own considerations to keep in mind as we plan for our speech, it is important to note that there is often crossover between each of them. In other words, a speech to inform can easily be entertaining, as well as present compelling information that leads the audience toward being persuaded. A speech to persuade can present an audience with fresh, new information while still managing to be engaging and entertaining. However, it is critical to our success as public speakers to keep our general purpose in mind at all times. All too often, novice speakers want to focus more on being entertaining, and as a result, their general purpose gets lost, as they focus more on laughs than on informing the audience. Similarly, a novice speaker might start out with a speech to inform, but end up attempting to persuade the audience by the end of the speech, in which case, the general purpose has failed. Therefore, it is absolutely critical that we remember our general purpose as we compose our messages, so that we remain focused on our primary goal.

Topic Selection and Refinement

Once we have our general purpose in mind, which usually takes place early in the planning stages, we can begin deciding on what specific topic area we want to use to inform or persuade our audience. This often presents one of the more difficult stages of speech development, especially if we do not have a limited or narrowed set of topics from which to choose. After all, when the sky is the limit, it is all too easy to feel overwhelmed and burdened by trying to figure out what to talk about.

To determine what topics are worthwhile, consider brainstorming lists of various topics, but do so without judging their value. For example, if you see a commercial on television that infuriates you because of the way it comes across, write down something like, "Manipulative media: How advertising controls our buying habits." If you run across a fascinating story on an elderly couple that survived the Holocaust and were reunited after 70 years apart from each other, consider writing down the following topic idea: "After the Holocaust: How Jewish survivors rebuilt their lives after WWII." Whether you keep a note-taking app handy on your smartphone, or an actual notepad handy in your bookbag, glove box, or purse, be sure to jot down ideas as they come up, so that when you are pressed for selection of a topic, you have a variety of ideas from which to choose.

Constant sources of topic ideas are easily found within current events. Pay attention to various stories in the media that grab your attention and make you want to read further. Exploring various news websites, particularly those that provide a wide sampling from diverse media outlets, such as Google News (news.google.com), provide a nearly limitless source of ideas.

Additionally, certain times of year provide timely, interesting topics, such as general election season (political candidate profiles, explanations of voting processes, persuading others to register to vote, etc.), holidays (how to make Christmas treats, history of Halloween, the truth behind Columbus, etc.), or seasonal-related topics (fun family summer activities, best places for skiing and snowboarding, the science behind the colors of autumn, etc.).

Lastly, consider covering a topic that might be new and unique to you, requiring a bit of research on your part. Often, topics that are new to us provide us with a built-in sense of curiosity. When we research these newer topics and begin learning more about them, the process of research can spark a sense of excitement in us, making us want to share that newfound information with others. We call this approach the **social media share test**, for if we run across new information that excites us to the point where we blindly click "Share" in order to spread that information with everyone in our social network, then it could very well present a fascinating topic from which to build a presentation.

Nested Brainstorming

Another technique for generating topic ideas is a more refined version of brainstorming. Try the following quick and painless technique for coming up with speech topic ideas off the top of your head, before taking it a step further and refining those ideas into something with which you can work.

Activity

For a fun topic-finding activity, go to Wikipedia.org, and on the main page (you may have to click on "English" first to get to the main page), near the top-left corner of the page, just under the site logo, you will see a link called "Random article." Click this link as many times as you want, until an article of interest appears that you can then research further.

- In 60 seconds or less, come up with a list of 10 general subject areas you would be interested in sharing with others. Pay no attention to their value and do not imagine whether or not your audience will like those subjects. We will deal with that aspect of speaking later. For now, simply come up with a list of 10 subject areas as seen here:

Creative Writing
Sci-fi Movies
Video Games
Mobile Apps
Cancer Research
Zombies
Auto Repair
Mindfulness
Fatherhood
Digital Music

- Next, take this list of 10 potential subject areas and circle 3–5 topics you love the most. How you define this is completely up to you. You might select topics that you know a significant amount about, you might select topics that you are passionate about, or you might select topics with which you have a great deal of experience. Regardless, narrow the list to 3–5 topics:

Fatherhood
Mindfulness
Sci-fi Movies

- Now, rank these remaining topics in order of *your* interest level. Which of these remaining topics would you be most interested in sharing with others? Again, do not worry (yet) about how the audience could feel about listening to these topics, as we will be studying that later.

Mindfulness
Fatherhood
Sci-fi Movies

- Once ranked, take your top-ranked item and break it into three subtopics. If you cannot successfully think of three additional subtopics, skip that topic and move to the next one on your list:

Mindfulness

1. Behaviors/activities to cultivate mindfulness
2. The effects of mindfulness on health
3. How mindfulness can develop better relationships

- Once again, as with before, take these three subtopics and rank them in order of *your* interest level (not what you think an audience might like). Your top-ranked subtopic may now become your primary speech topic. Once you have that topic, break it down further into yet another three additional subtopics, and these will become your three main points:

The effects of mindfulness on health

- Main point 1: Defining mindfulness
- Main point 2: Effects of mindfulness on mental health
- Main point 3: Effects of mindfulness on physical health

Topic Considerations

As you continue the process of narrowing and refining your topic, which you will likely continue doing throughout the process of composing and practicing for the delivery of your speech, there are certain considerations to bear in mind. First, keep your time limits in mind. If your allotted speaking time is on the brief end of the spectrum, such as 6–8 minutes, you will likely want to avoid selecting topics that are too broad in scope. Topics too general in nature run the risk of going well over the amount of time the speaker has been allotted, they may put the audience into a state of information overload where they no longer listen, and they may overwhelm you, the speaker, during the preparation phase. Conversely, avoid topics that are too narrow in scope, as they present the possibility for the opposite consequences: failing to reach the minimum amount of time assigned or presenting information that is well beyond the audience's comprehension level, which again, can cause attention spans to falter.

Ideally, in a speech to inform, your topic will have a fresh, unique, and innovative quality to it. You want to avoid trying to inform an audience of information they already know, but at the same time, you want to avoid going overly deep into a topic without presenting background information first. Finding the perfect topic, as well as the level of complexity for the information you plan on presenting, is part of the art of learning audience-centered speaking. In Chapter 4, we will examine methods for you to get to know your audiences, so that you can carefully tailor your information to their needs and information levels.

Specific Purpose

Once we have identified our general purpose and have a topic in mind, we can begin narrowing and refining our message using a **funnel approach**, moving from general information toward more specific information. One method of accomplishing this task

FYI

The average audiobook utilizes a conversational speaking rate of around 150 words per minute (Williams, 1998), so for every five minutes you are given to speak, stick to a length of around 750 words (if you wrote your speech out as a script). Naturally, when we get nervous, we speak a bit faster, but this number provides us with a good starting point for estimating how much writing we need for the time given. Knowing this helps with narrowing and focusing topic selection, so that we avoid choosing topics that are too broad to fit within the time constraints given.

is to re-frame the question "What do I talk about?" to "What do I want my audience to know or do, once they leave the room?" We can answer that question by filling in the unknowns left behind by the general purpose we discussed earlier: 1) To inform my audience about ______, or 2) To persuade my audience to ______. It is important to keep in mind that the specific purpose should only address *one* idea. If your specific purpose clumps together multiple, unrelated or distantly related concepts with an "and" or two, then you will know you have not sufficiently refined your topic. Using a specific purpose like this will likely result in a speech that comes across as choppy, disorganized, and confusing for your audience members to follow. However, if you used the nested brainstorming method mentioned earlier, then the last single topic you eventually wound up with could become your specific purpose, such as: "To inform my audience about *the effects of mindfulness on health.*"

Choose your specific purpose carefully and think critically, because from that point forward, everything you write will go toward fulfilling that specific purpose. Furthermore, as you write, you should return to this specific purpose often to ask yourself, "Does the information I am researching and writing further my attempt to achieve this purpose?" A great tip for accomplishing this task is to write down your specific purpose on a post-it note and then place it somewhere visible in your regular workspace. The specific purpose ultimately keeps us focused on a single goal, preventing us from getting off-track or off-topic, which, depending on the length of the speech, can be easy to do, especially with longer presentations.

Central Idea

Once your specific purpose has been identified, the next step is to figure out your central idea. The **central idea** is a single sentence that articulates the one thought you want your audience to remember at the end of your speech. If they remember nothing else you said other than this one thing, then what is that one key idea you want them to walk away with? You may be thinking, "That sounds an awful lot like a specific purpose," and many novice speakers confuse the two and use their specific purpose as their central idea, but they are not the same. To clarify the difference, try thinking of the central idea in a more familiar term, which you have likely heard before in a writing class: a thesis statement. A thesis statement is a single sentence that concisely presents an assertion or proposition that the speaker must then support with evidence. One method for determining your central idea is to answer the specific purpose as though it leaves a question unanswered, such as *why* or *what.* If my specific purpose, as mentioned in the example above, is "To inform my audience about *the effects of mindfulness on health,*" then the question unanswered by this statement is, *what*? What do you want the audience to know about the effects of mindfulness on health in a single sentence? In other words, what is the central idea behind this purpose that will ultimately lead to achieving that goal?

Keep the central idea simple, yet focused. If we were preparing a 6- to 8-minute speech informing an audience of the causes for the Industrial Revolution, we might not want our central idea to be, "The history of Western civilization is complex." Such a central idea is too broad and too vague, opening up the speech to far too much information than would be possible in that short a time. Instead, we would want a more specific central idea that more specifically summarizes the content of our speech as follows:

"Beginning with Gutenberg's printing press, the explosion of information-sharing in Western civilization led to rapid technological development."

Activity

Still struggling to identify your central idea? Try the "because" technique. Start by writing out your specific purpose, and then add "because" to the end of it. Whatever statement follows "because" may help you answer the *what* or *why* question left unanswered by your specific purpose. **Example**: To educate my audience about saving for retirement <u>because</u> *by adopting simple saving strategies that can be done on any budget, you will set yourself up to savor your retirement.* If you cut out the italicized segment, you have an example of a central idea or assertion regarding this specific topic.

Another way of looking at the central idea is to use a more familiar analogy. Think of our speech as a delicate and exquisite sauce that we need to make. In making a sauce, we gather together all of our ingredients (information from various sources); we mix it together in an orderly, careful, and measured fashion (the process of composition); and then we apply heat and simmer it, thereby reducing the liquid to a rich, powerfully flavored sauce that ignites the taste buds. The central idea is what is left over when we boil down the entire speech into just one carefully worded, yet rich, sentence, encompassing the whole of what we want our audience to know.

Based on our previously used sample of a specific purpose regarding the effects of mindfulness on health, here is an ideal central idea: *Developing mindfulness through regular practice produces benefits in all aspects of life, from mental health to physical well-being.* Note that the sentence is complete, grammatically correct, asserts a perspective, and includes just enough information from which to derive our main points. From this single sentence, we can write a speech about mindfulness, the practices that nurture it, and the physical and mental benefits we might expect from doing so. This central idea, once written, becomes the vehicle upon which we will accomplish our specific purpose. It is the hinge around which everything else in the speech will revolve. One piece of information you may want to remember, though, is that a central idea may need to remain flexible as you research your speech and tailor it further to your audience, but the specific purpose remains the same. Different audiences may require different methods to relay the same message, so keep your central ideas fluid.

Titling the Speech

While Shakespeare may have famously had Romeo ask Juliet, "What's in a name? That which we call a rose / By any other name would smell as sweet," the truth is, a creative and well-worded title potentially wins over an audience's collective attention span before the speaker even begins. Your speech's title may act like the cover to a book, and like it or not, most of us, despite suggesting that we should not judge books by their covers, decide what books receive further attention based on their initial impression. In most

Helpful Hint

Students often struggle to determine if they have effectively stated their central idea as an assertion. One way to figure out if you have accomplished this goal is to ask yourself if someone could disagree with your central idea or develop a speech on a different perspective regarding the same topic. For example, your central idea could be: "Even with limited space, growing your own vegetables is easy and has many mental and physical benefits." Using this central idea, someone could take a different perspective on this topic and propose an alternate central idea such as: "Growing your own vegetables is a complex and challenging process that requires immense time and ample space."

cases, you will be introduced by someone, who will, at the very least, tell the audience your name and speech title. Although, if you are utilizing visual aids, you may likely have a title slide projected onto the screen behind you as you make your way to the podium. Providing the audience with that first taste of what your speech promises to deliver—and doing so creatively—sets the stage, so to speak.

One student creatively titled his 6- to 8-minute speech to inform with visual aids, "How to Make a Baby in 8 Minutes or Less." Before the speaker reached the podium, his title already invoked laughter and giggles from his audience, thanks to the double entendre the title presented. However, his speech went on to inform the audience about contemporary fertility approaches for couples having difficulties getting pregnant. In an extremely well-researched presentation on medical science, the speaker found a way to use wry humor to win over his audience before he even spoke, but then followed that up with a charismatic, fresh, and innovative presentation that maintained their attention throughout the speech.

Another approach to developing a speech title involves looking at key phrases that may appear throughout your speech. If your speech contains a key phrase to be used repeatedly, such as Martin Luther King, Jr.'s "I Have a Dream" speech, consider using a shortened version of that phrase to reinforce it before you begin. A phrase could also be turned into a provocative question, such as "Could You Save a Life?" used as a title for instruction on the basics of CPR.

Chapter Summary

Remember that topic selection can make or break a successful speaker. Choose topics that you are passionate about or know extensive amounts of information about, because once you find that you are motivated to share information with others for some intrinsic reason, then that selection of a personally motivating topic can effectively cut anxiety in half. Consider a topic's "share test"—would you want to hear this information from others, or would you be willing to re-share or forward this information to others within your social network? If so, then that topic presents a viable choice with which to work.

Start your journey toward finding the perfect topic with thinking about the type of speech you will be giving. Will you speak to inform, to persuade, or to entertain? From there, begin brainstorming topics right away, and the sooner, the better. As you develop specific, narrowed, and focused topic ideas, start working to transform your general purpose to a specific purpose. What do you want your audience to know when you are done, or what is your persuasive goal? Identify your specific purpose first, and then start working on a draft of your central idea. Remember to keep everything fairly fluid and flexible, because, as you continue to develop your presentation, valuable information about what your audience members know (or don't know) and how they feel about your topic (or don't feel about it) may change how your purpose ultimately looks and subsequently, your central idea. In the next chapter, we will take a closer look at how you can get to know your audience, including methods for collecting data about their knowledge level, attitudes, opinions, and beliefs, all with respect to what you will be covering.

Part I
Speaking to Inform

Chapter 4

Analyzing Your Audience

> *"If the people in the audience are talking, you're being ignored. If the people are gazing at you, you've got something they want to hear."*
>
> —*Chuck Berry*

Once we have our topics selected and know both our general and specific purposes, the next place to turn our focus is our audience, for without taking our audience into consideration as we refine our message in preparation for delivery, we might as well stay at home and converse with ourselves in front of a mirror. Great communicators retain the integrity of their original message, but carefully tailor, shape, and mold that message to each audience's unique wants and needs. Speakers who fail to connect with their audiences often do so because they cared more about how they looked and whether or not their audiences liked them.

"Care deeply about your audience" is a piece of advice often given by veteran speakers as the number-one rule for effective public speaking. Unfortunately, many speeches are ineffective because the speaker is not mindfully present with their audience. Instead, they are more self-focused and preoccupied with distractions such as, "How do I look?" or "Does everyone like me?" This self-focused approach can amplify existing anxieties, interfering even more with successful communication, and rarely produces positive results. Caring deeply for your audience means preparing in advance, being mindfully present with your message and with the audience, and showing your genuine and authentic self.

Our goal, as effective and powerful communicators, is to create a speech that is **audience-centered**, adding value and meaning to the information we present by remaining mindful of what our audience members know about our topics, but also how they feel (attitudes, opinions, and beliefs) about them. To achieve this goal, we must, before every speech we deliver, analyze our audiences and adapt our communication to the results of that analysis. This process of analysis and adaptation, however, must never sacrifice the integrity of our original message. This is why topic selection and initial planning come first in the process, for the very reason we have chosen to stand up in front of an audience and speak is to have our voices heard. We must not forget that initial reason, despite what we think the audience may *want* to hear.

Collecting Audience Data

When we see the word "data," most of us picture an accountant's office or a research laboratory filled with beakers and vials, but data need not be purely numerical. Data may be **quantitative** (numbers and statistics), but it may also be **qualitative** (facts, stories, and observations). Collecting meaningful, purposeful data about an audience in relation to a speech topic is part science and part art. Planning and critical thinking play a large role in our success in this endeavor.

Before we can create a means to gather data, however, we must decide on what data matters to our speeches. A great place to start with data is demographics, or the most basic and quantifiable characteristics of a population of people. For example, we may want to look at demographics like gender/sex, age, socioeconomic background, and ethnicity/nationality/culture. Let's take a look at why any of these characteristics matter.

Gender and sex are not necessarily the same thing, and knowing the difference can make or break certain speech topics. Sex refers to the biological differences that make a person male or female, while gender refers to masculine or feminine qualities evident within a person of either sex. To determine how sex makes a difference to a speech topic, consider the following situation:

> You are scheduled to speak to an audience made up of 18 women and 2 men. Your speech topic is on early detection for breast cancer. Given that the sex breakdown of the room is 90% women and 10% men, the majority of your speech information will likely be directed to the women in the room, but at the same time, you absolutely *must* find a way to make a portion of your information appeal to the men in the room, such as by talking about how 1 in 1,000 men will get breast cancer, or how a man can assist a female partner with early detection measures. If you don't find a way to include the men in this conversation, then their attention spans will likely fade early in your presentation. By speaking inclusively and inviting men into the conversation using information that directly impacts those two men, you are effectively becoming an audience-centered speaker.

Age is another important demographic factor, because what one generation knows, is interested in, or the ways in which that generation listens and interprets information, varies greatly from one to the next. For example, if you needed to deliver two informative speeches on the dangers of social media, one to parents of high school students, and another to the high school students themselves, you would likely arrange your information in very different ways. For the first speech, with the parents of high school students, you might have to present more background information before you are able to cover the dangers of social media; whereas, with the students themselves, you are speaking to "digital natives" who have been raised on social media for the better part of their lives, allowing you to go much more in-depth with your topic.

Sex and age may be more outward characteristics that are relatively easy in most cases to spot without a lot of effort, but what about socioeconomic background, and how does it affect our speech preparation process? Socioeconomic background refers to one's position in society relative to others, which many will identify as "middle class," "in poverty," or "wealthy." Others may also refer to their position among the working hierarchy, such as "blue collar" or "white collar." To illustrate this point, consider the following student's example:

> *Shortly after graduating from my community college, I transferred to a prestigious private university, at which point, I was immersed into a student body of considerably*

greater wealth. One of my first experiences there was in a speech class, where a student delivered a speech on how to buy a used car, and her first main point discussed her real dilemma, which was whether to go with a BMW or a Mercedes. At that point, considering that I came from a high-poverty working-class background, I immediately tuned out.

Had the speaker, in this case, known her audience's background, rather than assuming it was homogenous (like-minded, with similar backgrounds), she could have provided more appealing options, thus inviting the whole audience into her presentation, which would have prevented losing a listener due to alienation or exclusion.

Lastly, a speaker must also know the intricacies of culture for a particular audience. A speaker discussing law enforcement abuses will cover information one way with a predominantly Caucasian audience and another way with an audience with a higher representation of minorities due to vastly differing viewpoints for each audience, but will ideally maintain the integrity of that message with both. Additionally, regional cultural expectations (i.e., a New York audience compared to an audience in Atlanta) can vary greatly, as will multinational audiences, so it pays for a speaker to prepare based on intercultural knowledge, as well as individual audience member characteristics. Being able to speak within cultural expectations and respecting cultural norms and customs can earn a speaker the respect and admiration of that audience, regardless of message content.

While demographics are a great place to start, we often need more detailed information about our audiences to be successful, which is where methods for both passive and active information gathering come into play.

If you needed to deliver a rousing persuasive speech in front of your city council members, how might you go about learning more about them? One place to start might be with a simple web search. Consider going to the city council's web page to read about each of the individual members, especially if, as the result of your speech, there is to be a vote on the outcome. Learn what their individual priorities are, what their backgrounds in the community are, and even, how they have voted in the past. Use this information to learn more about this specific audience and tailor your message to match those needs (we will discuss persuasive strategies in much more detail later, in Chapters 11 and 12). However, in addition to this research-based approach, another option might simply be to show up early to the meeting and try to talk to various people. Learn about this specific audience by listening to the various conversations, or by talking to people who know this audience well.

If, in another hypothetical situation, we were being hired as communication consultants for a relatively large organization, we might look through the organization's website, but also, search local papers and other news outlets for stories and press releases about the organization, so that we were able to speak to the various practices and activities of that organization (this is also excellent advice to conduct prior to a job interview, by the way). Interviewing the supervisor or human resources manager of an organization is another way to gather information about your audience. These key people can provide demographics, behaviors, knowledge, attitudes, and interest levels of the targeted

Types of Demographic Categories to Consider

- Gender
- Sex
- Age
- Education
- Occupation
- Religious affiliation
- Socioeconomic status
- Ethnicity
- Nationality
- Income level
- Birthplace

audience. The more we know and the more we can speak specifically toward topics and information that our various audiences find important, the greater rapport, or connection, we are able to make, resulting in greater listening ability as well as persuasiveness.

Survey Research

Passive information collection works well in many cases, but there are times when the stakes are higher, and we want to guarantee our chances for success even more. At this point, we may want to consider pursuing more active means of collecting data on our audiences, and this can be done through survey research.

Types of Questions

We can break down survey questions into two general categories: open-ended and closed-ended questions. Open-ended questions are questions that have no definitive answers, allowing the survey respondents to answer with anything they see fit, such as "What is your favorite movie of all time, and why?" Closed-ended questions are the opposite, considering that they limit the number of responses a respondent may offer, such as either-or questions (yes/no, true/false, etc.), multiple choice questions, and scaled questions ("On a scale from 1 to 10, rate your knowledge of...).

Both types of questions yield specific results, but only when applied to the appropriate data you are attempting to gather. Open-ended questions provide detailed information on each individual taking your survey, and as such, an open-ended question may provide you with as many different answers as you have people taking the survey. While this provides you with valuable information you might use later in your speech, to tailor your information to very specific members of your audience, it fails at providing you with a more basic snapshot of the audience as a whole, and this is where closed-ended questions work well. By limiting the number of responses to any one of your questions, you are able to more efficiently collect and analyze data about highly specific aspects of your topic.

Methods to Administer Surveys

In addition to question types, we have to consider how we will deliver, or administer, our surveys to our audiences, because each type of survey brings with it a different set of benefits and challenges.

First of all, one of the simplest ways to conduct a survey is to deliver it face-to-face in a sort of informal interview approach. We might write our questions out on a single sheet of paper, then walk around to each person in the room, asking them our questions and recording their responses. This is obviously cheap (only one piece of paper used), relatively quick—depending on our number of questions, but with those benefits come great drawbacks. If any of our questions are remotely personal or invasive, meaning that they dig a little too deep, those questions may activate what is called **social desirability bias**, or the tendency for most of us to want to bend the truth ever so slightly on surveys to make ourselves seem better than we actually are. For example, if I have a survey question that asks respondents face-to-face how many illicit drugs they have tried in the last month, I can expect that most people will answer with zero, even though statistics might suggest otherwise.

Another method of conducting a survey is to create a single sign-up or pass-around sheet that contains all of our questions, allowing each member of the audience to see how others before them have answered. While this is equally cost-effective, it also may activate the social desirability bias, but additionally, it adds the potential for **groupthink**, or the tendency for people to respond how the majority of others have responded before them, even if that isn't how they truly feel.

A third method employs technological means to create online surveys. A quick internet search for "free online survey tools" will turn up a wide variety of websites designed for the user to create surveys effortlessly, before providing a link (URL) that the user can then email to everyone in the audience. Additionally, such survey tools provide free analysis options, allowing you to automatically calculate a wide array of basic statistics (averages, distributions, percentages, etc.). Such surveys are quick to take, free to produce, and seem like they might be the best option available, but they come with their own unique problems, including the main one related to online surveys: response rates are notoriously low. Most online survey websites tell their users up front that response rates of around 20–25% are to be expected, so for every 20 people you poll, expect that a mere 5–6 will respond. Sadly, this does not provide a very representative picture of your audience to work with.

Finally, a survey option that may represent the best of all possible benefits is the old-fashioned paper survey. For an in-class speech, where you need to know as much as possible about your audience to effectively create an audience-centered speech, individual paper surveys present extensive benefits. First, depending on the length of the survey, one can copy and paste the same set of questions multiple times on a single page, thereby keeping printing cost to a minimum. Second, an individual paper survey provides anonymity and/or confidentiality to the survey-taker, thereby negating the social desirability bias, or at the very least, keeps it to a minimum. Third, individual paper surveys, if handed out to a captive audience, capture the highest possible response rate by taking advantage of physical audience presence. While paper surveys require the survey-asker to tabulate and analyze the results, unlike the online survey method, it does capture a large sample, resulting in the best possible snapshot of your audience.

Survey Length

A question often asked by Introduction to Public Speaking students is: How long should my survey be? Length of survey is highly determinate on your speaking topic. Consider the number of questions needed for the following topics:

- Caffeine intake of college students
- Differences between political parties
- Depression and anxiety

The first topic might need, at most, 3–5 questions to determine the audience's average weekly caffeine consumption. The second topic, however, is much more nuanced, requiring perhaps up to 20 or more questions to determine the audience's political views, while the third topic is much more broad and complex, perhaps necessitating 100 or more questions (and likely a lot more time than one might have in a speech class).

In addition to one's topic, context plays a large role. Your audience demographics might determine how many questions. For example, if you are to speak to a group of first-grade children, five questions are all you could probably ask before their attention spans are taxed. You may also want to consider the amount of time you have to deliver your survey, the size of the audience you are surveying, and how you are delivering the survey. All these factors and more may require you to choose your questions wisely.

Designing Questions

As mentioned previously, you will need to decide early on if you need open-ended questions for individual feedback or closed-ended questions to provide more generalized information on your audience. Among closed-ended questions are the question types of either-or, multiple choice, and scaled questions, but each type carries with it a different set of considerations.

Either-or questions include true/false, yes/no, or any other pair of polar opposite responses you can think of, but should be used when you *only* have two available options from which to choose. Consider the following poor examples of either-or questions:

- What political affiliation are you: Democrat / Republican
  - *People are more likely to identify as having tendencies toward both parties or neither, requiring this to be altered into a multiple-choice question with more options.*
- What religion are you: Christian / Other
  - *This question implies that any religion other than Christianity is not worthy of being named, but rather, lumped into a general category, unintentionally insulting some members of your audience.*
- Would you consider yourself: Healthy / Unhealthy
  - *Consider the social desirability bias here—who would rate themselves as unhealthy?*
- How often do you exercise: All the time / Never
  - *There are many more options than this.*

If we altered those questions into better uses of the either-or question type, they may look like the following:

- Do you generally describe yourself as: Left-leaning / Right-leaning
- Do you consider yourself strongly religious: Yes / No
- I can recite the Bill of Rights: Yes / No

Notice how the questions leading the respondents to the answers posed are much more generalized, providing two equally attractive options from which to choose.

Multiple-choice questions are helpful because they allow you to provide your audience with a limited number of responses, but a poorly designed question might unfairly lead your respondents to answer in a way they normally would not answer. Avoid unintentionally inserting bias into the lead-in question or statement, and with your response choices, be sure to give each response as equal a chance of being selected as the others. Avoid inserting one improbable response for the sake of humor, because then people may choose that response in an attempt to be funny, at which point you have lost out on a data point from that person. Be sure you are not giving preferential wording to the answer(s) you want your audience to select. The more honest they are with their responses, the better you are able to tailor your message to them.

Scaled questions provide us with the best possible resolution for audience responses. We might ask the audience to place their knowledge or interest level on a scale from 1 to 10, and once the surveys are returned, we can analyze the results to provide an overall picture of that audience. For example, if, on a knowledge-level question, the audience surveys result in an average of 7.2, then we know they are reasonably knowledgeable already, requiring us to go a bit deeper with our topic than initially thought. Other uses of scaled questions include Likert Scale questions, which are questions that have responses on a qualitative scale of agreement, such as those having "Strongly Disagree" on one end of the scale, "Strongly Agree" on the other end, and "Neutral/No Opinion" in the middle of the scale. These types of questions are particularly helpful for determining audience attitudes, beliefs, and opinions.

However, as with any other type of survey question, be sure to keep any potential bias out of the question prompt, as well as the scale itself. For example:

> *Poorly worded scaled question prompt: "The president's speech last night was full of lies and deceit."*
>
> *Re-worded scaled question prompt: "The president delivered an effective and informative speech last night."*

In the first example, the survey taker knows immediately that the person who wrote the survey is not the president's biggest fan. For a fellow critic of the president, that could lead to an answer of stronger agreement than normal, and for a fan of the president, that could lead to greater disagreement than normal. By rephrasing the question as shown, the initial statement sets up a survey respondent with the best possible opportunity to agree or disagree, thereby capturing the most honest and accurate responses possible.

Question Types	
Open-ended	Describe how the thought of exercising every day makes you feel: ____.
Either-or	Do you exercise on a regular basis? ☐ Yes ☐ No
Multiple choice	How often do you exercise each week? A. Not at all B. 1–2 times C. 3–4 times D. 5–6 times
Scaled questions	Exercising is an important part of maintaining my health: Strongly Agree Agree Neutral Disagree Strongly Disagree
Checklists	What types of exercise do you engage in regularly (check all that apply)? ☐ Running ☐ Biking ☐ Hiking ☐ Weight training ☐ Yoga ☐ Team sports ☐ Other ________________
Ranking	Which of the following exercise types would you say you most enjoy? Rank in order from 1 (most liked) to 5 (least liked): ______ Running ______ Biking ______ Hiking ______ Weight training ______ Yoga

Figure 4.1. Types of Survey Questions

Maintaining Surprise

As we design surveys to test an audience's knowledge level or gauge their overall opinions and feelings about a certain topic, it is important for us to remember our general purpose in designing and distributing these surveys: to collect information. If, however, a survey effectively gives an audience the best parts of our information by unintentionally either informing them about our topics or by arousing their curiosity to the point where they pull out their phones to do a quick search, then why give the speech at all? Great surveys seek to collect information, not give it away before the presentation. Consider the following story, as told by a former student in COMM-101:

> *For my speech to motivate others to act, I decided that I wanted to persuade my audience to think more critically about stories they hear in the media, but to accomplish this goal, I decided it would be best to show them how easy it is to be fooled. So, I decided to give the time-honored Dihydrogen Monoxide (DHMO) speech. Of course, DHMO is just another name for water; however, in my presentation, I didn't reveal that DHMO is another name for water. Instead, I continued using the acronym DHMO and described what happens when someone comes into contact with DHMO in its gaseous state (a steam burn); 2) what happens with prolonged exposure to DHMO in solid form (frostbite); and 3) how there are "secret" government pipelines that carry DHMO beneath our very feet (water mains). After making my case for the dangers of this chemical, my audience, for the most part, was simultaneously disgusted and terrified, or at least, they were until I revealed that "Di" is the prefix for 2 and "Mono" is the prefix for 1, meaning 2 hydrogen atoms and 1 oxygen atom, better known as* H_2O *or water. At that point, my case was made and my speech was successful, but that would not have happened if I had asked a question on my audience survey like, "Have you ever heard of Dihydrogen Monoxide?" Someone would have looked it up, blurted it out, and the surprise would have been ruined. Instead, I asked my audience about things like their knowledge of chemistry or of Latin/Greek roots. Once I knew who those experts were, I was able to ask them to remain silent while I spoke, to maintain surprise.*

While it is perfectly acceptable for the audience to know a speech topic by reading a survey, be sure that your purpose remains focused on collecting information, not on giving the audience too much information in advance.

Survey Analysis and Usage

Once the audience has responded to the surveys and we have collected them, what do we do with all the data? One approach to survey analysis is to perform simple averages. Tally up the total number of responses for each question, and then divide by the total number of surveys returned. Multiply this by 100, and that gives us the raw percentage for that answer. For Likert Scale questions, simply assign a number to each response along the scale to determine the audience average along that scale.

As we continue working on the speech, audience survey results provide us with an excellent way to let the audience know how they measure up to the rest of their peers, which can create an effective way to relate to members of the audience. In other words, it tends to keep them listening. For example, if we were working on presenting information on outdoor activities in the summertime, we might insert a statement into the speech like, "According to my audience survey, 15 out of 18 of you like to go camping in the summer, while the remaining 3 would rather stay at a resort." Information such as this can be extremely helpful in relating the topic to specific members of the audience, but also, these statements help show people how their responses to the survey compare to others in the same audience, satisfying a natural element of curiosity.

Beyond inserting survey results into our presentations, the audience survey also helps us more specifically tailor the information we ultimately choose to use within the speech. If the speech starts to grow beyond the scope of time we have been given, then the survey provides us with a window into what the audience truly needs to know. For example, if the amount of time given is only 6–8 minutes, and we have enough information for a 10–15-minute presentation, then we would consult the survey results to determine more accurately what information could effectively be cut from the speech without negative impact to our central idea. Conversely, if we only had enough information to make 4–6 minutes worth of talking time, then we could also use the survey to determine what information could be expanded or elaborated on, based on what we felt the audience needed to hear the most.

Chapter Summary

After selecting and refining the speech topic, the next most important consideration is to determine how that topic will be received by the intended audience, for without such consideration, we may as well stay home and speak to ourselves in the mirror. This is the principle of audience-centered speaking, or the act of carefully and mindfully tailoring one's presented information to the knowledge levels, beliefs, values, and opinions of an audience. As a means to tailor our information to an audience in this manner, we must first start with collecting information from that audience. This data collection can happen passively (eavesdropping, public information, conversations prior to the speech, etc.) or actively (interviews, surveys, etc.), but ultimately, we must find out what the audience knows or does not know about the topic, and also, how they feel about the topic (attitudes, opinions, beliefs, values, etc.). Once we know what they know and how they feel about our topic, then we can work further to refine what information makes it into our presentation, as well as how we present it so that the audience memorably understands it as we originally intended.

Chapter 5

Gathering Information

"Research is to see what everyone else has seen and to think what nobody else has thought."

—Albert Szent-Györgyi

By this point in the speech-building process, we have selected our topic, refined it, drawn up some initial plans (general purpose, specific purpose, possibly ideas for main points to cover), and considered the intricacies of our audiences, but now is the time to add pizzazz to our speech, and that is done through research. At first glance, you might think, "Pizzazz and research? There's two concepts I never thought I would see together!" However, research is the process of systematically investigating a subject or topic area as a means to gather new facts and information, so in a sense, it is research that helps us make our speeches fresh, unique, innovative, and ultimately, interesting.

However, as mentioned earlier, in Chapter 1, looking for information in the Information Age is like trying to quench one's thirst by taking a drink from a fire hose. At least, that's generally how it feels as we begin the arduous task of gathering information to use in a speech. One of the main keys to effective research is to keep our specific purpose in mind as we begin to look. A great tip is to write out or print out the specific purpose and keep it next to us while we begin our quest for new and innovative information. Doing so will inevitably keep us on track and prevent wasted time or effort. For each piece of information we gather and each source we identify, we should consistently ask ourselves two important questions in addition to this consideration of the purpose: "Does this evidence support the goal of the speech?" and "Is this evidence important to and appropriate for this audience?" Lastly, a critical piece of advice is to begin early. As soon as the topic has been refined and we have considered our audience's needs regarding their knowledge and interest levels, we should begin gathering information as soon as possible. Of all the tasks involved in preparing an effective presentation, the two portions requiring the most time and dedicated effort are the research process and rehearsal or practice (covered in Chapter 8).

Where to Look

Let's face facts. When embarking on a research endeavor, most (if not all) of us likely head for the student's best friend: Google. While we will dedicate plenty of time to discussion of how to effectively, efficiently, and accurately search electronic sources, we would be remiss if we did not first discuss more traditional means of gathering information. There are times when it is actually more effective *and* efficient to use these means than what might seem faster and easier, so take some time to challenge yourself regarding these time-honored traditions of research.

Traditional Sources

Traditional (AKA, non-internet) research sources include:

- Books
- Magazines
- Newspapers
- Interviews with credible experts
- Peer-reviewed academic journals
- Documentaries

Note: All of the above *technically* can also be found by way of internet research. Books, magazines, and newspapers are all available online, as are many interviews with experts, academic journals (using your college library's search engines), and documentaries via sources such as YouTube or Netflix.

Popular Literature is defined as news articles, magazine articles, and other exposé pieces written by journalists who are either employed by the entity for which they write or are freelance contractors hired for a specific assignment. These pieces cover current events, profiles of people and places, highlight in-depth reporting, investigative reporting, or other items of interest to the general public. Popular, in this context, does not refer to how many people buy the magazine or read the article online, but for whom the material is written. If the intended audience is the "general population" for the purpose of providing news, entertainment, or information, then the article is considered popular.

stockfour/Shutterstock.com

In the not-so-distant past, all of the above sources were often considered automatically credible, but with more recent developments in communication technology (as discussed in Chapter 1), some of the above sources may require careful consideration. Take, for instance, the fact that anyone with a computer and internet access can publish a book. So-called "vanity publishers" such as Lulu.com offer users the ability to upload document files and have them professionally printed and bound. These organizations are referred to as "vanity publishers" because they were once reserved for authors who "couldn't cut it" in the traditional publishing market, but merely wanted to see their names on book jackets. However, more and more authors are finding this avenue of publishing a viable alternative, as self-publishing often offers authors a much higher percentage of royalty revenue. As this is considered, take into account that contemporary publishers may not as carefully verify information being printed in their books as was the case in the past. There may even be an unscrupulous motive for providing misinformation, such as driving book sales. Be sure to research author reputations and credentials, for in public speaking, the responsibility sits with the speaker to *show* the audience why a source should be considered credible. Simply stating that an author published a book is not enough to demonstrate validity.

Similarly, with respect to magazines and newspapers, an author of an article in the *New York Times* or *Time* may have automatic credibility, considering how widely known and respected those publications are, but at the same time, certain media outlets are widely known for their bias in publication. For example, it is widely known that *Fox News* is a predominantly conservative organization, while *MSNBC* is widely known as having a liberal bias. It is also helpful to know what other publications are associated with those larger parent companies. Rupert Murdoch, the current head of News Corp., the parent company of *Fox News*, also owns the *Wall Street Journal*, and upon further review of articles within that paper, one can easily see the alignment of bias with the parent company. Knowing these biases and how an audience might perceive them helps the speaker know what research to use and what to avoid. If an audience survey reveals that the audience is more of a left-leaning audience (slightly more liberal than conservative), then the speaker should probably avoid using sources like *Fox News*, and instead, look for the same or equivalent information via a publication that the audience is more likely to perceive as credible and trustworthy.

Trade and Professional Journals are published by and for specific industry insiders and professionals. Most often written by industry experts, but sometimes by journalists, these publications are often weekly or monthly and are designed to provide industry leaders and practitioners with trends, news, political analysis, commentary, and other information that specifically relates to their specific interests.

Federico Rostagno/Shutterstock.com

Interviews with credible experts are, for the most part, highly credible, but also come with the caveat that the speaker must know how an audience may perceive that expert. For example, if we were to find an interview with Dr. Phil published online, we would probably want to know whether or not the audience felt he was a credible source to use. Objectively, Dr. Phil McGraw is a credentialed psychologist, leading one to believe that his testimony would be accurate, but again, the act of communication with an audience requires that our audience *perceive* the testimony as credible for it to have a positive effect. Otherwise, we lose credibility with our audience and our communication falls upon deaf ears.

Finally, we turn our attention to peer-reviewed academic journals, such as *Communication Monographs* or the *Journal of the American Medical Association*. These periodic publications are among the most trusted and widely revered sources of information regarding credibility, and for good reason. The process of peer review makes being published in one of these journals a gargantuan feat for many would-be contributors. As soon as an article is submitted (often a research study or a theoretical article), the article is sent out to a team of expert volunteer reviewers, all of whom are renowned authorities on the subject for which they are reviewing. Those peer reviewers know nothing about the author of the article (called a **blind review**), and they proceed to read, fact-check, and provide suggestions for editing as needed. While the rate of rejection varies depending on the reputation of the publication, such rejection rates are generally high. It is not uncommon for an author to receive stacks of rejection letters before finally finding a home for an article to be published. By the time such an article achieves publication, we can rest assured that it has been carefully scrutinized by experts and edited thoroughly, making this source among the most credible possible.

Scholarly Literature
Generally written by people who are considered experts in their field, the authors of this type of literature are researchers, scientists, or professors. They usually are employed by universities, colleges, or other research institutions. Articles submitted for publication are peer-reviewed using a painstaking and thorough process that evaluates the article for accuracy, quality, and appropriateness for the publication.

Sergei25/Shutterstock.com

Although this section is labeled "traditional" sources, it is useful to note that all of the above can be found online if one knows where and how to search. Google Books and Amazon both provide helpful previews of books, most magazines and newspapers provide access to their articles free of charge, interviews with experts are often published online, and yes, even scholarly journals can be found online via the college library's website. However, such searching can be considered an art form, and as with any other art form, may require outside assistance. For that reason, it is highly recommended that you spend time consulting with your college reference librarians once you have a topic and general direction in which to begin your research. These highly trained and well-educated specialists exist for your benefit and should be utilized to not only uncover the most credible and beneficial information, but additionally, their expertise in knowing where and how to look for credible information, once tapped, can save enormous amounts of time!

Internet Sources

Okay, let's go back to what most of us will likely start with: a quick and easy Google search. However, as Abraham Lincoln notes on the following image, "Don't believe everything you read on the internet just because there's a picture with a quote next to it." Most, if not all, sources found online will require further review and careful consideration before accepting that source as the primary one we wish to cite within the context of our presentations.

Domains

A common misconception is that a website's **domain** (the letters after the "dot" such as .com, .org, etc.) cues us as to whether the information may be deemed credible or not. In 1985, the world saw its first .com domain, Symbolics.com. At this time, there were only six top-level domains in existence: .com, .org, .mil, .gov, .edu, and .net. During this period, for-profit corporations received the .com designation, non-profit organizations reserved .org, federal and state government entities used .gov, military branches used .mil, higher education institutions used .edu, and .net was generally reserved for networking purposes only, such as email servers or internet service providers.

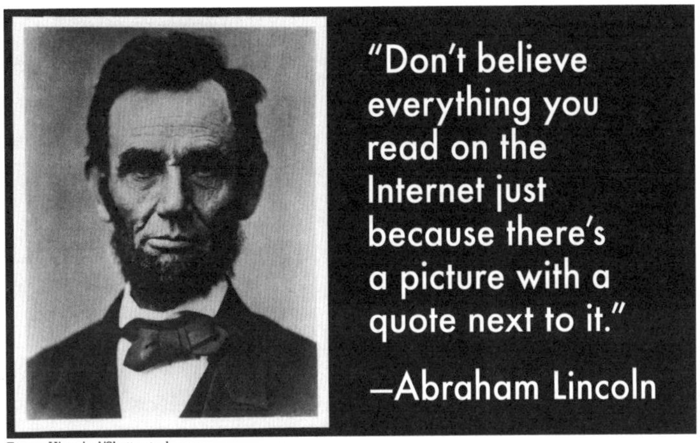

Everett Historical/Shutterstock.com

However, as the internet began to expand rapidly around 1991 and beyond, many of these were never enforced, especially those wishing to register with a .org domain. Today, anyone (without accountability or oversight) can register for a .com, .org, or .net domain, while .gov, .mil, and .edu continue to be more carefully regulated. A vast array of top-level domains have sprung up, almost as a cottage industry. Nearly every country has their own unique domain (.ca, .jp, .uk, etc.); there are topic, interest, and industry-specific domains (.cloud, .link, .club, .bike, .hotel, .church, etc.); and there are even domains aimed toward interpersonal relationships (.family, .dad, .home, etc.).

An example of why the domain should not be a primary factor in determining credibility can be seen in the website www.martinlutherking.org. In 1995, Grand Wizard of the Ku Klux Klan (KKK) Don Black, leader of the controversial white supremacist group Stormfront, purchased the rights to this site, along with mlking.org and mlking.com. Since then, Stormfront has resisted repeated attempts to take over the domain, both through court action as well as through outright purchase, and instead, continues to present information such as stating that the renowned civil rights leader had, in fact, been a drunken philandering con-man, or proposing that the federal holiday marking King's birthday should be repealed. If a student were to utilize information from this site without carefully verifying or vetting the information by checking sources, that student could end up with a potentially hostile audience due to the grossly inaccurate and factually incorrect information being displayed.

Who Runs the Site?

To vet such information on common websites, look for links marked as "About us" or "Hosted by ___." Explore those links, for they usually take the viewer to at least a brief paragraph explaining the mission of the organization and why they are in existence. Such links often exist for author names on popular news article websites, such as *Huffington Post* or *Time*, providing the researcher with additional information about selected authors. Often, if there is an agenda being pushed by that author, quickly Googling that author's name will return enough information to make an educated decision as to whether or not she or he should become a credible source in our speech.

What Ads Do You See?

In addition to vetting the author(s), look at the advertisements present on the site. Granted, in many cases, you might see automatically generated ads along the sides (sometimes marked as Google ads), and these are ads that are generated based on **cookies** stored on our individual computers. A cookie is a small piece of data sent by a website and stored in a user's web browser while the user is browsing. Every time the user loads the website, the browser sends the cookie back to the server to notify them of the user's previous activity on that site. Other ads, those that are permanently loaded to the specific site, tell us a lot about the organization presenting us with the information we are seeing. As the old saying goes, "money talks," which means that advertisers are paying revenue to the owner of that site for the opportunity to place their message amid the site's information, and as a result, depending on the revenue, an advertising company could easily sway the owner of the site to alter the tone or content of said information.

How Old Is the Information?

Next, be sure to look at the age of the information being presented, particularly if the information you are looking for is at all date-sensitive, such as technology-related topics. Take, for example, the following student account, as to why dates are important:

> *I was in a class my senior year, called Communication Consulting. In this class, we split into groups of 4 students each, and each group had to present a different consultation project summary. A group got up to speak before mine, and their topic was "How to handle yourself at an international business dinner." One of the students in their group was covering people from Eastern Europe and their customs, and as she started speaking, she said something that struck us all as odd: "First thing you guys need to know is that you never want to call them Russians, as they prefer to be called Soviets." Everyone in the audience started looking around at each other in disbelief, but she continued: "Also, don't talk about the Iron Curtain, the arms race, or Communism. Instead, talk about topics like Glasnost or Perestroika." Our eyes widened, because at that moment, we knew she was serious. We knew there was some pretty sketchy research here. Everyone started looking at our professor, whose face was turning redder by the minute. At the end of their presentation, the prof asked to see her sources, at which point, he pulled one of them up on the big screen, in front of the whole class. Imagine her shock when he pointed out that one of her sources, on the Soviet Union, was a snapshot of the* World Book Encyclopedia *from 1983!*

The student in this example failed to look for a date reference of any kind, and instead, accepted everything she read as contemporary fact, and in the end, she ended up feeling humiliated in front of her peers. Always check for a date, and if one cannot be found, consider moving on to another source that includes one.

Wikipedia

No conversation about research would be complete without everyone's favorite information villain, Wikipedia, which also happens to commonly be the #1 ranked search result, regardless of what information we are researching. The common argument against Wikipedia is that anyone can change information in any article at any time, so whatever information we happen to be looking at could be manipulated and false. While this is true, it only presents a small fraction of what really goes on behind the scenes of a Wikipedia article, so let's look deeper, using a hypothetical case study:

Case Study: "Asphalt Aaron"

Hi, I'm Aaron, and to say that I am passionate about asphalt paving is an understatement. It is my life, my livelihood, and all I care about. You might suggest I need a better hobby, but I wouldn't listen. One day, after work, I am surfing the web, looking up new and innovative advances in asphalt paving technology, when I decide to see what Wikipedia has to say about my passion, but lo and behold, there is no such article. Emboldened by this oversight, I take it upon myself to create one.

I then have to sign up to create the article in the first place, which presents very little difficulty, but then I have to learn the Wikipedia interface as a means to create my article and do it justice. Unfortunately, learning to create this article requires some advanced understanding of coding and programming lingo, but I am passionate about this, so I remain convinced that it is my duty to bring this article to life. Eventually, I learn my way around, craft a well-composed article on asphalt paving, and I submit it for publication.

At this point, the article goes to a volunteer editor at Wikipedia. Think, for just a moment, about the *type* of person who volunteers their time to edit articles for Wikipedia—for free. These people are the aptly named "grammar police" who are quick to point out inconsistencies and errors in our daily writing otherwise, so getting an article accepted by them could prove difficult. Many articles require sources to back up assertions, high quality writing, and uniqueness of topic to make it to the light of day, otherwise, they are swiftly deleted by these editors, who ultimately have the final say.

However, throughout a process of editing and revision back and forth between the editor and I, my article finally goes live. The next day, however, my mortal enemy, Concrete Chris, decides to play a cruel joke on me and edit my article to suggest that concrete paving is superior to asphalt. He signs up, enters my article, and makes the edits, proud of his work to undo everything I have done. At that point, I receive an email notification telling me that someone has edited my pet project. Given the amount of time and effort put into my article, I am likely to try to find a computer quickly to see what has been changed. As soon as I see my nemesis' writing, all I need to do is click a button to notify those same volunteer editors that the edit is disputed, at which point, my article reverts back to the last saved version prior to Concrete Chris' edits while the issue is resolved.

As we can see from this story (loosely based on real events), while it is true that anyone can edit a Wikipedia article, the process to do so is rather rigorous and regimented. Although this does not provide full accountability, this, combined with previous studies on the accuracy of Wikipedia, which show that it is just as accurate (if not more so) than print sources such as *Encyclopedia Britannica* (Giles, 2005), goes on to demonstrate the validity of utilizing it as a research tool.

However, it should be noted that Wikipedia is not considered an author, as it is an aggregate of information that has been compiled by millions of individual authors. For this primary reason, we should never quote Wikipedia as though it is a primary source. Doing so would be like reading a book from your college library, and then, in your speech, stating, "According to the library…" Wikipedia is merely a collection of information, not an author. What we want to use within the context of our speeches is not "Wikipedia," but the articles that are cited within a Wikipedia entry. For example, take a look at the following excerpt from a Wikipedia entry on the reliability of Wikipedia:

An early study in the journal *Nature* said that in 2005, Wikipedia's scientific articles came close to the level of accuracy in *Encyclopædia Britannica* and had a similar rate of "serious errors".[4] The study by *Nature* was disputed by *Encyclopædia Britannica*,[5] and later *Nature* replied to this refutation with both a formal response and a point-by-point rebuttal of *Britannica*'s main objections.[6] Between 2008 and 2012, articles in medical and scientific fields such as pathology,[7] toxicology,[8] oncology,[9] pharmaceuticals,[10] and psychiatry[11] compared Wikipedia to professional and peer reviewed sources and found that Wikipedia's depth and coverage were of a high standard. Concerns regarding readability were raised in a study published by the American Society of Clinical Oncology[12] and a study published in *Psychological Medicine* (2012),[11] while a study published in the *European Journal of Gastroenterology and Hepatology* raised concerns about reliability.[13]

Take note of the hyperlinked numbers, and we see a source cited for the first sentence. When we click on that number, we are taken to the following entry in the bibliography at the bottom of the article:

4. ^ a b c d e Giles, J. (2005). "Internet encyclopaedias go head to head: Jimmy Wales' Wikipedia comes close to Britannica in terms of the accuracy of its science entries". *Nature* **438** (7070): 900–1. Bibcode:2005Natur.438..900G. doi:10.1038/438900a. PMID 16355180. The study (which was not in itself peer reviewed) was cited in many news articles such as this: "Wikipedia survives research test". *BBC News* (BBC). December 15, 2005.

In our speech, this is the source we would want to cite for our information, such as, "According to a study done by the journal, *Nature*, in 2005…" However, even this should be verified. It is critically important to follow the trail to the original source, read it, and verify that the source truly says what the Wikipedia author contends. The last thing we want, as speakers, is to cite false or inaccurate information and end up with an audience member who knows that it is false, for that will be the person whose hand goes up first when it is time for questions!

Blogs

Since 1994, when Justin Hall created the first online journal while attending Swarthmore College (Chapman, 2011), weblogs, or "blogs" as we know them today, have become popular places for personal insights, journals, and information sharing.

Scotusblog.com is a blog started by renowned attorney, author, Harvard Law professor, and Supreme Court advocate Tom Goldstein in 2002. The blog has become a highly respected comprehensive source for what is going on at the Supreme Court. The blog contains commentary and analysis by credentialed and well-respected experts in the legal community. The blog is used by attorneys, students, and professors as a trusted resource.

Blogs can be written by anyone for any reason. They pre-date social media applications like Facebook, Instagram, and Pinterest, so many of them are simply people who wished at one time to communicate their thoughts to the world. When conducting a web search with Google, Bing, or any other search engine, you will likely have dozens, if not hundreds, of blogs appear in the search results for nearly any topic or search string. Blogs can be a single person's opinion, a scholarly journal of a researcher, or a collection of like-minded individuals sharing their perspectives on a topic. Major news outlets like the *New York Times*, the *L.A. Times*, and others, have blog sections in their publications where knowledgeable journalists and credentialed individuals are asked to opine on a subject or present deeply researched current event information. You must look carefully at blogs, just as with any website, and evaluate the accuracy, trustworthiness, and credibility of the author and the information presented before you use it as a source. Key questions you should ask when evaluating blogs include:

- What kind of blog is it?
- What is the overall purpose of the blog?
- Can you find the credentials of the blog author?
- Are there source citations and links to supplemental information within the blog?
- Is the blog current?
- Does there seem to be a bias to the blog (rhetoric, selective facts, etc.)?
- Does the information in the blog contradict information found in another source?

Just remember that not all blogs are created equal. Know your source before you use it to avoid the embarrassment of losing credibility with your audience.

Using Research in a Speech

When writing, an author who uses outside information has specific rules guiding the explicit citing of someone else's work. Whether utilizing MLA, APA, Chicago, or any other formalized set of citation and referencing rules, the guidelines are clearly laid out for an author. In verbal communication, such as a public speaking context, however, rules are not as readily apparent, if existing at all, but a speaker still has the ethical responsibility to let listeners know where certain outside information originated, so how is that accomplished?

As mentioned, in writing, the rules are clear. For example, in this book, so far, we have used APA style and formatting (APA, 2016), such as that example of an in-text citation. While styles like MLA and Chicago may have differing rules to format these citations, they all perform the function of letting the reader know specifically where to go look for more information, should something resonate with the reader. The in-text citations point to references, usually located at the end of a paper, chapter, or book, so that the reader can go look up the reference if she or he chooses. In a speech, the responsibility to let listeners know where information came from works a bit differently.

As a speaker delivers the message to the audience, there will be times where information will need to be supported by outside sources. At those moments, the speaker has an ethical responsibility to let the audience know where the information came from, just as in writing, but with a subtle difference. A speaker also has the responsibility of letting the audience know *why* the source should be perceived as credible. The reason for this is because a speaker, unlike a writer, does not have the luxury of providing an instantaneous way for the audience to pause the act of communication and look up the source in question.

This begs the question: How much information does a speaker need to share with the audience to demonstrate credibility? The answer, of course, depends on the audience, which is yet another justification for the speaker to get to know the audience as much as possible prior to the presentation. While this presents some difficulty in assuming how much information is enough, it is typically best to err on the side of caution and present more information, but not so much as to become distracting. Take a look at the following two examples:

> Oral citation 1: *"According to Dr. Shann Ferch, touch is an integral component in acts of forgiveness."*

In this first sample, the citation is too brief. As an audience member, presumably unfamiliar with the expert being cited, all we would know is that the person is a doctor, but we would not know his area of specialty. For all we know, Dr. Ferch could be a chiropractor, which does not suggest he knows nothing about the topic, but we definitely need more information. However, if the audience was familiar with Dr. Ferch's work, such as delivering a presentation to students and staff at Gonzaga University, then the first citation could be the perfect amount of information.

> Oral citation 2: *"According to Dr. Shann Ferch, author of the 2011 book* Forgiveness and Power in the Age of Atrocity, *published by Lexington Books, as well as professor of forgiveness and leadership studies at Gonzaga University, touch is an integral component in acts of forgiveness."*

In this second sample, the citation is way too lengthy. While it does provide ample information (in fact, it provides nearly the entire full citation one would see in a bibliography), by the time the speaker is done relaying all of Dr. Ferch's information, the audience has forgotten where this information is heading!

> Oral citation 3: *"According to Dr. Shann Ferch, a leadership professor and forgiveness researcher at Gonzaga University, touch is an integral component in acts of forgiveness."*

This third sample provides the perfect amount of information for the average audience unfamiliar with our source. By providing the audience with just enough information to establish the source's credibility, we effectively support the claim we are making with respect to our information. Commonly known and understood sources do not need much in the way of credibility, however. For example, a mainstream and well-known publication like the *New York Times* needs no initial explanation as to the credibility of the author, so the best rule to follow is to include only as much information as necessary to make the case for a source's credibility.

Another consideration to keep in mind as a speaker trying to relay the sources of research is to think about where to insert bibliographic information. There are generally two approaches to this: front loading and back loading. Take a look at the following samples:

> **Back loading:** *"More than 90% of our communication is sent through nonverbal channels, such as facial expressions, eye contact, vocal tone, posture, and gestures. Marketers are keenly aware of this fact and often manipulate actors in commercials to provide maximum persuasive effects. I found my information on nonverbal percentages from a book on public speaking by Hamilton Gregory, and I found the information on marketing in an article in* Time Magazine."
>
> **Front loading:** *"According to a book on public speaking by Hamilton Gregory, more than 90% of our communication is sent through nonverbal channels, such as facial expressions, eye contact, vocal tone, posture, and gestures. A recent article in* Time Magazine *suggests that marketers are keenly aware of this fact and often manipulate actors in commercials to provide maximum persuasive effects."*

In the back loading example, we can see that research information is provided up front, and the source for that information is shared later. In this type of citing, the audience is initially left to assume that the speaker created the factual information being shared. It is only after the source is revealed that the audience realizes that it is from an outside source. In the front loading example, we can see that, not only is the audience cued to hear that the information comes from outside sources, but it is also done in 11 fewer words, allowing a more conversational tone to develop.

Now that we have seen how to construct an oral citation, how do we know when and where to insert them? Generally speaking, any time we are relaying information to the audience that we gathered from an outside source, we want to give credit where credit is due. This is the rule we will follow the vast majority of the time, but there are certain, more specific instances where a citation becomes absolutely necessary:

- Any time you are using numbers: dates, statistics, total counts, etc. Never leave a number hanging without stating where it came from.
- Any time you state a testable, observable, verifiable fact, use your source citation to provide support for that fact. For example, "According to recent reports by NASA, there is evidence to suggest that another planet lies just beyond Pluto."
- Any time you are stating information that could be deemed questionable by your audience, use a credible source to back up your claim. Example: "Cleopatra lived closer to the invention of the iPhone than she did to the building of the Great Pyramid." According to whom?

While these guidelines provide a starting point for where, when, and how to cite your outside research, keep in mind that one of your goals as a public speaker is to remain conversational and engaging. If your speech begins to sound like a book report and subsequent bibliography, your audience may very well tune you out. Be sure to find ways to insert this information as support material, but remember to do so as conversationally as possible.

Thinking Critically About Information

To think critically about the information we use in a speech, we must learn to put in the effort and "leg work" to obtain the most accurate and up-to-date information possible. As mentioned previously with vetting our sources, there are times when we need to just as carefully review the information itself. To discern the difference between questionable information and credible information, we must train ourselves to watch for clues along the way.

- Is the information well supported, or is it based on hearsay? Hearsay is essentially rumor. If the information you are finding sounds like it might be true, but does not have sources to back up the claims, you might be looking at anecdotal evidence or hearsay. For example, it is a commonly held belief that suicide rates skyrocket on Christmas Day, and at first glance, this makes sense, partly because we have heard the claim anecdotally (or through hearsay) so many times, but also, because the rationale seems plausible. A 30-second Google search, however, produces credible information proving this wrong, as suicide rates peak in the springtime "because the rebirth that marks springtime accentuates feelings of hopelessness in those already suffering with it" (Burton, 2012, para. 3).
- Is the information based solely on the testimony of non-experts or on opinions alone? Beware of claims made by many sources of information that a product or service changed someone's life for the better. Be sure to read the fine print, which usually states something along the lines of, "Results not typical." Additionally, we should generally avoid using weblogs (AKA, blogs) for most intents and purposes. Blogs are rarely peer-reviewed, nor are the bloggers running them typically held accountable for misinformation. Of course, there are exceptions to almost every rule, including this one. Certain blogs may provide a wealth of information, particularly if the blog is written and managed by an expert in a particular topic-related field. Always take a few extra moments to double-check information found in a blog with outside sources. The extra effort will pay off in self-confidence that the information we are employing in our presentations is accurate.
- Are you looking at opposing perspectives? It is not enough to merely research one-sided information, because frequently, audience members will not be in 100% agreement with your topic, so it is important to know the opposition to a topic to be prepared to address it adequately. For example, if we were giving a presentation on stricter gun regulations, it is critical to research the positions of advocates for fewer restrictions and less gun control, even in a purely informational speech. Doing so provides a more well-rounded presentation, but additionally, there are times where expanding one's perspective can also create a much richer, more deeply layered message, relatively free from bias.

Using Outside Information Ethically

Plagiarism is defined as the practice of taking someone else's work and passing it off as one's own original work. However, plagiarism is not always so simple, as it can take several forms.

The first and most severe form of plagiarism is the practice of blatantly copying someone else's original work. While this practice is relatively commonplace in writing, blatant copying with respect to a speech actually presents *more* work, rather than reducing it. It is significantly easier to learn what to say in one's own speech by crafting it all along than it is to try to memorize someone else's "lines," similar to the way an actor memorizes a script. Additionally, memorization presents problems with delivering a speech conversationally, which we will discuss later, in Chapter 8.

Second, and somewhat less severe, would be the practice of piecing together others' works from multiple sources, without any sort of effort to synthesize these works into an original presentation. We might think of this as the copy-and-paste approach, but it also creates difficulty in delivery as mentioned above.

Third, and possibly most common, would be taking someone else's work and lazily paraphrasing it just enough to be considered not a direct or blatant copying of another's work. For example, if a source has the following statement: "Plagiarism is one of the greatest transgressions in all of academia and should warrant a public flogging," and the speaker changes it to, "Plagiarism is one of the gravest sins in education and deserves a public beating," then the speaker really has not created original work, but instead, has used a thesaurus to aid him or her in stealing another's ideas. While the words themselves were not completely stolen, the original ideas certainly were stolen. If the original source is not given credit, instances like this can constitute plagiarism.

Chapter Summary

Speakers ultimately have an ethical and moral responsibility to both their basic message as well as to their audiences to use credible and accurate information in the presentation of their messages. Supporting one's message with information in this fashion begins with critically evaluating the sources of one's information, followed by critical evaluation of the information itself. As the speaker delivers the message, the audience must be made aware of the outside sources that contributed that information, but furthermore, the audience must also know *why* those sources are to be perceived as credible authorities on said information. By following these practices, speakers build credibility and believability among their audiences, lending to the desired goal of making the message memorably understood as originally intended, thereby fulfilling the general and specific purposes of one's speech. Additionally, these practices help eliminate the scourge of plagiarism by encouraging ethical communication practices. Learning to research critically, evaluate information carefully, and communicate it clearly is an art form that, in the end, results in the creation of innovative, original thought, but also provides for the dissemination of ideas among others. For more information, please see Appendix H for the "CRAAP Test," a handy guide to evaluating information for use in academics (and life).

Creating an APA Reference Page

(based on guidelines from *APA*, 6th Edition)

General Guidelines

- All lines after the first line of each entry in your reference list should be indented one-half inch from the left margin. This is called hanging indentation.
- Authors' names are inverted (last name first); give the last name and initials for all authors of a particular work for up to and including seven authors. If the work has more than seven authors, list the first six authors and then use ellipses after the sixth author's name. After the ellipses, list the last author's name of the work.
- Reference list entries should be alphabetized by the last name of the first author of each work.
- For multiple articles by the same author, or authors listed in the same order, list the entries in chronological order, from earliest to most recent.
- Type out the journal title in full.
- Maintain the punctuation and capitalization that is used by the journal in its title.
    - For example: *ReCALL,* not *RECALL* or *Knowledge Management Research & Practice,* not *Knowledge Management Research and Practice.*
- Capitalize all major words in journal titles.
- When referring to books, chapters, articles, or web pages, capitalize only the first letter of the first word of a title and subtitle, the first word after a colon or a dash in the title, and proper nouns. Do not capitalize the first letter of the second word in a hyphenated compound word.
- Italicize titles of longer works such as books and journals.
- Do not italicize, underline, or put quotes around the titles of shorter works such as journal articles or essays in edited collections.

Books

Basic Format for Books

Author, J. M. (Year of publication). *Title of book: Capital letter for first word of subtitle.* City, State: Publisher Name.

Note: For "Location," you should always list the city and the state using the two-letter postal abbreviation without periods (New York, NY).

Edited Book, No Author

Author, J. M., and Author, A. B. (Eds.). (2016). *Title of book: Capital letter for first word of subtitle.* City, State: Publisher Name.

Edited Book with an Author or Authors

Smith, J. (2000). *Title of work.* A. B. Jones (Ed.). City, State: Publisher Name.

A Translation

Ulvang, M. (2016). *Title of translated work.* (J. M. Jones, Trans.). City, State: Publisher Name. (Original work published 1814)

Note: When you cite a republished work in your text (like the one above), it should appear with both dates: Laplace (1814/1951).

Edition Other Than the First

Author, M. E., Author, R. S., and Author, R. D. (1997). *Title of work* (4th ed.). City, State: Publisher Name.

Article or Chapter in an Edited Book

Author, A. A., and Author, B. B. (Year of publication). Title of chapter. In A. A. Editor and B. B. Editor (Eds.), *Title of book* (pages of chapter). Location: Publisher.

Note: When you list multiple pages in parentheses, use "pp." before the numbers: (pp. 1–21).

Multivolume Work

Smith, P. (Ed.). (1973). *Title of multivolume work* (Vols. 1–4). City, State: Publisher Name.

Academic Journals and Periodicals

Basic Entry

Author, A. A., Author, B. B., and Author, C. C. (Year). Title of article. *Title of Periodical, volume number*(issue number), pages.

Article in Journal Paginated by Volume

Author, H. F. (2016). Journal article title. *Journal of Samples, 55*, 893–896.

Article in Journal Paginated by Issue

Jones, R. (2016). Article title. *Journal Sample, 15*(3), 5–13.

Article in a Magazine

Smith, W. A. (2015, May 9). Magazine article title. *Magazine Title, 135*, 28–31.

Electronic and Online Sources

Article from an Online Periodical

Online articles generally follow the same guidelines for printed articles. Include all information the online host makes available, including an issue number in parentheses.

Author, A. A., and Author, B. B. (Year/Date of publication). Title of article. *Title of Online Periodical, volume number*(issue number if available). Retrieved from http://www.periodicalwebaddress.com

Online Newspaper Article

Author, A. A. (Year, Month Day). Title of article. *Title of Newspaper.* Retrieved from http://www.someaddress.com/full/url/

E-Book

Author, J. W. (n.d.). *Title of online book.* Retrieved from http://www.website.com

Kindle Book

Stoker, B. (1897). *Dracula* [Kindle DX version]. Retrieved from Amazon.com

Chapter/Section of a Web Document or Online Book Chapter

Author, A. A., and Author, B. B. (Date of publication). Title of article. In *Title of book or larger document* (chapter or section number). Retrieved from http://www.someaddress.com/full/url/

Dissertation/Thesis from a Database

Smith, S. (2008). *Title of dissertation.* Retrieved from ProQuest Digital Dissertations.

Online Encyclopedias and Dictionaries

Often encyclopedias and dictionaries do not provide bylines (authors' names). When no byline is present, move the entry term to the front of the citation. Provide publication dates if available or specify (n.d.) if no date is present in the entry.

Modernism. (n.d.). In *Encyclopædia Britannica Online.* Retrieved from http://www.britannica.com/art/Modernism-art

Online Lecture Notes and Presentation Slides

When citing online lecture notes, be sure to provide the file format in brackets after the lecture title (e.g., PowerPoint slides, Word document).

Jones, A. (2016). *Title of file* [PDF document]. Retrieved from Online Web site: http://www.webaddress.com

Smith, K. F. (2016). *Title of presentation* [PowerPoint slides]. Retrieved from http://www.webaddress.com

General Web Page

List as much of the following information as possible (you sometimes have to hunt around to find the information; don't be lazy. If there is a page like http://www.website.com/page.htm, and somepage.htm doesn't have the information you are looking for, move up the URL to the primary domain: http://www.website.com/):

Author, A. A., and Author, B. B. (Date of publication). *Title of document.* Retrieved from http://www.webaddress.com

E-mail

E-mails are not included in the list of references, though you parenthetically cite them in your main text: (E. Robbins, personal communication, January 4, 2001).

Nonprint Sources

Interviews, Email, and Other Personal Communication

Do not include personal communication in your reference list. Instead, parenthetically cite the person's name, the phrase "personal communication," and the date of the communication in your main text only.

(E. Jones, personal communication, June 5, 2016).

Motion Picture

Kennedy, K. (Producer), and Abrams, J. J. (Director). (2015). *Star Wars: Episode VII—The Force Awakens* [Motion picture]. USA: Lucasfilm.

Television Broadcast or Series Episode

Writer, W. W. (Writer), and Director, D. D. (Director). (Date of broadcast or copyright). Title of broadcast [*Television broadcast or Television series*]. In P. Producer (Producer). City, state of origin: Studio or distributor.

Single Episode of a Television Series

Writer, W. W. (Writer), and Director, D. D. (Director). (Date of publication). Title of episode [Television series episode]. In P. Producer (Producer), *Series title*. City, state of origin: Studio or distributor.

A Television Series

Smith, D. L. (Producer). (2016). *Cool drama show* [Television series]. Hollywood, CA: Columbia Broadcasting Syndicate.

Music Recording

Songwriter, W. W. (Date of copyright). Title of song [Recorded by artist if different from song writer]. On *Title of album* [Medium of recording]. Location: Label. (Recording date if different from copyright date).

Creating an MLA Works Cited Page

(based on guidelines from *MLA Handbook*)

General Guidelines

- Use double-spacing for each entry and between entries. Indent second line of each entry.
- Do not start entries with a number or a bullet.
- Alphabetize entries by first letter. (Don't categorize entries by media type.)
- Spell out months of three to four letters; use three-letter abbreviation for all others.
- Use italics for all titles of books, magazines, newspapers, movies, etc. (no underlining).
- Use quotation marks for titles of poems, short stories, articles, pamphlets, brochures.
- Use --- in place of author's name when it is the same as previous entry.
- Replace missing information with an appropriate abbreviation, such as *n.d.* for *no date* or *n.p.* for *no publisher* or *no publication date.*
- For online sources, include a location to show the source. Many scholarly databases use a DOI (digital object identifier). Use a DOI in your citation if you can; otherwise, use a URL. Delete "http://" from URLs. The DOI or URL is usually the last element in a citation and should be followed by a period.

Books

Basic Entry

Author's Surname, First Name. *Title: Subtitle.* Place of publication: Publisher (shortened), Year of publication. Medium of publication.

Single Author

Wollstonecraft, Mary Shelley. *Frankenstein.* New York: Penguin Classics, 2000. Print.

Two or Three Authors (List authors in order on title page; only first author listed with last name first.)

Jones, Jeff, and John Smith. *Title of Book.* New York: Publisher, 2004. Print.

More than Three Authors (List authors in order on title page; only first author listed with surname first.)

Jackson, Finn, et al. *Title of Book.* New York: Publisher, 2014. Print.

Editor with No Author (List title first, then list editor or editors.)

Title of Book. Eds. J.W. Smith and S. Jackson. New York: Publisher, 2008. Print.

Author with Editor (List author first and editor after title.)

Jones, Jennifer. Title of Book. Ed. Chase A. Smith. New York: Publisher, 2008. Print.

Sacred Text (Editors' and translators' names follow title.)

The New Oxford Annotated Bible. Ed. John Smith. 4th ed. New York: Publisher, 2007. Print.

Pamphlet or Brochure

"Donating to Charity." New York: Organization, 2008. Print.

Periodicals

Basic Entry

Author's Surname, First Name. "Article Title." *Journal Title volume.issue (year): pages.* Medium of publication (i.e., print, web, etc.).

Article in Magazine (Provide publication date and pages, but not volume or issue.)

Published monthly:

Jones, Debra. "Title of Article." *Publication May 2016: 24–34.* Print.

Published weekly:

Smith, Lisa. "Article Title." *Magazine Title 9 Jun. 2016: 01.* Print.

Article in Scholarly Journal

Jackson, Percy, and Skye Walker. "Article Title." *Journal Title 24.6 (2012): 27–29.* Print.

Article in Newspaper (Include section and page number after date of publication.)

Vader, Annie. "Article Title." *Newspaper Title 11 Jan 2015: B20.* Print.

Editorial in Newspaper (List title of article first.)

"Article Title." Editorial. *Newspaper Title 11 Mar. 2015: C20.* Print.

Article in Newspaper (Accessed through Database) (Include database name and date accessed.)

Kenobi, Ben. "Article Title." *Newspaper Title 10 Aug 2015: A20. LexisNexis.* Web. 2 Dec. 2016.

Electronic Sources

Basic Website Entry

Author Last Name, First Name. *Website Title. Site sponsor, Publication date or date last update.* Medium of publication. Date accessed.

Article in Newspaper (Include website name and sponsor.)

Amidala, Patty. "Article Title." *TheTimes.com. Generic City Times, 28 Nov. 2010.* Web. 2 Jan. 2009.

Entire Website

Organization Title. *Page Title. 4 July 2014.* Web. 21 Jan. 2016.

Page from Website

Binks, J. J. "Page Title." *Site Title. Organization Name, n.d.* Web. 20 Apr. 2016.

Article in Online Magazine/Newspaper

Windu, Macy. "Article Title." *Page Title. Site Title, 14 Jun. 2012.* Web. 3 Mar. 2016.

Home Page (Academic)

Jensen, John. "Page Title." *Dept. of Philosophy. North Idaho College, Spring 2016.* Web. 17 Apr. 2017.

Audio and Visual Sources

Video or Film (Emphasize specific director, narrator, and performer as necessary with "Dir.," "Narr.," or "Perf.")

Star Wars: A New Hope. Dir. George Lucas. Lucasfilm, 1977. DVD.

Podcast or YouTube

Organa, Lee. "Title of Video." Project: Report. YouTube, 9 Dec. 2014, Web. 19 Mar. 2016.

Miscellaneous Sources

Lecture or Public Address

Teplin, Linda. "Early Violent Death in Delinquent Youth: A Prospective Longitudinal Study." Annual Meeting of the American Psychology-Law-Society. La Jolla, California. March, 2005. Presentation.

Interview (Use *Personal, Telephone,* or *Email* to designate medium of interview.)

Jinn, Qui Gon. Personal interview. 11 Dec. 2001.

For assistance with either APA or MLA formatting, you may want to visit the following websites. Keep in mind that using online citation generators does not guarantee your page will be formatted correctly, as you must input the correct information in the correct field. Always check your final draft against the above guidelines.

- owl.english.purdue.edu
- www.easybib.com
- www.citationmachine.net

Chapter 6

Organizing Ideas

> *"Mostly I make lists for projects. This can be daunting. Breaking something big into its constituent parts will help you organize your thoughts, but it can also force you to confront the depth of your ignorance and the hugeness of the task. That's okay. The project may be the lion, but the list is your whip."*
>
> *—Adam Savage, Mythbuster*

While the process of preparing a speech or presentation begins with topic selection, followed by audience analysis and gathering research, something must be done with all that raw information. This is where learning to organize information comes into play. Remember, our goal as public speakers is not to memorize our speeches (scripted speaking), nor is it to improvise what we say, but to speak *extemporaneously*, meaning that we compose a plan for what we want to say, then learn that plan, create notes to keep ourselves on track, and then speak conversationally according to our plans.

To illustrate this point, take a look at the following example. How much time would it take you to memorize and repeat the following 41 letters: *y-m-s-e-c-p-h-e-i-s-a-u-t-o-b-m-u-s-o-a-t-e-p-o-r-x-e-e-n-n-o-r-o-t-a-a-i-n-i-z-g?* Unless you are one of those rare and fortunate individuals blessed with a photographic memory and can easily recall everything you see, then odds are, memorizing this seemingly random string of letters may prove nearly impossible. What if we eliminated the dashes and reorganized the letters as follows: *My speech is about extemporaneous organization?* Notice that none of the letters changed. We did not add, nor did we delete, any of the letters. All we did was place the letters into meaningful and manageable chunks. The same holds true for our information within a speech, whether we are to speak for 5 or 50 minutes. Besides our benefit of being able to recall our information, a well-organized speech is easier for an audience to understand and recall, which is, of course, the end goal for an effective communicator.

Audiences can quickly tell the difference between an organized and a disorganized speaker. Disorganized speakers often bounce between unrelated points, detour into irrelevant stories, lose their connection to the audience, and generally seem unprepared. Such disorganization, at best, turns away an audience's collective attention span, and at worst, can create a hostile, irritated, or insulted group of listeners. This is not to suggest that a little disorganization is bad, however. A speaker can be engaging, entertaining, and informative, and a hint of disorganization may almost seem welcome, as it makes the speaker seem more fluid and conversational. On the whole though, organized speakers are perceived as more knowledgeable, articulate, and believable, ultimately gaining the audience's trust and respect.

To commence our organization of information, we will use the process of **outlining** to arrange the ideas for our speech. Outlines help us arrange the larger ideas into a manageable order, but then also help us fill in those larger ideas with supporting information to help expand and refine our points. Outlines also help us ensure that our introductions and conclusions effectively frame those larger ideas into a memorable format for our audiences. The remainder of this chapter will be divided similar to the outlines you will create for your speeches. We will first cover the importance of introductions, followed by how to create the body of the speech, and then we will wrap up by discussing how to compose memorable conclusions. At the end of the chapter, you will find several helpful sample outlines that will serve as models for your later work.

Why Not Memorize?

Most novice speakers operate under the assumption that they should memorize their speeches, word-for-word, but that couldn't be further from the truth. The best speakers do not memorize, but rather *learn* their speeches in a process similar to learning directions from your home to somewhere unfamiliar. Rather than obtaining a map and memorizing step-by-step, turn-by-turn directions, we pull up a map and *learn* the major milestones we need to watch for. We get to know where to turn, roughly how far between turns, and what to look for along the way. Creating an outline is similar, as the outline acts as our roadmap, showing us the highlights we need to cover and providing us with just enough detail to get from start to finish, but it is up to us to fill in the rest with conversational speaking. In another analogy, think of a familiar story from your life, such as when you learned to ride a bike. Could you tell that story without creating an outline and note cards? Of course you could, since you *know* the story. You might tell it differently from one retelling to the next, but the highlights of the story (the main points, central idea, etc.) remain the same. Avoid memorizing speeches. Leave that to actors!

Similar to a written essay or composition, there are three main sections to an informative speech: the introduction, the body, and the conclusion. Each section serves an important purpose in crafting a memorable speech. These three sections align perfectly with a saying that is often credited to Dale Carnegie: "Tell them what you are going to tell them, tell them, then tell them what you told them." Though there may be disagreement on who said this quote first, there is broad consensus among communication professionals and educators that these three things are all you need to know to craft a memorable speech or presentation regardless of length and complexity.

Tell Them What You Are Going to Tell Them

This is the introduction of your speech—the opening component that serves to engage your audience and get their attention. The introduction has several specific roles to fill in your speech, and is generally no more than 10–15% of your speech and includes not only a glimpse for your audience of "coming attractions," but also grabs their attention and gives them a reason to sit up and pay attention. We will cover the introduction of your speech in great detail later in this chapter, but suffice it to say that if you don't give your audience a roadmap early in the speech, you will probably lose their attention before you even hit your first main point in detail.

Tell Them

This is the substance or content of your speech. This is the body, where you pour out the detail of your content and the research, support, and evidence to back it up. Organize this section into the most important points that you feel will most clearly and effectively deliver your message to your audience. This is the biggest section of your speech, consuming 70–80% of your speaking time.

Tell Them What You Told Them

Reiterate, summarize, and add punctuation to your speech. Like the introduction, the conclusion of your speech is only 10–15% of the total time of your delivery, but it is a critical piece in achieving highly effective results. Reminding the audience about the three important points you detailed in the body, and ending your speech with a memorable closing statement solidifies your message in the minds of your audience, and gives them a completed thought circle. Humans, by nature, hate to be left hanging. Abruptly ending a speech will nearly guarantee that your audience will remember less of it and for a shorter period of time—if at all.

The Purpose of the Introduction

Though the introduction is a small portion of the time allotted for delivering your speech, there is a significant amount of work being done. You will never get your message across to the audience if you don't first get their attention. Once you have their attention, you don't want to lose it, so you need to be sure that you "set the hook" by capturing their interest. Interest is great, but that's still not enough to insure they are going to listen to you. The audience needs to know that the information will be of use to them in some way, but they also want to know how you are invested in the topic and feel that you know something about the topic you are covering. Finally, your introduction is your first opportunity to deliver your core message to the audience (your thesis or central idea) and give them a preview of the most important elements of that idea. If your speech is less than 10 minutes long, that's a lot of things to accomplish in only a minute or two, so let's begin by dissecting the four major portions of the introduction: 1) Grabbing attention; 2) Relating to the audience; 3) Relating to yourself or establishing credibility; and 4) Providing the core of the speech, including a preview of what is to come.

Creating the Introduction, Step 1: Grab Attention

"It was a pleasure to burn." —Ray Bradbury, Fahrenheit 451

"It was the best of times, it was the worst of times." —Charles Dickens, A Tale of Two Cities

"Mr. and Mrs. Dursley, of number four Privet Drive, were proud to say that they were perfectly normal, thank you very much." —J.K. Rowling, Harry Potter and the Sorcerer's Stone

If you were to ask well-known authors, they will tell you that the opening line of a book is possibly the most important line in the entire book. Authors, like any other profession, need to make a living to maintain their profession, but unlike other careers, to do so and sell copies of their books, authors must be able to hook a reader within only one or two short lines. Most of us, when searching for a new book to read, look first at the covers, and then to the first line of the story, and if it sufficiently grabs our attention, we continue perusing the pages. However, if those first lines fall flat, the book jacket is closed, set down, and forgotten forever.

A similar phenomenon occurs within the first few seconds of a speaker's message. The first words uttered or the first actions that may communicate a message to an audience are absolutely critical. Borrowing from our previous analogy of a speaker to an author, imagine picking up a book that began with, "Hi, everyone. My name is Stephen King, and today, I'd like to share a really scary story with you about homicidal clowns." Such a book promises as much excitement as watching grass grow or paint dry, and most of us would likely put it down without hesitation. In a similar light, a speaker who gets up before an audience and "warms up" with a casual greeting, small talk, and an awkward announcement of the topic being covered, tends to put off most audiences' attention spans. Considering that the average human transient attention span (temporary response to a stimulus) is around 8 seconds long (Dukette & Cornish, 2009), a speaker has an extremely brief window of time in which to grab the audience's attention and subsequently, sustain it for the duration of the speech. In fact, the shorter the time the speaker has to speak, the more important this initial **attention getter** becomes. If you have been given a limited amount of time to speak, don't waste it on anything that does not further your purpose for speaking.

To grab an audience's attention, there are several time-honored techniques that continue to work today, despite all our various advances in technology, and they include: quotations, stories, rhetorical questions, providing shocking or unexpected information, and providing a compelling visual aid or demonstration.

Quotations

A great quotation, related to your speech topic, often provides wisdom from a well-respected source that says something valuable or profound in much fewer words than most of the rest of us can manage in much more. Quotes should be selected for their elegance, eloquence, or clever wit, but should always be selected for their relevance to your topic. Avoid using quotations that are fun or humorous, but irrelevant to the topic, for then the audience may feel cheated. Consider pulling quotations from websites, like BrainyQuote.com or GoodReads.com, literature, poetry, film, or even from people you know. Few lines are more valuable than a well-selected and well-read quote to kick off your speech.

Stories

Providing a story or a **narrative** helps a speaker frame the topic with which she or he is working. Stories provide us with a way to personalize a topic by helping audience members identify with the characters, events, or places within the story being told. Also, stories can be entertaining and engaging, further reinforcing the idea of an attention getter at the beginning of a speech. Stories can be "what if" scenarios that give us a hypothetical situation that helps paint a picture, but they can also be real-life anecdotes from ourselves, others, or even from fictional works like television, film, or literature. A good story should be selected for both its relevance to the topic, as with quotations, but more importantly, a story should resonate, or strike a familiar chord, with the audience.

Knowing the audience in advance becomes critically important when selecting the perfect story to illustrate or frame a point.

Asking Questions

"According to the U.N., roughly 2.7 billion people live on less than two dollars a day. Could you?" This is an example of a **rhetorical question**, or a question designed to evoke a thought or emotive response from an audience, but not be answered. Starting a speech with a question like the one above immediately cuts to the point, while simultaneously giving the audience concrete information and getting them to think about the main idea of the speech. Delivering a rhetorical question effectively requires skill, though, so it is advised that beginning speakers avoid using rhetorical questions until they gain a bit more experience. The question must be delivered slowly, deliberately, and followed by a brief pause that allows the audience to consider the question being asked. Too short a pause, and the audience does not have adequate time to think, while too long a pause runs the risk of having the audience actually start responding to the question. Finding the right balance of time can be an art form, but once perfected, gives the speaker a powerful opening tool for grabbing attention. In addition to this deft use of pause, the speaker should also follow up the question by showing how the rest of the speech will go into addressing the nature of the question.

Another form of question is the **quick poll**, where the speaker poses a question that requires little commitment from the audience, other than raising a hand. For example, using the topic above, the speaker might start by saying, *"Can I get a quick show of hands for everyone in this room who currently has a job?"* Gaining a small showing of audience involvement like this is a highly effective way to grab attention, and the critically thinking speaker can combine this technique with the rhetorical question to further drive home an important point. For example, following the question above, the speaker could say, *"Now, keep your hand up if you make less than two dollars a day at your job, just like the other 2.7 billion people in the world who make the same wages, according to the U.N."* Such strategies can be risky though, especially when they backfire, such as when audience members do not raise their hands as expected, or when a speaker ends up with more audience involvement than previously desired. Use discretion, and always have a backup plan.

Unexpected Information

"Just how big is a billion? To put this in perspective, let us look at a single second. Now, let's figure out how long ago one billion seconds was in our history. Any guesses? It is currently 2016, and one billion seconds ago takes us all the way back to 1984!" Using a set of statements like this to arrive at an unexpected conclusion would be a great way to kick off a speech explaining a concept like the federal deficit, especially if the speaker wished to put into perspective the scope of the federal budget. Statements such as these stimulate audience members' curiosity and keep them listening for more useful information. Another way of approaching this, but also combining the technique with gaining audience involvement, would be to have the speaker have every other male in the room raise his hand and then ask every third female in the room to raise her hand as well. Then, explain to the audience that, according to Change4Cancer.org, the statistics show that the people with their hands in the air represent the odds of being diagnosed

with some form of cancer. While sobering and somewhat macabre, such involvement causes the audience to feel invested and personally related to the topic being presented from that point forward.

Visual Aids and Demonstrations

While visual aids will be discussed in much more detail in Chapter 10, it is worthwhile to note here that visual aids can provide a speaker with powerfully gripping opening techniques. Additionally, demonstrations may provide an audience with a visually compelling reason to listen as well. A student delivering an informational speech on the martial art of tai chi may walk slowly and deliberately out into the center of the room, take a deep breath, and, in silence, begin performing various forms and poses inherent to the art. Without saying a word, such a demonstration effectively captures an audience's interest to hear more.

Refer to Current or Historical Events

> *"Last week we noted the founding of this great college in 1886, with a big celebration in the campus commons. The first students to graduate were nursing students, and they received their diplomas in 1890. Since then, there have been thousands of nurses who got their education right here."*

The above example refers to both the past and the present and would be a good attention getter for a speech by a student from this school who might be a nursing major, delivering a speech to her/his speech class about some element of nursing or the medical field. It is generic, yet personal, in that it immediately engages the audience and brings them personally closer to the topic and its relevance.

Creating the Introduction, Step 2: Relate to Audience

Once the audience members are primed and ready to listen because you have effectively hooked their collective attention, you must do something to promise that their investment in time and attention will continue to be worthwhile for the remaining amount of time you have the floor. This is done by explicitly and carefully relating your topic to the audience. This is not done on a general basis, but in a highly controlled and specific manner, wherein you demonstrate that you have carefully tailored your topic to their needs. This is where your previous audience analysis will become absolutely critical to your success as a speaker.

Consider this portion of the introduction the "What's in it for us?" phase, where you must clearly and explicitly answer this question for the audience. Rather than merely telling the audience why your topic should matter to them, *show* them how it relates to them. For example, if the speech topic was on early detection for breast cancer, you might state the statistics on how many women will be diagnosed with breast cancer in their lifetimes, but then, you might also state the odds of the men in the room being diagnosed as well, in addition to talking about how spouses and partners play a critical role in early detection, thereby connecting your topic clearly to each and every individual in the room.

Creating the Introduction, Step 3: Relate to Self (Establish Credibility)

Much research has been done on the concept of what Aristotle called "ethos," or credibility. You could be the most knowledgeable, well-educated, competent, caring, and trustworthy person on the planet, but if your audience doesn't know that, or if they perceive you as anything but those qualities, then all the work you did to prepare, all the passion and experience you have, will not matter. Your audience will stop listening or won't believe what you have to say.

After grabbing the audience members' attention and showing them how your topic relates to them personally, it is time to relate the topic back to yourself and answer the questions: "Why me? Why now?" To establish your credibility as a speaker, this step is absolutely necessary, because audiences want to know up front why they should trust or believe you as you deliver all subsequent information to them in your presentation. For example, you may be an expert or an authority on your chosen topic, but you may also have nothing more than a vested interest in the topic and a genuine desire to share the information with them.

The late James McCroskey, a communication professor at the University of Alabama–Birmingham, and Jason Teven, a professor at California State University, Fullerton, spent years researching the concept of credibility. They identified three components of individual credibility: competence, trustworthiness, and caring/goodwill (1999). This step in your introduction should provide three important pieces of information:

1. **Competence:** The degree to which an audience perceives a speaker as being knowledgeable or expert on a given topic. What are your credentials, if any, regarding your relationship with the information you are about to present? Have you researched the topic extensively? Have you taken coursework in this area of study? Does your work experience relate to the topic? Without giving the audience your resume and work history, make this connection clear, yet brief. Explain just enough to establish credibility.

2. **Trustworthiness:** The degree to which an audience member perceives a speaker as being honest and sincere. Why do you want to speak about this topic? What is your vested interest in conveying this information to your audience today? Do you have a specific inspiration that might show us why you care about this topic? What is your motivation?

3. **Caring/Goodwill:** The degree to which audience members perceive a speaker as genuinely caring about them. Let your audience know that you are speaking on this topic because you care about them and are concerned for their welfare and not trying to manipulate them or mislead them. If the audience members believe you have their best interest in mind, they may overlook imperfections in your style, delivery, or even other lingering competence and trust questions.

Here's an example of how you could relate a topic to yourself that combines these three aspects:

> *"I'm a biology major, so talking with you about the potential for a pandemic relates pretty heavily to my future career goals* (**Competence**). *Pandemic diseases fascinate me, which is why those goals include pursuing a career in medical research* (**Trustworthiness**). *I believe that we should all have a basic understanding of what a pandemic flu could do to us as a society, so that we can better prepare ourselves for it, when the next pandemic does strike* (**Caring/Goodwill**)."

Be careful with this step, though. Try not to seem boastful or arrogant regarding your qualifications. Instead of stating, "I have a Ph.D. in this subject, so I'm the most highly educated person in this room," you might state, "I have extensive training and education on this subject, and since it was the topic of my doctoral studies, I feel well prepared to share some of my findings with you today." Again, keep this section relatively brief, but long and detailed enough to provide the audience with a reason to trust you as their speaker for this particular message.

Creating the Introduction, Step 4: The Core of the Speech

The last step of the introduction before we transition into the body of the speech involves showing the audience what they can expect to hear throughout the body. The core of the speech can be broken down into three parts: the central idea (thesis), the specific purpose, and the preview of main points. For novice speakers, this step may seem at first glance to be a bit repetitive—and it is. The thing about human listeners is that we are remarkably inept at remembering what we hear, so effective speakers know to cover their most important points at least three times throughout a speech. Showing the audience this core in the introduction is the first point at which you will share your central idea and main points, but it won't be the last.

Central Idea

Imagine collecting all of the information you are about to present to your audience, placing it into an imaginary pot, and heating it up to a boil. After a while, you have boiled all those ideas down into just one declarative sentence, and that sentence is your central idea. Another way of looking at this concept is by asking yourself what one piece of information is more important for your audience to know and remember above all other information. Your central idea should be able to tie together all of your main points and their supporting points, for everything throughout the rest of your speech points to this central idea. Still another way of looking at it is to think of it as your thesis statement. The following examples show you what a good central idea might look like, in comparison with central ideas that need a bit more revision:

> **Needs work**: *"How to shoot a basketball."*
>
> **Why**: First, this is an incomplete sentence. Second, it makes no assertion or declaration. Third, it more resembles the topic of a speech or its title than a central idea or thesis.

Better: *"Learning how to shoot a basketball may seem difficult but can be perfected through practicing fundamental techniques."*

Why: This is now a complete sentence and makes an assertion that can be proven or disproven through research and fact. As an audience, we can expect to hear the speaker talk about the difficulties of learning how to shoot, fundamental techniques, and how we might incorporate those into practice.

Specific Purpose

After stating your central idea, it is a good idea to let your audience members know what your specific purpose will be. Remember that we discussed how to move from a general purpose ("To inform") toward a specific purpose ("To inform my audience about the benefits of practicing mindfulness") in Chapter 3. This is the point in your speech where you will try to work this specific purpose into your message as a means to let the audience know what they can expect to learn from your presentation.

We can use the basketball example from above to illustrate how the central idea and specific purpose might sound together:

> *"Learning how to shoot a basketball may seem difficult but can be perfected through practicing fundamental techniques, so today, I would like to inform you about how to develop the perfect jump shot."*

In most cases, the specific purpose will naturally roll off the tongue after asserting the central idea, but essentially, its purpose in the speech is to show the audience what they can expect to hear.

Preview of Points

In the final step of the introduction, we may consider this as the "tell them what you are going to tell them" stage. After relaying your central idea and your purpose in speaking with this particular audience, you will then *briefly* tell the audience what points they can expect to hear about during the following presentation. Note the keyword, "briefly" here. An effective preview can often be accomplished with a single sentence, but rarely should a preview require you to say more than three sentences or so.

The purpose of the preview is to provide the audience members with a set of mental bookmarks to organize your information in their minds. This way, as you speak and transition between your main points, the audience members effectively know what to expect and this knowledge maintains their attention spans. Additionally, this step proves to the audience that you are well prepared and organized, further cementing your credibility as a speaker.

Example of an effective preview, beginning with our earlier central idea and specific purpose statements:

> *"Learning how to shoot a basketball may seem difficult but can be perfected through practicing fundamental techniques, so today, I would like to inform you about how to develop the perfect jump shot. I will first cover the importance of a strong stance,*

then secondly, I will show you the steps of an effective shot, and finally, I will talk about methods for practicing to improve your accuracy."

Notice that the speaker in this case adds certain words to demonstrate to the audience the order in which these points will come: "I will *first* cover...*secondly*, I will show you... *finally*, I will talk..." Including these verbal signposts continues organizing your points to make them more memorable later on.

The purpose of an introduction is threefold: 1) orient your audience to your topic; 2) set the tone for the remainder of your speech; and 3) hook their attention and show them that their investment of time and energy spent listening to you will be worth it in the end. An effective introduction for a speech that is 6–10 minutes long will likely take you about 1½–2 minutes to deliver. Obviously, time will vary depending upon the overall length of your presentation, as an hour-long lecture may require much more time than that to effectively orient audience members to your information. Great introductions fulfill these purposes without giving away too much of the "good stuff," which you keep in your back pocket until the body of the speech, which is our next stop on this tour of speech composition and organization.

Composing the Body of the Speech

The body of the speech will likely comprise about 80% of your total speaking time or more, depending on the length of time given to speak. Depending on your learning style and approach to writing, it might be beneficial to compose the introduction and conclusion sections of the outline after you complete the body. For some, it is easier to summarize and introduce content once it has been constructed. As speaking time lengthens, that percentage will increase, but for the most part, 75–80% of your speaking time should be devoted to the body of the speech, for this is where the bulk of your information is placed. As such, it is important for us to discuss how to organize that information.

The first place most speakers start when composing the body is with devising the main points. On average, most people can comfortably take in about 2 to 7 main points in a presentation, but a good place to start with a classroom speech is with 3 points. Three points provide a variety of information without overwhelming the audience, but at the same time, keeps information manageable, given the average classroom speech time limits.

As main points develop, it is important to keep certain guidelines in mind, as these guidelines will not only develop a higher quality oratory but will help the speaker manage information to be presented. The first guideline to remember is to restrict each of your main points to a single concept or idea.

Don't: *Main Point I: Engineers are important to our society, but the role of the engineer is one of the least understood.*

Do: *Main Point I: Engineers are important to our society.*

Main Point II: The role of the engineer is one of the least understood.

Avoid combining too much information into a single point when a point could effectively be split into two main points. Additionally, your main points should be expressed using complete sentences, similar to your central idea. A main point makes an assertion that subpoints will then add information to support.

As you arrange your information, you will need to consider the order in which it is presented. Keep in mind the **primacy effect** and the **recency effect**. Listeners have their best recall for information presented first (primacy) and last (recency), while information in the middle is less likely to be recalled later. Therefore, place the most important information for your audience at the front and/or closer toward the end of the body for better retention.

There are several options available for how to arrange your information, and each should be considered as you determine the best order for your particular topic:

- **Chronological Pattern:** In this organizational pattern, you arrange your information in a time-based sequence. If you are presenting anything historical, this pattern often makes the most sense, but you might be teaching kids how to make chocolate chip cookies, in which case, your information could be presented in a thorough step-by-step breakdown that follows a sequential order.

- **Spatial Pattern:** Using this format, you would arrange your information according to physical proximity to one another, such as in explaining how an internal combustion engine operates. In such a speech, you might move from the bottom to the top of the engine, or from the inside to the outside. Such a pattern could also be helpful when trying to inform new students on where to find services on campus.

- **Cause-Effect Pattern:** In this speech pattern, you might want to show the relationship between certain causes and their effects. For example, you might want to discuss the topic of drug addiction by presenting three unique stories and showing the audience what caused their addiction, as well as the effects it had upon their lives.

- **Problem-Solution Pattern:** A pattern frequently used in more persuasive speeches, with this pattern, the speaker presents a problem, followed by a solution to that problem. In an informative speech, the speaker could break up each main point into a problem and its corresponding solution, followed by another problem and corresponding solution for the next main point.

- **Topical Pattern:** In one of the most common patterns found within informational speeches, this pattern involves breaking up your topic into smaller topics, such as seen in our previous example of learning how to shoot a basketball. This is often the "default" pattern when none of the others seem to be a better fit.

Once you have your main points selected and written up, it is time to start thinking about supporting points, nested beneath each main point. To illustrate this portion of speech composition, let's use a sample speech topic of examining various classes one could take in communication studies, wherein the central idea for the example is: *Communication is a diverse field of study that touches nearly every portion of everyone's daily lives.*

Main Point I: *Public speaking provides us with a way to learn about how to communicate in front of groups.*

Main Point II: *Interpersonal communication gives students the opportunity to learn about one-on-one communication in a variety of contexts.*

Main Point III: *Intercultural communication courses allow us to explore how our culture and background affects the way we interact with one another.*

At this point, we need to take each of our main ideas (underlined) and break them down further in an effort to expand these ideas and add supporting material. Notice that each main point is related closely to the central idea, arranged in a declarative assertion, providing us with the opportunity to "prove" or support that idea with research.

For the first main point above, we might break it down like so:

Main Point I: *Public speaking provides us with a way to learn about how to communicate in front of groups.*

A. *Most of us suffer from varying degrees of public speaking anxiety, requiring us to learn how to overcome this anxiety so that we might effectively communicate our ideas with others.*

B. *Many of the lessons we learn in public speaking impact our ability to write, as well as interact with people on a daily basis.*

Note

As a rule of outlining, you must have a minimum of two subpoints, or else a single subpoint may then become an additional main point. You cannot have a solitary subpoint.

Notice that each of our supporting points (subpoints) is outlined using a capital letter, whereas main points are indicated by Roman numerals (I, II, III, etc.). If we needed to break down our supporting points further, we would add another indentation and begin them with a numeral (1, 2, 3, etc.).

Also, each supporting point falls within the topical area of our main point, rather than becoming another main point of its own. While the other two main points are related to other fields of communication studies, these two subpoints relate directly to the study of public speaking, demonstrating how they support the main point of public speaking.

To continue our example, let's take a look at how the other two main points can be broken down:

Main Point II: *Interpersonal communication gives students the opportunity to learn about one-on-one communication in a variety of contexts.*

A. *Interpersonal communication may include interaction with friends, family, romantic relationships, and even coworkers.*

B. *Learning about interpersonal communication combines the fields of psychology, sociology, and communication theory into a fascinatingly complex and interwoven area of study.*

Main Point III: *Intercultural communication courses allow us to explore how our culture and background affects the way we interact with one another.*

A. *Culture goes much further than merely ethnicity or nationality, as many of us might initially think of when considering our culture.*

1. *Gender affects listening ability.*
2. *Age affects relevance to certain topics.*
3. *Religious preference may affect one's internal priorities.*

B. *Learning about one's own culture provides a greater foundation from which to study others' cultural backgrounds.*

Transitions

As your outline continues to fill in with main points and supporting information, you should begin seeing how your information "flows" together. However, before going much further, we need to consider the elements of speech composition that help tie each of these various points together seamlessly, and those are your transitions. Ideally, transitions should be conversational, so as to make the speech feel effortless as your audience listens, and at the same time, must guide and direct listeners toward where your information is headed. One of the most obvious ways to do this is to explicitly announce that you are transitioning to a new point: "For my second main point, I would like to cover…" However, you should avoid doing this. It sounds mechanical, stiff, and adds a proverbial speed bump to the flow of information. While effective and clear, as mentioned, you want your transitions to be seamless and conversational.

One helpful technique for transitioning between points involves creating a single sentence that links prior information with a preview of upcoming information, often called a **bridge**. To do this, create a sentence with two parts, or clauses, where the first half of the sentence is a summary of whatever was said last, and the second half of the sentence provides a brief preview of where you are headed next. For example:

Main Point I: *Public speaking provides us with a way to learn about how to communicate in front of groups.*

A. *Most of us suffer from varying degrees of public speaking anxiety, requiring us to learn how to overcome this anxiety so that we might effectively communicate our ideas with others.*

B. *Many of the lessons we learn in public speaking impact our ability to write, as well as interact with people on a daily basis.*

Transition: *Speaking in front of groups can truly be nerve-wracking, but there are times when speaking to just one person can be equally daunting.*

Main Point II: *Interpersonal communication gives students the opportunity to learn about one-on-one communication in a variety of contexts.*

In this example, we can see that the first half of the sentence, "*Speaking in front of groups can truly be nerve-wracking...*" summarizes the supporting point the speaker just made, while the second half of the sentence, "*...but there are times when speaking to just one person can be equally daunting*" previews the next point regarding interpersonal communication studies. As your public speaking skills develop, these types of transitions can easily become second nature to you, and you may even be able to compose and use them on the spot!

Another form of transition is called the **signpost**, and just as with an actual signpost on a road, these phrases signal listeners, in a literal or explicit sense, where you are taking your information. For example, if your preview of points states that your speech will inform your audience about: "First, public speaking, second, interpersonal communication, and third, intercultural communication," then between each of those main points, you could signal where you are headed by inserting a signpost such as, "Moving on to our second topic of the day..."

Finally, the last transitional device for us to cover is the **spotlight**, which we can think of as similar to the eye-catching headline on a viral social media article: "What this public speaking class taught me was more important than anything I had ever learned before." Note that this sentence builds curiosity through suspense, but at the same time, spotlights the upcoming information as being about public speaking.

Signal the End

The final transition of your speech, as you conclude your last supporting point within your final main point, must cue the listeners in your audience that your speech is about to conclude, and we refer to this as **signaling the end**. One of the simplest and most obvious ways to signal the end is to state, "In conclusion..." Don't do that. As with mechanical, robotic, and awkward transitions, you probably cannot imagine using "in conclusion" in daily conversation. If you did, you probably would not be invited back into those conversations in the future. Instead, get creative! Many speakers choose to employ a time-related reference, such as "I could go on all day, talking about all the benefits to taking additional communication classes, but my time here is limited." Some speakers choose to employ a more creative and topic-based approach, such as a student's speech on how to build a fire, where he stated, "Now that I'm done talking about extinguishing your fires, it's time to extinguish this speech." Adding creative touches like this, especially near the conclusion of your speech, often works well among listeners, considering that they have just put in a lot of mental effort in digesting all of your presentation's unique and innovative information.

A great way to gather end signals in your daily life is to pay attention to your various instructors, as they near the end of each class session. What is it that they say, that cues everyone's backpack zippers to start unzipping, books to be closed, and materials to be put away for the day? Sometimes, such statements are very subtle, such as, "As you all leave here today..." (which cues us that it is almost time to go), and other times, they may be more explicit. Either way, they can give you great creative fodder for your own speeches.

Concluding the Speech

The conclusion is written out in a highly similar fashion to your introduction, so you might be tempted to ask, why the repetition? Remember, most of us make relatively poor listeners, in that we are only capable of capturing and retaining portions of what we hear, and that fact is only multiplied by increasing the length of a speech and depth of material being presented. Signaling the end cues your listeners to prepare for your concluding remarks, and so the conclusion essentially represents your last opportunity to reinforce the most important portions of your speech, which includes your central idea, restating your main points, and leaving the audience with a memorable statement, or clincher.

Restate Your Central Idea

In many cases, immediately after signaling the end of your speech, you can flow straight into restating your central idea, and many speakers restate it word-for-word or *verbatim*. However, if this "feels" too repetitive for you, and you are concerned about your audience feeling the same way, paraphrase it in a slightly different verbiage, but be careful not to change the meaning of the central idea. Be direct and clear, so that the audience knows, without a doubt, what the primary idea of your speech has been.

Recap Main Ideas

Following a restatement of your central idea, your conclusion should have a recap of your main points. This is basically the "Tell them what you told them" portion of your presentation. Again, even though it may feel repetitive to preview your three points in the introduction, detail those points in the body of the speech, and recap the main points yet again in the conclusion, remember that this repetition is for your listeners' benefit. The recap drives home your most important points one last time, so make it count. This summary of your main points should be abundantly clear, yet brief, and never include new information at this point. An example of an effective recap of main points, based on our prior example is (main points identified for reference):

> *We now know that 1) public speaking helps us with our confidence when talking to groups, 2) interpersonal communication helps us with our daily interactions, and 3) intercultural communication helps us learn how to interact with people from different backgrounds than ourselves.*

Clincher

Following this brief recap of your main ideas, we need to find a way to close out the speech. Ideally, our last few statements should reinforce the central idea you just reminded your listeners of only moments ago, as well as provide some form of verbal punctuation, letting the audience know beyond any doubt that the speech is now done. You also are providing closure for the audience, completing a thought circle, if you will, by leaving them with a feeling of completion and not confusion. A **clincher** is similar to an attention getter but at the end of the speech instead of the beginning. This last statement could very well be the last thing the audience remembers about your message, so make it count!

An effective clincher can be accomplished using a variety of methods:

Use a Quotation

Finding great and powerful quotes to illustrate your topic but also reinforce your central idea is as good a way to close the speech as it is a technique to introduce it and grab attention. For example, in our prior speech example, we could end it as follows:

> *I would like to close today with the words of composer John Powell, who said, "Communication works for those who work at it."*

Use a Narrative

Speakers often begin their introductions with a story that illustrates one of their points or the central idea. If you are using this technique, consider utilizing a **story split**, which is where you introduce the story in the beginning of your speech, but then save the dramatic ending for the conclusion. For example, using our earlier example, let's say that the story in the beginning of the speech talked about a student who walked into the first day of his speech class, nervous and feeling sick to his stomach because of extreme anxiety. Such a story could have been used to help students in the audience to relate with the character in the story, especially the extreme nerves the student experienced. Then, in the conclusion, we could end the story as follows:

> *Remember the deathly afraid student from my story in the beginning of this speech? I'm proud to tell you all that I was the student in this story. Today, I teach public speaking, for I learned how important it is to connect the passion behind my message to the power of the human voice. You all hold that power and potential in you today.*

Reference the Introduction

In addition to story splits, think of how you can bring your speech around full circle to whatever you said within your introduction. If it was a quote, consider bringing the audience back to the wisdom from that quote, or even consider sharing another quote from the same person. If it was a startling fact or statistic, how can you bring their attention back to the significance of that fact? Referencing the introduction helps put your entire message into a nice, neat package for them to remember.

Important Guidelines for Conclusions

- **Avoid lengthy conclusions.** A good, effective conclusion should probably not take longer than a minute to a minute and a half. There are, of course, exceptions to this, but use your discretion.
- **Never include new material.** The conclusion is to recap your points and reinforce your central idea, so there should not be any additional information here.
- **End strong.** Many newer speakers experience difficulty with strong conclusions, as they are so excited about the prospect of being able to sit down and finally get out of the spotlight that they rush it. Others fail to effectively practice the delivery of their closing lines and struggle to find the right tone, usually resulting in the speaker uttering a desperate, "Thank you" or "That's all, folks." This is the public speaking equivalent of an acclaimed author placing "The End" at the conclusion

of an award-winning novel. It is unnecessary, for if the conclusion has done its job, the audience will automatically know the speech is over.

Chapter Summary

Creating an outline provides our speech with a skeleton. We could just as easily switch out the metaphor for any of the following: scaffolding, framework, or roadmap. All of these essentially make the same point. An outline provides us with a foundation from which to prepare our spoken remarks. The outline does ***not*** represent a transcript of what will be spoken, though. Creating a transcript for a speech is something one would employ for a memorized or scripted talk, not an extemporaneous speech, which is the focused style of speaking within this book. Extemporaneous speaking, if you recall, is one in which we start with a basic plan (the outline) and then prepare for free-flowing, yet guided conversation with our audience using that outline as our plan.

The outline covered in this book uses a five-step process: introduction, three main points, and a conclusion. Within the introduction step, there are four primary components: 1) the attention getter, 2) relate to audience, 3) establish credibility or relate to self, and 4) the core of the speech, consisting of our central idea, specific purpose, and preview of main points. The body of the speech consists of three main points, each of which is supported by a minimum of two subpoints, and between each main point, we employ a smooth and seamless transition. The conclusion of the speech consists of three parts: 1) signal the end, 2) briefly recap the main points, and 3) conclude with a clincher that reinforces the central idea.

Outlines should be written in such a way as to capture the essence of what you intend to say to your audience. Ideally, you create an outline for a speech that could be redelivered to multiple audiences over great periods of time. While the phrases you use and elaborations of points may differ slightly, the outline is what provides us with the core of that presentation, so that we can effectively deliver the same essential information to a variety of audiences.

Activity

Power Statement

The next time you are rehearsing your closing statement, consider trying this activity. As you speak your concluding lines, close your eyes and imagine yourself pounding your fist on the podium with each and every word. As you do so, you will notice that your vocal rate slows down, you dwell a bit longer on each word, and you utter the words with more strength and power. During your speech, don't actually hit the podium, but do so in your mind, as a means to remind yourself to slow down and add verbal punctuation.

Sample 1A: Speech to Inform

Name: Cassidy Kobialka

Audience Analysis

Answer in complete sentences and use examples from your audience analysis questions.

A. How much does your audience already know about your topic and how will you design your speech regarding their level of knowledge? **No one could define for me what an engineer does, so I'll have to cater my explanations to this group's basic knowledge level.**

B. How much interest did the audience have in your topic? How will you make the topic interesting to them? **Over 30% of my class is interested in the social sciences, so they have not thought about engineering, but we are all still considering our career choices now.**

C. What is your audience's attitude regarding your topic? How will you address that attitude in your speech? **Most of my audience considers engineers to be nerds. I will show them the wide variety of professional careers that engineers go into to dispel this myth.**

D. How will the audience demographics (not what you learned on your Audience Analysis) impact the development of your speech? **We have more females than males, and engineering is usually considered a "guy" career.**

Title: *It Ain't Rocket Science!*

General Purpose: To inform

Specific Purpose: To inform my audience about the career of an aerospace engineer

Introduction

A. **Grab Attention:** Have you ever wondered what an *aileron* does or what a *winglet* is? Have you ever heard the term "transonic" and wondered what it means?

B. **Relate to Audience:** Okay, I know what you're thinking—what the heck is she talking about? Or maybe you're thinking, no...not really—all of that sounds just too complicated. Well, to tell the truth, this stuff "ain't rocket science!" You could say it takes one to know one. Those strange terms are actually important to you, too, but you just don't know it yet.

C. **Relate to Self (Establish Credibility):** Well, I "ain't no rocket scientist" myself, but considering the fact that five of my family members are engineers, I feel qualified to talk to you about this career. Don't worry, that doesn't mean I'm going to explain what an *aileron* does or what a *winglet* is. That stuff I'll leave to the rocket scientists. I do think I want to become an engineer, however.

D. **Central Idea:** Aerospace engineering is one of the most progressive, challenging, and rewarding fields that can be studied today.

E. **Specific Purpose:** Today, I would like to inform you all about the career of an aerospace engineer.

F. **Preview Main Points:** I will cover...

   I. What engineers do

   II. Why aerospace engineers are important to us

   III. The skills needed in engineering—not the least of which is communication

Transition to #I: So what is engineering?

Speech Body

I. The role of the engineer is perhaps one of the least understood in society, according to Jeff Lenard of the American Institute of Chemical Engineers.

   A. The comic strip creator, Scott Adams, debunks the mystery of engineering through his famous character, Dilbert; when you read Dilbert, you actually have a pretty good idea of what an engineer does.

   B. Engineering is not a science; engineers generally don't "do" science.

   C. "Scientists discover the world that exists; engineers create the world that never was."

   D. Engineering is all around us; as a career it may be the best way to make the biggest contribution to society.

Transition to #II: Let's talk more about those contributions now.

II. Aerospace engineers are very important to us.

   A. The settings in which aerospace engineers work is varied because of their demand.

   B. Aerospace engineers are needed in NASA, the Department of Defense, with private defense contractors, and aeronautical firms. (NASA)

Transition to #III: One does not simply wake up one day and decide to work for NASA, though.

III. To be successful in this rewarding career, engineers are required to have excellent skills—especially communication.

   A. Entry-level aerospace engineers require at least a BA in aerospace engineering or mechanical engineering.

   B. Courses in propulsion, thermodynamics, aerodynamics, chemistry, physics, and calculus are typical for the aerospace engineer.

   C. There is a tremendous need for engineers to have excellent verbal and written communication skills.

Signal End: I could go on talking about engineering all day, but my time is limited, so now it's time to wrap up.

Conclusion

A. **Restate Central Idea:** Today, we learned about how aerospace engineering is one of the most progressive, challenging, and rewarding fields that can be studied today.

B. **Recap Main Points:** I explained to you what an engineer does, why we specifically need aerospace engineers, and the skills needed to become an engineer—especially those skills we learn in this course.

C. **Clincher:** Who knows? One of you may become a rocket scientist. It really is a high-flying career!

Works Cited

Blain, Celeste. *Is There an Engineer Inside You? A Comprehensive Guide to Career Decision in Engineering.* (2nd Ed.) New York: Bonamy Publishing, 2015. Print.

"Careers in Aeronautics." National Aeronautical and Space Administration. *NASA.gov.* n.d. Web. 5 Feb. 2018.

Garder, Geraldine. *Careers in Engineering.* (2nd Ed.) New York: The McGraw-Hill Company. 2013. Print.

Sample 1B: Speech to Inform

Name: John Raines

Audience Analysis

Answer in complete sentences and use examples from your audience analysis questions.

A. How much does your audience already know about your topic and how will you design your speech regarding their level of knowledge? **Everyone is familiar with fear in general, so I'll try to focus on aspects of it that are specific to my topic.**

B. How much interest did the audience have in your topic? How will you make the topic interesting to them? **The audience was curious about the direction this speech would take, so I'll try to build on that and give them specific, solid examples that they can integrate into their lives.**

C. What is your audience's attitude regarding your topic? How will you address that attitude in your speech? **The attitude was mostly positive, so I'll try to use that to my advantage.**

D. How will the audience demographics (not what you learned on your Audience Analysis) impact the development of your speech? **The majority of the audience is 18–20 years old, so I'll try to word my information in such a way that it is received as constructive advice from a fellow student with a little more life experience. Gender shouldn't be an issue.**

Title: *A Fearless Life*

General Purpose: To inform

Specific Purpose: To inform my audience about the nature of fear

Introduction

A. **Grab Attention:** Frequent urination, dry mouth, excessive sweating...these are but a few of the many symptoms of phobic anxiety.

B. **Relate to Audience:** Many of you are standing at the thresholds of your adult lives, with an excitement about the unknown.

C. **Relate to Self (Establish Credibility):** I have always been a bit of a risk taker, looking fear square in the eye, and it hasn't always been easy.

D. **Central Idea:** But, to live without risk, is to risk not living.

E. **Specific Purpose:** Today, I want to inform you about the nature of fear.

F. **Preview Main Points:** I will cover...

I. What fear is

II. What fear does

III. How to master your fears

Transition to #I: "Courage is resistance to fear, mastery of fear—not absence of fear." (Mark Twain) So let's begin by talking about what fear is.

Speech Body

I. Fear is a complicated emotion.

   A. Fear is a perspective. (PsychCentral.com)

   B. It's a response to the unknown and uncontrolled.

   C. Fear is a controlling emotion. (MedicineNet.com)

Transition to #II: Now, let's look at how this plays out in our lives.

II. Fear controls our actions.

   A. Fear greatly reduces our options. (Encarta)

   B. Fear limits experience to the safe and the known.

   C. Ultimately, fear makes life dull and routine.

Transition to #III: There is no reason we have to live that way. We can master our fear.

III. Mastering our fears can be a way of life.

   A. First you must see fear for what it is.

   B. And by seeing it, develop a hatred for its controlling nature.

   C. Then love it, for the passion and excitement it brings to life.

Signal End: So before I close, let me recap.

Conclusion

A. **Restate Central Idea:** Remember, that to live without risk, is to risk not living.

B. **Recap Main Points:** Today, we talked about what fear is, what it does, and how you can master it.

C. **Clincher:** Now you have the tools to understand how fear might be affecting you. In the words of Philip Adams, "It seems to me that people have vast potential. Most people can do extraordinary things if they have the confidence or take the risks. Yet most people don't. They sit in front of the telly and treat life as if it goes on forever." (Philip Adams)

Works Cited

"Generalized Anxiety Disorder." *MedicineNet.com*. 2009. Web. 10 Mar. 2019.

"Phobia." *Encarta Encyclopedia.com*. 2008. Web. 11 Mar. 2019.

"Social Anxiety Disorder Symptoms." *PsychCentral.com*. 2009. Web. 10 Mar. 2019.

Sample 2A: Speech to Inform with Visuals

Name: Cory Williamson

Audience Analysis

Answer in complete sentences and use examples from your audience analysis questions.

A. How much does your audience already know about your topic and how will you design your speech regarding their level of knowledge? **The audience knows very little about the actual science of attraction, so I'll need to keep the terminology very basic and not lose them with big, technical terms.**

B. How much interest did the audience have in your topic? How will you make the topic interesting to them? **The audience is very interested already, but I'll try to maintain that interest with some humor and some explanations of human nature that might surprise them.**

C. What is your audience's attitude regarding your topic? How will you address that attitude in your speech? **My audience seems to be mostly interested in how to use my information to get a date, improve relationships, etc. I'll try to use that inherent connection to the material as a way to keep them interested in the actual scientific explanations.**

D. How will the audience demographics (not what you learned on your Audience Analysis) impact the development of your speech? **Most of my audience members are traditional college freshmen in age, economic status, etc. This means they probably have dating/attraction on their minds quite a bit.**

Title: *Are You Lookin' at Me?!*

General Purpose: To inform

Specific Purpose: To inform the audience about the science of attraction

Introduction

A. **Grab Attention:** Are you lookin' at me? Well that's alright...well...I like to write...I like classical music...I dress nice...I enjoy Mexican food...and on occasion I like to beat the person I'm with...Now hold on! That is an exaggeration. But that is how attraction works sometimes. You initially see someone and you are attracted in some way, but as you get to know someone that attraction could change for better or worse.

B. **Relate to Audience:** Every human has experienced attraction in one way or another.

C. **Relate to Self (Establish Credibility):** I am greatly interested in why humans are attracted to one another and have experienced the feeling of attraction toward another, so I decided to look into the matter.

D. **Central Idea:** Human attraction is a scientific process that begins many kinds of relationships.

E. **Specific Purpose:** Today, I want to inform you all about the science of attraction.

F. **Preview Main Points:** I will cover...

   I. The visual aspects of attraction

   II. The biological aspects of attraction

   III. How attraction affects relationships

Transition to #I: Experiment number one: Sins of the Flesh.

Speech Body

I. Part of attraction is due to what our mind perceives as physically appealing.

   A. The human body is the first thing we notice in another human.

      1. Females are generally attracted to males that are sexually appealing and have good fatherly traits such as height, muscles, facial features, some hair.

      2. Males are generally attracted to females that have sexually appealing features such as large breasts, waist-to-hip ratio, face, legs, and butt.

   B. Symmetry plays a role in figuring out if the person has good genes.

      1. When we see a person we are subconsciously analyzing if they have the features that would make for good offspring. (*Science of Sex Appeal* DVD)

      2. The better the symmetry the more it shows that a person doesn't have any visible gene defects.

Transition to #II: Now to take a look at how human biology takes action in attraction.

II. The biological aspects of attraction are the natural human responses that trigger sex appeal in a person.

   A. Pheromones are the chemically secreted odorless molecules that trigger sexual responses from animals. (*Pheremoneking.com*)

   B. Females are more vulnerable to these pheromones.

   C. Females find different males more attractive depending on if they are ovulating or not.

Transition to #III: Attraction is both what we see and what we feel. Those experiences could lead to relationships or simply sex.

III. Attraction has the possibility of leading to relationships.

   A. According to Dr. Fisher (*The Brain in Love and Lust*), love is divided into 3 categories.

      1. Sexual cravings are sometimes mistaken for love.

2. Attraction is craving for the individual.

3. Attachment is when you are at peace and comfort with the one you're with.

B. Getting to know someone can change where they belong on the love scale—up or down.

C. Lust is the sexual drive of attraction.

1. When humans experience an orgasm while having sex a chemical oxytocin is released that gives the feeling of attachment between males and females. (*mcmanweb.com*)

2. Love is what you make it. It varies amongst all people, so love as you want to be loved.

Signal End: Enough about love. As I close, let us take a look back at what attraction is about.

Conclusion

A. **Restate Central Idea:** We now know that human attraction is a scientific process that begins many kinds of relationships.

B. **Recap Main Points:** We saw that physical appearance plays a major part in initial attraction as well as biological occurrences in our body. Attraction has the possibility of leading us to sex and/or love in a relationship.

C. **Clincher:** The ideas of what I have said aren't meant for you to overanalyze a relationship you are in or could be in. Allow attraction to flow naturally and experience where it could take you...Let me leave you with one last thing. The next time you visit the strip club take a look around and see lust and attraction working at their finest.

Works Cited

Science of Sex Appeal. Perf. Alan Dunn, Farrah Shaikh. Discovery Communications, LLC, 2009. DVD.

"The Brain in Love and Lust." *McMan's Depression and Bipolar Web.* n.d. Web. 21 Mar. 2019.

"The Science of Attraction." *Pheremoneking.com.* n.d. Web. 21 Mar. 2019.

Sample 2B: Speech to Inform with Visuals

Name: Matt Kelso

Audience Analysis

Answer in complete sentences and use examples from your audience analysis questions.

A. How much does your audience already know about your topic and how will you design your speech regarding their level of knowledge? **Everyone knows a little bit about fire, but most don't know how to start one without the luxury of matches and lighters. I will try to focus the majority of the speech on information they don't already know.**

B. How much interest did the audience have in your topic? How will you make the topic interesting to them? **A couple audience members were avid outdoorsmen who didn't seem that interested, but several others seemed anxious to improve their fire skills. I'll try to maintain interest by stressing how useful fire-starting skills are for everyone.**

C. What is your audience's attitude regarding your topic? How will you address that attitude in your speech? **Only a couple seemed turned off by the topic, while the majority seemed curious and open to it. I will feed that curiosity with useful information.**

D. How will the audience demographics (not what you learned on your Audience Analysis) impact the development of your speech? **Most members of the audience are typical, college-aged students from North Idaho. This implies that they are somewhat interested in the outdoors and will find themselves camping, hunting, etc. at some time in the near future.**

Title: *Man's Best Tool*

General Purpose: To inform

Specific Purpose: To inform my audience about fire

Introduction

A. **Grab Attention:** (magnesium block demonstration) These little sparks that you see have mesmerized mankind throughout history. Imagine a world without heat, cooked food, boiled water, and light sources after dark. Fire provides all of this and more.

B. **Relate to Audience:** Everyone in this class will at some time use fire for enjoyment, cooking, and possible survival. It is extremely important that we all know how to effectively create a fire with the tools available to us in any given circumstance.

C. **Relate to Self (Establish Credibility):** Obviously, I'm an outdoors fanatic, and as such I have created literally hundreds of fires. Last year I took a survival course that taught me how to make a fire from scratch using primitive sources.

D. **Central Idea:** Fire-building knowledge is crucial for everyone and could even save a life.

E. **Specific Purpose:** I want to inform you about fire today.

F. **Preview Main Points:** I'll do that by covering...

  I. The various uses of fire

  II. Both modern and primitive methods to create fire

  III. Steps needed to create a successful and safe fire

Transition to #I: Let's begin by discussing the history of fire use.

Speech Body

I. Our history has shown many uses for fire.

  A. Fire has been used for cooking and as a heat source.

  B. Fire has been used in blacksmithing.

  C. Many myths and stories have been created around the subject of fire.

Transition to #II: Fire has obviously played a huge role throughout the history of mankind, but let's turn to examining the different methods for its creation.

II. Fire can be created by using a number of methods.

  A. Primitive methods, such as magnesium flint and a bow drill, are still used today.

  B. Some modern methods include matches, lighters, lenses, or batteries. (*AAA Wilderness Survival*)

  C. Both sources require the use of good tinder material as the starting point.

Transition to #III: Now that we know how to create a fire, let's look into the steps needed to create a successful and safe fire.

III. Creating a successful and safe fire is essential.

  A. The teepee and log cabin style are both easy and safe.

  B. Use a shovel to clear a patch of land on which to build it.

  C. For safety purposes, always stay with your fire and maintain it.

  D. A fire of any size should be extinguished thoroughly. (Ken Long)

Signal End: It is now time to extinguish this speech.

Conclusion

A. **Restate Central Idea:** Fire-building knowledge is crucial to each and every one of you.

B. **Recap Main Points:** Today, we have discussed the importance of fire and its various uses. We have gone over some basic ways to create a fire with limited resources available, and we have discussed how to build a safe fire and extinguish it properly.

C. **Clincher:** There is only so much experience you can get from learning about fire, but to really hone your skills it takes nothing but repetition, practice, and experimentation. Now get out there and let your pyro side run wild!

Works Cited

"AAA Wilderness Survival: How to Light a Fire." *GeoCities.com*. n.d. Web. 4 Nov. 2018.

"Fire." *ComingBackAlive.com*. n.d. Web. 4 Nov. 2018.

Long, Ken. Fire Chief. Personal Interview. 3 Nov. 2018.

"The Truth About the History of Fire." *Buzzle.com*. n.d. Web. 4 Nov. 2018.

Chapter 7

Using Language to Frame Your Message

> *"The difference between the right word and the wrong word is the difference between lightning and a lightning bug."*
>
> —*Mark Twain*

On December 7, 1941, President Franklin D. Roosevelt addressed a joint session of Congress following the Japanese attack on Pearl Harbor. The first sentence he uttered would later become one of the most well-known phrases from just about any speech within the 20th century. As with any president, FDR had a staff of advisors and speechwriters, and one of his assistants began the speech as follows:

December 7, 1941: A date which will live in world history.

Just before he addressed Congress, FDR crossed out the words "world history" and scribbled the word, "infamy," which led to him starting his famous speech with:

December 7, 1941: A date which will live in infamy.

Today, this phrase has become one of the most famous in American history. Would it have had the same impact if the original line had been used? We will never know for certain, but one thing is clear: Roosevelt's last-minute edit demonstrated his understanding of the concept inherent within the Mark Twain quote above. "World history" technically communicated the same idea, but the substitute word of "infamy" added color and emotion to the phrase at a time when the president needed it most. FDR's purpose in this speech was to request a declaration of war on Japan from Congress, effectively launching the U.S. into World War II, and he understood that his words would indelibly have an outcome on that decision. As such, FDR chose "infamy" because it carried with it a more ominous tone, highlighting the furor and anger felt by the American people, as they watched the attack on Pearl Harbor in horror.

As we consider our audiences for any given presentation, we must also consider how our language will impact the perceptions of our messages, for we must remember that communication is the act of being memorably understood as we originally intended. If we are speaking at a pep rally or a motivational speaking event, the language we select should be moving and uplifting. If we are delivering the eulogy at a funeral, our words should be respectful, yet somber. We must choose the right words, for the right audiences, based on the needs of the situation.

Know What to Avoid

"When in doubt, throw it out."

Being a mindful communicator, especially with respect to public speaking, means considering your audience when deciding what words, terminology, and phrases to use. Keep in mind that the primary goal of communication is to ensure your message is memorably understood as you originally intended it, so being cautious and mindful about the language you use is much more than being what some may call "P.C." or politically correct, which has become a loaded term in contemporary politics. If the language you use triggers a negative response from certain members of your audience, then it is highly likely that those audience members are no longer listening with the intent to understand, but have either turned off their attention spans or are listening with the intent to defend themselves against you later.

In keeping this goal in mind, we must be mindful of the language we use and use language that resonates with our specific audiences. Some categories of language to consider avoiding include political, religious, racial, ethnic, or sexual references that some may consider offensive or at the very least, off-putting. For example, words that may have once been acceptable may need slight edits before using them in front of a potentially diverse audience, including words such as "stewardess" (flight attendant), "fireman" (firefighter), "cleaning lady" (housekeeper), etc.

Varied Meanings

Be aware that there are two types of meanings to keep in mind when composing language for a speech: **connotation** and **denotation.**

The denotation of a particular word refers to its factual/literal meaning or common dictionary definition. When using a word for which you are not 100% sure of the denotation, be sure to look it up, as some words could potentially have more than one denotation, or certain terms or phrases may mean something completely different to various audience members. If you look up the word *snake* in a dictionary, you will discover that one of its **denotative** meanings is "any of numerous scaly, legless, sometimes venomous reptiles having a long, tapering, cylindrical body and found in most tropical and temperate regions."

Alternatively, connotation has more to do with the additional emotional or cultural meaning associated with the word, term, or phrase. The connotation for the word *snake* could be "danger" or "evil." Here's another example: consider the two terms, "swamp" and "wetland." One word conjures images of bugs, snakes, and foul stenches, while the other causes us to imagine a picturesque scene with graceful birds and beautiful foliage. However, they could easily be used to refer to the same scene, since they both have similar denotations. The connotations of some words—or the attitudes we associate with them—can easily be seen when we examine pairs of words that are essentially similar in meaning, but different in the favorable or unfavorable attitudes they evoke in most people. For example:

- refreshing—chilly
- plain—natural

- clever—sly
- terrorist—freedom fighter
- snob—cultured
- assertive—pushy
- skinny—slender
- statesman—politician
- smile—smirk
- domineering—assertive

Be aware of the potential connotation your choice of language may have on diverse audiences. Simply the word "diversity" implies race or gender to some listeners, when the actual dictionary definition is simply "difference"—without any connotation whatsoever.

Describing a group of people gathered on the street as a "rally" suggests a gathering of passionate, happy, and celebratory participants, but calling it a "mob" connotes a darker, angry, or perhaps violent gathering. You need only go as far as newscasts and articles to find a single event interpreted differently. The connotation applied by media is subtly imprinted in one's mind and shapes public opinion about such events.

Loftus and Palmer (1974) conducted an experiment to illustrate the impact that the connotation of one's chosen words can have on memory. Two groups of students were shown a video of a car accident, and then, some time later, were asked questions about what they had seen. The first group was asked how fast they thought the cars were moving when they "hit" each other, and the second group was asked the same question with a subtle change: the word "hit" was substituted with "smashed." The results showed the group that was asked how fast the cars were moving when they "smashed" into each other estimated the speeds to be much higher than those who were asked with a much more passive or neutral verb. Additionally, the group using the word "smashed" also reported seeing broken glass at the scene, yet there was no broken glass in the video.

Lastly, when using words for which you are unfamiliar, be sure to review their meaning carefully so as not to accidentally communicate the wrong message, and most importantly, be sure you can effectively pronounce the word with ease. This may take some practice and repetition, particularly for tough medical terminology, but you can easily find online pronunciation guides that will show you how to pronounce such words. Many online dictionaries include an audio clip of the word being pronounced.

Clarity

Simply put, less is more when it comes to word choice. We have probably all endured at one point or another a speech in which the speaker attempted to use "big words" to make themselves seem smart, when in reality, it only ended up frustrating the audience and turning off their attention spans. Complex ideas can easily be conveyed using simple, everyday language. For example, Shakespeare's famous soliloquy from Hamlet ("To be or not to be...") contains 261 words, and of those, 205 of them are only one syllable each. Avoid using big words unnecessarily, as this can result in an audience viewing you as pretentious or disingenuous. For example, one might say, "It is important to take immediate and expeditious action to vacate the premises," when a simpler and more direct way to say the same thing in a speech might be, "Tell everyone to get out of the building quickly!"

Concrete Language

In addition to keeping things simple, be sure to use words that clearly convey what you mean. In other words, avoid being overtly abstract or vague. For example, when describing a person's net worth, don't say, "He is very wealthy." Instead, use concrete figures, such as, "He is currently worth $1.2 million and owns homes in four countries." This is your opportunity to practice the age-old writing advice, *show, don't tell.* Language can be utilized to vividly describe people, places, and things, so use concrete, illustrious language to make your points more memorable. Also, be precise with your language. Avoid overusing pronouns (he, she, it, they, etc.). It has often been said that the most quoted "source" in the world today is "They." For example, "They say we're going to get rain soon" or "I hear they're predicting an early spring!" Going back to our previous idea of citing where your information comes from, be sure to provide concrete, precise sources for your information.

Accuracy

The credibility of a speaker is often judged by grammar, as well as usage. Grammatical errors are annoying to some listeners and may give the impression that the speaker is less intelligent than she or he actually is. Avoid common slang and regional dialect in a formal public speaking event. Words like "orientate" or "irregardless" may be common vernacular, but they aren't correct grammar. Likewise, incorrect tenses and pronouns can be equally annoying. To sound articulate and polished, use "himself" instead of "hisself," "you were" instead of "you was," or "I went" rather than "I had went." To people in their 60s or older, "busted" may mean having no monetary resources; whereas to someone younger, it could imply getting caught doing something embarrassing or illegal; while to someone else, it might mean simply, "broken."

Euphemisms

Beware of misusing euphemisms, which are indirect methods of restating an unpleasant, blunt, or even offensive statement, for they can quickly become misleading. For example, if I suggested, "The proverbial excrement will strike the wind oscillating device," it may sound more polite initially, but when we take a closer look at what is *really* being stated, it is easy to see that it is a slightly nicer way of restating the old adage having to do with serious trouble. Euphemisms have their place, though; for example, we often refer to someone as having "passed away" rather than saying that person is dead, because it softens the blow of the terms, especially if we are referring to one of our loved or respected ones.

There is a "dark side" of euphemisms that should be avoided. This occurs when euphemisms are used to manipulate, distort, mislead, or obfuscate the true meaning of words and phrases. The term **doublespeak** was coined to describe this kind of language after publication of George Orwell's novel, *1984*, where those in power created a language they called "newspeak." Doublespeak is commonly used by politicians and corporations when it is desirable to equivocate, to avoid the emotional impact of more accurate language. For example, a politician referred to a controversial pipeline bill in Congress as the "Keystone jobs bill." In another example, NASA and other government officials referred to the coffins of deceased Space Shuttle *Challenger* crew members as "crew transfer containers." Use of this kind of language with the intent to deceive or distort is considered manipulative and should be avoided.

Inflated Language

In a similar vein to euphemisms, inflated language has a similar tendency to come across as disingenuous. Inflated language is when we rename something to make it sound greater than it really is, such as when Rosanne Barr famously referred to herself as a "domestic goddess" instead of a stay-at-home wife and mother. Other examples of inflated language include: "corrosion control specialist" (car wash operator), "reutilization marketing facility" (junkyard), or "price integrity coordinator" (sales clerk).

Jargon

Jargon is the technical language that is specific to a certain field or profession. We might also say that it is "esoteric" (words intended to be understood by a small group of people with highly specialized interest or training). For example, the military is well known for its dependency upon acronyms. In the film, *Good Morning, Vietnam*, Robin Williams' character, Adrian Cronauer, pokes fun at this practice with the following illustration:

> *Excuse me, sir. Seeing as how the V.P. is such a V.I.P., shouldn't we keep the P.C. on the Q.T.? 'Cause if it leaks to the V.C. he could end up M.I.A., and then we'd all be put out in K.P.*

Of course, jargon like this is perfectly acceptable if your audience is familiar with the jargon being used, but someone delivering a speech that is full of such acronyms, to an audience that is completely unfamiliar with them, would have trouble communicating, as well as maintaining their attention. Most industries, such as restaurants, the military, or medicine, have terminology that is specific to members of that group. Jargon can also be regionally specific. In North Idaho, it is not uncommon to hear people refer to their truck as a "rig." This is in addition to the age-old debate surrounding the use of the interchangeable terms, pop, soda, or coke. This jargon is regionally specific. Southerners prefer coke; in the Southwest and East, they use soda; and, in the Northwest and Midwest, people prefer to say pop. Knowing the specific jargon of the group you are talking to is critical. Jargon can be especially confusing to people who are speaking English as a second language, as slang and jargon are not as easily translated and understood.

Vivid Language

Regarding the art form of creating imagery using language, American hip-hop artist, Mos Def, said:

> *The ability to have somebody read something and see it, or for somebody to paint an entire landscape of visual imagery with just sheets of words—that's magical. That's what I've been trying to strive for—to draw a clear picture, to open up a new dimension.*

Abstract ideas and concepts can be brought to life through the use of vivid imagery, which is an art form in and of itself. Take a look at the following passage, written by North Idaho College communication instructor, Dr. Josh Misner, in an attempt to poetically capture the feeling of experiencing a fleeting moment while out on a hike with his two young children:

> *...then there are those magical moments between worlds, when we wait upon the silence and cast our gaze into the lights. The wind serenades us with the melody of a thousand years and trees dance to a rhythm of immemorial joy. Our palms caress crusted tips of wild grass as we comb through the meadow without words, yet mysteriously hearing their meanings echo among the chatter of nature. A smile and bright, wondrous eyes light the path ahead while we leave our cares behind for another day, another moment, but not this one. Today, we soak it all in, unfettered by definition or explanation. Today, we roam. Today, we marvel. Today is ours.*

The exact same event could have been captured in a more factual manner as follows:

> *We paused to take in the silence of the forest around us. The wind blew gently through the trees, while we ran our hands across the overgrown wild grass. We smiled at one another and continued our hike.*

The difference between the two descriptions of the exact same event provides the reader (or listener, in the case of public speaking) with a wholly different experience of the same account. In the first passage, the imagery of bringing wind to life, along with painting a picture of the scene, almost places us there on the hike with them. While the second passage effectively does the same job, the first is clearly more effective at capturing the *feel* of the moment, through the use of vivid imagery.

In addition to vivid imagery, consider using **similes** and **metaphors** to illustrate your concepts and points. A simile is a comparison between two seemingly dissimilar items that uses *like* or *as* to draw the comparison. For example, "That class session felt like a thousand years long!" A metaphor is similar to the simile, but does not use *like* or *as*, effectively making a more direct comparison, such as, "That class session was a thousand years of my life I'll never get back!" Be careful not to use **cliché** metaphors or similes, which are phrases and comparisons that are far too overused in regular conversation, such as "last but not least," "better late than never," or "stuck out like a sore thumb." These do not add variety or spice to your speech, and, when speaking to a foreign audience, these types of metaphors may end up creating confusion, since their intended meaning often gets lost in translation.

Rhetorical Devices

A rhetorical device is a way to arrange our language in an artful way, so as to make the conversation more engaging and subsequently, more memorable for audience members. There are many rhetorical devices that professional speech writers employ (Table 7.1).

Table 7.1. Rhetorical Devices

Figures, Definitions, Illustrations			
Alliteration	Allusion	Anadiplosis	Analogy
Anaphora	Anesis	Antimetabole	Antithesis
Aposiopesis	Appositio	Assonance	Asyndeton
Catachresis	Climax	Conduplicatio	Diacope
Distinctio	Enthymeme	Enumeratio	Epanalepsis
Epistrophe	Epitheton	Epizeuxis	Eupemismos
Exemplum	Expletive	Hyperbole	Hypophora
Metaphor	Oxymoron	Paradox	Parallelism
Personification	Polysyndeton	Rhetorical Question	Scesis Onomaton
Sententia	Simile	Symploce	Synecdoche

Most rhetorical devices were developed and identified by Greek and Roman teachers in the classical period. Four of the most popular ones are: **alliteration**, **antithesis**, **parallel structure**, and **repetition**.

Alliteration

Alliteration is the occurrence of the same letter or sound at the beginning of adjacent or closely connected words. We can easily see alliteration used in everyday uses of language, such as television shows (*Mad Men*), sporting events (*Final Four*), company names (*Dunkin Donuts*), and in famous phrases (*Home sweet home; Right as rain*). When used sparingly, alliteration can spice up the language of your delivery, such as "We owe it to our city to help the hungry, the homeless, and the helpless among us." However, alliteration can easily be overdone, turning an otherwise innocuous statement into an exercise in pure silliness: "Nick's nephew needed new notebooks now." Of course, if it is your intention to bring an element of silliness to your presentation, then by all means, continue, but do so with caution.

Antithesis

An antithesis is a rhetorical technique in which two dissimilar or contrasting ideas are juxtaposed (placed side-by-side for contrasting effect). Consider President John F. Kennedy's famous example: "Ask not what your country can do for you—ask what you can do for your country." Or, we can use Neil Armstrong's famous quote, as he took his first steps on the moon: "That's one small step for man, one giant leap for mankind." You might consider this technique when trying to draw attention to an important point:

- Many are called, but few are chosen.
- We are taught to speak, but rarely how to listen.

Parallel Structure and Repetition

Parallel structure is the technique of arranging phrases or clauses of a sentence in parallel form, such as in the following examples:

- Dogs make great pets; they are loyal, they are obedient, and they are loving.
- Our coach told us that we should get a lot of sleep, that we should eat well, and that we should think positively about tonight's game.

Martin Luther King, Jr. was a master at the use of parallel structure, combined with repetition to add engagement to his oratory. Consider his famous *I Have a Dream* speech:

> *I have a dream that one day this nation will rise up and live out the true meaning of its creed: "We hold these truths to be self-evident, that all men are created equal."*
>
> *I have a dream that one day on the red hills of Georgia, the sons of former slaves and the sons of former slave owners will be able to sit down together at the table of brotherhood.*
>
> *I have a dream that one day even the state of Mississippi, a state sweltering with the heat of injustice, sweltering with the heat of oppression, will be transformed into an oasis of freedom and justice.*
>
> *I have a dream that my four little children will one day live in a nation where they will not be judged by the color of their skin but by the content of their character.*
>
> *I have a* dream *today!*

Repetition is where we repeat certain words or phrases to garner emotional effect. Those repeated phrases are pleasant to the human ear, because they carry with them a certain rhythmic quality, adding emphasis and aiding in memory retention. Repetition is an element of public speaking that is different from written communication. In public speaking, repetition is *desired* as a means of helping the audience remember key ideas. In written communication, repetition is not as necessary because a reader can review the text for memory and comprehension.

Chapter Summary

With language, there is power, and as such, the words we select to use for our speeches should be chosen mindfully as we consider our audiences. Select the right language and tone for those words based on the context in which you will be speaking; be sure your tone matches the expected tone for the situation.

The language chosen when composing your speech should take into account both the denotation (dictionary definition) and connotation (emotional implication) of the words being spoken. Aim for clarity in your choice of words. Keep them simple, concrete, and avoid overusing abstract language. Be aware of language to avoid, such as euphemisms, inflated language, or jargon. Finally, be sure to employ vivid language through the use of metaphor, simile, and rhetorical devices such as alliteration, antithesis, and parallel structure or repetition to keep your audiences engaged and listening.

Chapter 8

Practice, Preparation, and Delivery Techniques

> *"Take advantage of every opportunity to practice your communication skills so that when important occasions arise, you will have the gift, the style, the sharpness, the clarity, and the emotions to affect other people."*
>
> —*Jim Rohn*

As a general rule of life, learned skills require practice to refine, develop, and perfect. Any dedicated athlete will confirm this fact. The average person off the street cannot pick up a textbook on the fundamentals of basketball, study it during a caffeine-fueled all-nighter, and then show up for tryouts with an NBA team, expecting a starting spot on the team. The same is true of foreign languages, hobbies, crafts, and trades. For skill to be developed, it takes time, it takes effort, and it takes a vigorous commitment to the process of trial and error.

Communication in general, but especially public speaking, is essentially a set of learned skills that must be developed through regular, dedicated practice. Some people have a seemingly natural talent for public speaking, while others on the opposite end of the spectrum are crippled by the mere thought of standing up in front of an audience. If we were to poll a large enough number of people and graph their anxiety levels regarding public speaking, we would likely see a natural bell curve, with about 60–70% of the population possessing relatively mild anxiety levels, 15% or so having little to no anxiety, and 15% would report extreme anxiety over public speaking, a fear that can become crippling, leading to communication apprehension.

Why Practice?

As mentioned previously in Chapter 2, one of the primary sources for public speaking anxiety is the element of uncertainty. We are afraid of all of the possibilities that could go wrong, including saying the wrong thing, forgetting what we need to say, or having our audience turn against us or view us as incompetent speakers. Practicing helps us eliminate many of those sources of uncertainty, and with that practice, we start developing self-confidence with respect to the message we are about to deliver. Practicing effectively trains our mouths to say the words, our bodies to deliver the accompanying nonverbal communication to supplement our message, and our brains to perform under pressure.

Getting Started

Successful and effective practice sessions begin with the outline, for a great speech depends on the quality and completeness of your written foundation. Remember that the outline will be acting as the roadmap for how we get from our attention getter (opening statement) to our clincher (final statement), so as with an actual road map, we want our directions to be as clear, complete, and concise as possible. Once you feel that the rough draft of your outline is as complete and audience-centered as possible, then that is the time to begin practicing.

Food for Thought

Items missing from an outline will not magically appear as you deliver your speech in front of the audience. For example, if your outline was missing your central idea, and your outline is what you used to practice your speech, then you have trained yourself to deliver a speech without a central idea. Be sure your outline is complete, proofread, and as close to your final draft as possible before you begin to practice.

Starting Tips for Practice

Above all, the one thing to avoid when deciding on a practice strategy is the practice of "cramming." While this strategy may work on a history exam when trying to memorize dates and facts at the last minute, so that you can effectively regurgitate those facts before you forget them, this strategy will fail you as a communicator. Remember, public speaking is a learned skill that is developed and refined in the same way as a golf swing, a free-throw shot, or learning a new language. Practice should begin well in advance of your speech and should also be spread out over time, rather than concentrated all in one or two sessions. Practice is most effective when undertaken in brief yet frequent sessions over time.

As you begin practicing, you must understand that there is a vast, yet subtle difference between memorization and learning. For example, if you were asked to tell the story of your first kiss, the time you learned to ride a bike, or the first time you flew in an airplane, you could most likely recall and tell others that story with relative ease. Those stories were not memorized. You did not write down lines for those stories, study them, and then repeat them until you could recite them perfectly each time. Those stories are easy for you to tell without much advance preparation because they are **learned**. You know the material; telling the story is a matter of putting the concepts you know into words. At most, your notes for telling those stories would consist of a few keywords and phrases to jog your memory and keep you on track.

Memorization, on the other hand, is the process of storing and recalling exact phrases and words. This is a process utilized by actors who need to recall exact lines in prewritten scripts, but for a public speaker, whose primary goal is to have a fluid conversation with an audience, it will not suffice. Audiences, first of all, can easily see through a speaker with a scripted speech. From eye contact to vocal tone, rate, and variety, everything about that speaker's delivery will seem canned or manufactured, anything but genuine and authentic. Additionally, what would happen if you forgot a line? Potentially, that could cause what some might refer to as a "speech fatality"—an unrecoverable error that causes extreme anxiety, resulting in panic and possibly failure. When a speech is learned instead of memorized, there is always a backup plan, because you know the **concepts** you are trying to convey, so the words you choose to convey those concepts may vary, but the essence of the message remains the same. For that reason, avoid rote memorization at all costs, and instead, get to know your material and use notes to help guide you as you make your way through that material.

As you practice, it is also important to remember to practice your phrases differently each time you run through your speech. Not only does this prevent memorization as a result of your practice, but it also effectively "trains" you to deliver your message in a variety of ways, developing multiple phrases for saying the same thing. That way, if you get stuck trying to remember how you were planning on phrasing a certain point, you will have numerous options from which to draw, keeping your speech fluid and conversational.

Remember that, during practice sessions, you should practice in the exact same way you intend to present when in front of your audience. This means that, if you are going to be standing up and moving around, do not practice from a seated position, staring at a computer screen, and going through your lines in your head. You will want to stand up, move around, gesture, and practice your phrases out loud, projecting your voice just as you will in front of the audience. What this practice method provides is training for your body (the delivery vehicle) via **muscle memory**. In the same way a professional golfer practices a drive a thousand times to develop and refine the swing, a public speaker needs to train the muscles of the body, including the neck to move the head around the room, effectively maintaining eye contact with the entire room, but also, the diaphragm to expel enough air through the vocal cords to project the voice to the back of the room. If, instead, you practice from a seated position, then when you get up to speak, standing to deliver your message will feel unfamiliar to you, and if you recall from earlier chapters, uncertainty and unfamiliar situations are what generate natural anxiety. In the same way, practicing phrases in your head instead of speaking them out loud only teaches you to remain quiet and reserved. Lastly, you should practice at least once with a full dress rehearsal, wearing what you plan to wear for your presentation. The last place you want to discover that your heels are hurting your feet or that your shirt doesn't fit quite right is when you are in front of an audience and trying to concentrate on delivering your message.

Positive visualization (also called **positive imagery**) is a valuable technique used by athletes, musicians, actors, dancers, or other performers who perform their craft in front of spectators. This technique involves engaging one's imagination to visualize a positive outcome from the upcoming performance. For example, a basketball player preparing to take a crucial free-throw shot to win the game at the last minute will dribble the ball a few times, then pause and *visualize* the shot being taken, imagining the ball going through the air in a perfect arc and sinking through the hoop, touching nothing but the net. Only after that visualization will the player physically take the shot. For a public speaker, he or she should imagine himself or herself successfully delivering the speech as close to an ideal reality as possible. One of the worst things a speaker can do prior to the speech is engage in negative self-talk, such as thinking, "I'm not ready for this," or "This is going to be awful!"

While everyone will have a different "best practice" number of practice sessions to effectively learn a speech, it requires some trial and error to find out what will work best. Some people are fortunate enough to possess photographic memories and can recall written information effortlessly, and for them, perhaps one practice session is all they need. Others may end up on the opposite end of that spectrum, requiring 30 or more practice run-throughs before they feel comfortable enough to deliver their speech. Despite most of us falling anywhere along this spectrum, many novice public speaking students suggest that the following three practice "sessions" provide a recipe for success.

Practice Session #1

As mentioned previously in this chapter, before practicing at all, you absolutely *must* have a solid foundation in your outline. Prepare the outline as fully and completely as possible before beginning practice, but in addition to the outline, you will want to locate a timer. Most cellular phones have stopwatch apps readily available, but in a pinch, one could easily find a relatively cheap stopwatch or use the kitchen timer function on just about any microwave.

There are two approaches to the timing during practice sessions. One way is to start the stopwatch, deliver the speech, and then see how much time has elapsed, adjusting as necessary from that point. Another method is to use a countdown-style timer, setting the timer for the maximum amount of time allowed and delivering the speech after starting the countdown. If the timer beeps before the speech is finished, this allows the speaker to make a note on the outline regarding how much material is remaining, so they know how much needs to be cut from the final draft. Regardless of how you choose to use your timer, it is critical to your success that you utilize one. Practicing with a timer trains your brain to recognize how much time has elapsed, helping you to develop almost a "sixth sense" regarding the time, so that you will automatically know how long your speech has lasted while delivering it in front of your audience. One of the reasons we stress development of this sense of time is that, when we are under high stress and anxiety, our perception of time becomes distorted. After a ten-minute speech, one student may sit down and feel like only two minutes have passed, while another student may sit down after three minutes and think that more than eight minutes went by. Using this method provides us with critical **biofeedback**, teaching us how much time has elapsed, so that we finish our message within the time we have been allotted.

In this first practice session, once you have your timer set up how you want it, and your outline is in front of you, start the timer and deliver the speech from the outline, vocalizing it as closely as you imagine yourself giving it in front of your audience.

> **Important Note: If you mess up, stumble over your words, or forget to say something, *keep going*! When you begin speaking in front of an audience, it is highly likely that, at some point, you will mess up or stumble, so it is important to train yourself how to adapt and recover.**

After the conclusion of your first run-through of the speech, stop the timer to determine whether you are under time, over time, or if you fall within the range allowed for this specific speech. Ideally, you will fall within the upper-middle point within the time range you have been allotted. For example, if your speech should be 6–8 minutes, aim for the 7:30–7:45 mark. For most of us, as we get increasingly nervous, our vocal rate has the tendency to follow our heart rates. So, if our hearts are pounding and feel like they are going to burst out of our chest, it is very likely that we will be talking considerably faster than we did at home, during practice. Taking this into consideration, it is best if we give ourselves a little extra room, just in case.

If this practice session ends up over time, go back through the outline and determine what information can be edited out of the speech. Use what you now know about your audience to make editing decisions, and always remove the information that does not seem to fit with the audience's needs. If you are under the time limit, go back to the outline and consider elaborating further on some of your points. Again, utilize the audience analysis to determine which points would better suit their needs.

Continue practicing your speech in this manner until you confidently deliver your speech while making sure the timing comes out consistently. At that point, put the speech aside and walk away. There is a point of diminishing returns when it comes to practicing a speech. Practice too much, and it will become too rote and rehearsed. This first practice session serves only one purpose: testing the time limits and determining if the amount of information included fits within the parameters of the speaking engagement. Once that has been accomplished, any further practice could actually damage your ability to remain conversational.

Practice Session #2

By now, your outline should be nearing final draft status and very few changes will need to be made to it, but we still require it for this practice session. Additionally, we need the timer once again, but we will also need note cards. Begin transcribing your outline to your note cards at this point using only short phrases and keywords that will jog your memory regarding what information needs to be delivered. To demonstrate what this could look like, let's borrow a main point from one of the sample outlines in Chapter 6:

I. Part of attraction is due to what our mind perceives as physically appealing.

  A. The human body is the first thing we notice in another human.

    1. Females are generally attracted to males that are sexually appealing and have good fatherly traits such as height, muscles, facial features, some hair.

    2. Males are generally attracted to females that have sexually appealing features such as large breasts, waist-to-hip ratio, face, legs, and butt.

  B. Symmetry plays a role in figuring out if the person has good genes.

    1. When we see a person, we are subconsciously analyzing if they have the features that would make for good offspring. (*Science of Sex Appeal* DVD)

    2. The better the symmetry, the more it shows that a person doesn't have any visible gene defects.

A note card for this main point could look like this:

— Attraction = physical appeal
- Body noticed first
  - Women → Men with height, muscles, face, hair
  - Men → Women with large breasts, waist/hip, face, legs, butt
- Symmetry = genes
- **Science of Sex Appeal DVD** → subconscious analyzing
  - Good symmetry = no gene defects

Notice that this speaker has deliberately written the notes on the card almost cryptically. Part of the trial-and-error process of learning to be an effective public speaker involves learning what the most basic keywords and phrases will jog the memory in the midst of high anxiety. One thing, however, is certain and must be remembered at this stage:

> **The more text you write on a note card, the more likely you will be to read directly from it, instead of maintaining eye contact with your audience.**

Include only the minimum amount of text to jar your memory so that the majority of your time is spent making meaningful eye contact with your audience. The only time you should write full sentences is when you are transcribing a full quote, at which point, the audience almost expects you to read from the card, to do justice to the original source.

Also worthy of note is that this speaker highlighted the source for his facts. Using color, symbols, bold font, etc. is a great way to ensure that, when necessary, you can look down at your notes and immediately find the information you need, when you need it. The longer you look down at your notes, hunting for the material you need, the greater the chances are that anxiety could begin welling up inside you.

Pro Tip

Use only one note card per section of information within your speech. For example, use one card for your introduction, one card for each main point, and one card for your conclusion. Not only does this minimize the number of cards to keep track of, but think about what you are saying as you rotate to a new card: a transition. Flipping to a new card as you state your transition provides your audience with a subtle nonverbal cue that suggests you are moving on to new material.

Another great idea for you as a novice public speaker is to include notes to yourself regarding delivery of the speech. For example, as long as the information in your speech is not heavy, serious, or depressing, consider drawing smiley faces on your cards to remind you that it is okay to smile once in a while. A smile has numerous benefits, from relaxing you in a moment of stress, to showing the audience that you are friendly and care about your topic. You could also draw arrows, pointing to the sides of the room, to remind yourself to move around and ensure you cover the entire audience with your eye contact. You will likely be amazed at how easy it is to forget such seemingly simple bodily functions during a speech, but it is truly remarkable.

Once your notes have all been transcribed to the cards, deliver your speech from the note cards, but have your outline nearby. Should you become stumped as for what to say, make a note of it, and come back to it later, using the outline as your guide. If certain areas consistently prove problematic, edit your note cards to ensure they are as clear as possible. Check your time after each practice round to ensure your timing remains steady and toward the upper-middle range. As soon as you can effectively deliver your speech from the note cards alone, without the outline as a backup, stop there and practice no further until the next session.

Practice Session #3

For this practice session, you will only need the timer and your note cards. Start the timer, and just as with session #2, deliver your speech solely from the note cards, but the twist in this session is to challenge yourself to look up, pretending that you have an audience in the room. It is even more effective for you to have previewed the venue where you will be speaking and imagine yourself in that room, looking at how you expect your actual audience to be seated. Continue your practice run-throughs, challenging yourself to wean away from the notes as much as possible. Ideally, you will spend a minimum of 70% of your speech *not* looking at your notes, but instead, at your audience. Remember to vary your phrases, so as not to memorize, but to *learn* your material well enough to be able to deliver it as conversationally as possible. At this point, your note cards effectively become like a parachute, and less like a crutch. The more you push yourself to get away from the notes and use them only when you forget what to say next, the more you will learn your speech and give off the impression of credibility, preparedness, and confidence.

During this third practice session, you may choose to incorporate the following:

- Deliver your speech to a test audience of family or friends. Outside perceptions can offer feedback that we may not necessarily see ourselves.
- Deliver your speech in front of a full-length mirror, without looking away. This helps to desensitize the part of our emotional brain (the limbic system) that controls our natural aversion to eye contact. The longer you are able to make awkward, uncomfortable eye contact with yourself in the mirror, the easier the audience will become.
- Record yourself delivering the speech using a phone, camera, or webcam and watch it for self-review. It is true that we are our own worst critics, and you will likely notice things about yourself that nobody else will notice. As uncomfortable as this feels, it provides truly valuable feedback, leading to greater development as a speaker.

These three practice sessions will provide you with a good starting point with which to work. Some people may require more than these three sessions, while some people may be able to get by with less, but this much is certain:

> ***The sooner you begin practicing and the more time you allow yourself to develop a speech, the more prepared you will feel and the more confident you will become. This preparedness and confidence will translate to credibility in your audience's eyes.***

Planning Your Delivery

Once you have learned the content portion of your speech, the next consideration is to think about how you can use the delivery of your message to give it more impact among your audience members. Remember that the goal of an effective communicator at all times is to be memorably understood as you originally intended. The best and most well-written speech in the world will still fall short if not delivered effectively, so as you practice, you must take into account how to manage first impressions, as well as nonverbal communication, including: personal appearance, eye contact, vocal quality, and movement.

First Impressions

The first place to start with generating a positive rapport is with setting a good first impression with the audience. It is always important to show up early and to be prepared. Arriving at the last minute, frantic and nervous, sets a negative tone among audience members that may be difficult, if not impossible, to overcome. Before being introduced, ensure all visual aids are set up and ready to go, and the room is arranged to your liking. If you are being formally introduced, and if the audience can see you (i.e., you are not backstage, but visible to the audience as you are being introduced), be sure to manage your nonverbal cues. Stand tall and exude confidence, even if you are not feeling confident. When it comes to confidence, great speakers "fake it until they make it," which eventually transforms nerves into confidence. After you are introduced or called on, and it is time to "take the stage," walk tall and slowly up to the podium, all the while reminding yourself that nothing else matters but the message in this moment. Remember all the preparation and practice that has led up to this moment and remind yourself that you are ready. As you take your place at the podium (or wherever you plan on beginning), pause for a moment and smile, ensuring you have the audience's attention.

Take a deep, cleansing breath and exhale slowly before you begin, and then begin strong. Avoid warming up into your speech by saying unnecessary phrases like, "All right…" or "Okay…" Also, avoid greeting the audience or reintroducing yourself if you were already introduced. If you have a limited amount of time to convey your very important message to the audience, then every last word you say should go toward delivering that message. Pausing before commencing your introduction demonstrates self-control and respect for your audience.

Appearance

In addition to first impressions, as stated above, our appearance should set us apart as the speaker, rather than as an audience member. To achieve this goal, keep two general rules of personal appearance in mind: 1) Anticipate what your audience will be wearing and dress about one or two steps more formally than how you expect them to be dressed. Your goal with this first rule is to project a professional, credible image to your audience; 2) If your appearance is related to your visual aids, then what you wear becomes a visual aid that enhances your topic. When in doubt with respect to rule #1, aim for business casual by wearing what you would expect to wear to a professional job interview, such as an interview for an office manager, a supervisory position, or a marketing specialist. Additionally, avoid wearing anything that might distract your audience from focusing on your message, such as hats (again, unless related to your visual aids), or shirts with text of any kind and/or flashy logos.

Finally, take the following aspects into consideration when planning your personal appearance: the occasion, your audience, your topic, and the image or persona you are trying to display. First, regarding the occasion, you can imagine that what you might wear to deliver a commencement address to a graduating class would be totally different than what you might wear to a funeral or a wedding, so the occasion sometimes dictates what you need to wear. Second, considering your audience, there are times when dressing one level more formally may involve wearing jeans and a t-shirt, especially if your audience is going to be wearing shorts, sandals, and tank tops. Generally speaking, plan on dressing at least as nice as the nicest-dressed person in your audience, but when in doubt, err on the more formal side. Thirdly, there are times when your topic will suggest what you need to wear. For example, a Hawaiian print shirt, shorts, and sandals would be perfect attire for explaining tourist attractions on Oahu, while yoga pants and no shoes might be more appropriate for demonstrating yoga poses. Lastly, take into account what type of persona you want your audience to see. If you are going for more power and authority, dress more formally in darker colors. If you are going for more lighthearted humor or an upbeat, positive tone, wear lighter colors. If you are normally perceived as the class clown and you want to be taken seriously in this speech, dress more formally to help dispel your previous persona.

Eye Contact

Eye contact, according to Andersen (2007), performs several interactional functions, including the following:

- Regulates and monitors our interaction
- Signals cognitive activity (such as when we roll our eyes up when thinking about something)
- Expresses a desire for involvement
- Signals attentiveness

The number-one reason novice speakers fail to engage their audiences with sufficient meaningful eye contact is due to relying too heavily on their notes. Such speakers are likely to use their notes even when they are well prepared, simply because it is more comforting to look down at the notes, rather than at all those pairs of eyes staring. A lack of eye contact with an audience damages the possibility to create rapport because, as mentioned above, if eye contact is poor or inconsistent, it cannot regulate or monitor interaction, nor can it generate a desire for involvement or engagement with the material being presented. Audiences are likely to tune out a speaker who fails to engage them with consistent eye contact.

Eye contact is much more than merely scanning the audience, however. Eye contact must be meaningful, meaning that, for each person in the audience, you "lock on" to that person for at least a couple of seconds before moving on to the next person. It is recommended that you do this randomly throughout the audience, so as to feel more natural in your interaction with them. One technique that may help you with this is to look at the person in the front corner of the room, then move to the audience member in the opposite rear corner, then the other rear corner, then the opposite front corner, and then fill in the gaps between them all randomly. The most important consideration is to aim to reach every audience member meaningfully at least once.

Vocal Quality

In a speech, obviously, the human voice is the vehicle delivering the majority of the message. While other nonverbal qualities may complement or supplement that message, the vast majority of the literal message is being delivered via the voice, and as such, we must consider all of the qualities of the voice, to ensure the most effective and memorable delivery possible.

Volume vs. Projection

Have you ever gone to a concert one night, only to find out the next morning, when you woke up, your voice was so hoarse, you could barely speak? This is most likely due to a strain being placed on your vocal cords due to increasing your volume, rather than projecting your voice. Actors refer to projection as having a "stage voice" and do so using the diaphragm and their breathing, rather than shifting that strain to the vocal cords. Most of us, when we want to be heard loudly, simply increase our volume. Do this often and sustain it long enough, and you will feel it in your throat. Learning to project the voice, however, involves feeling your diaphragm (the muscle below the lungs that is responsible for filling and contracting the lungs during breathing) actually expel more air through the vocal cords as they work, effectively *projecting* your voice throughout the room. Projection saves our vocal cords and prevents having a tired, hoarse voice the next day.

To develop projection, you can practice this by trying to deliver your speech to a partner, while the partner slowly increases the volume of background music. As the volume of the music increases, try to project your voice over the music, concentrating on feeling your diaphragm expel more air through your voice.

Clarity

During conversation, most of us are relaxed enough not to have to think about the clarity of our enunciation, and as a result, we tend to slur our words, drop syllables off the ends of words, and mumble. During practice, it is important to slow down enough and pronounce our consonant sounds sharply and crisply. Exaggerate your enunciations in practice, so that when it comes time to deliver the speech, you have effectively trained your voice to articulate the sounds more clearly.

Additionally, if there are words that present problems with pronunciation, such as the word, *phenomenological* (go ahead, try to say it five times fast), be sure to devote extra time to ensuring you can pronounce these words effortlessly and correctly. Look up the words using a tool such as YouTube, so that you can actually hear others saying the words first. Be sure to look up several sources in this manner, to ensure you are gaining the correct pronunciation. This is especially important when using foreign language-based words or medical/science-based terminology, for the sake of your credibility as a speaker.

Pitch and Intonation

The highs and lows in your vocal tone are called **pitch**, while varying your pitch is referred to as varied **intonation** patterns. When a speaker reads an entire speech off of a prewritten manuscript, things like pitch and intonation often fall by the wayside, while in everyday conversation, our pitch and intonation vary widely, leading to often engaging conversations that draw us in and keep us hooked. Think about it. If you had a staggering statistical fact to provide to your audience, such as, "Our basketball team powered their way to a 30–0 undefeated season last year," and as you stated it, you sounded more like Ben Stein's character in the film, *Ferris Bueller's Day Off* ("Bueller... Bueller... Bueller..."), your fact would end up lost on the audience, falling with a thud. However, if you provided this fact with the pitch and intonation it deserved, adding enthusiasm and the right amount of emphasis, your audience would recognize the sheer importance of such a feat.

Intensity

Intensity can be demonstrated by varying the loudness and softness of your voice. To experience this, try saying the following aloud, as directed:

> *(Softly)* "Are we going to put up with this?"
>
> *(Switch to loudly)* "No! Today, we fight!"

As you tried this exercise, did you notice the meaning change as you altered your intensity? Playing with intensity can drastically alter the mood or feel of your message. Try to vary your intensity, starting softer at first, but then build toward a climax near the end of your speech. This technique works especially well when utilizing narratives (stories) to convey important points.

Rate

Most of us speak at a conversational rate of around 150 words per minute (roughly two words for every heartbeat), and as our heart rate increases, so will our rate of speaking. Auctioneers are capable of speaking up to 300 words per minute, but in doing so, they sacrifice clarity and complexity of the messages they are capable of delivering. For public speakers, we want to keep our rates down to around the 150-word range. Keeping our rate of speech conversational like this helps demonstrate confidence to the audience, showing them that we are in control, rather than letting our nerves get the better of us, so one way of achieving this is to control the heart rate through breathing. Novice speakers often forget to breathe, and instead, take short, choppy breaths that often lead to an oxygen deficiency that quickens the heart rate, leading to an increased rate of speaking. By controlling the breath and using pauses in between sentences to take deeper, more controlled, and purposeful breaths, we will be able to keep our rate of speaking where it needs to be.

Pauses and Fillers

During regular conversations, it is normal for us to insert filler words, such as *um*, *uh*, *you know*, and so on. Filler words serve as a sort of placeholder for our conversation, so that if we are talking to someone and need to retreat into our minds to think of a word or what to say next, we insert those filler words (sometimes called **paralanguage**, or the sounds we make that are not necessarily language) to let the other person know we are not done finishing our thoughts yet. In a speech, however, such words are unnecessary, since the audience will not interrupt you while delivering your speech (or at least, they won't if they are a polite audience). While some filler words are to be expected and make the speaker come across as more natural and conversational, at some point, too many of them becomes a distraction from the message.

Instead of filler words, allow silence to fill the void between thoughts and sentences. Silence is much more eloquent and provides the audience with the impression that you are in control of your delivery, helping you to exude confidence. To reduce your use of filler words, the first step is to become aware of what fillers you use and at what points in your speech you use them. One effective exercise is to have a friend bang on something or make a loud noise whenever you use a filler word while practicing. This kind of feedback, though somewhat jarring at first, is invaluable because, as you become more aware of the fillers, you quickly become more able to control them and use pauses instead.

Pauses can be used to augment your message and should be used regularly. Short pauses (1/2–2 seconds) add emphasis by using the silence to draw brief attention to what you just said, and can also be used to separate ideas, almost as a nonverbal transition. Long pauses (3–4 seconds) should be used more sparingly, such as following a rhetorical question (a question not designed to be answered, but to draw attention to a point made by considering the question) or after making a powerful or provocative point. Long pauses command audience attention in dramatic fashion, but used too frequently, can give the audience the impression that you are unprepared or overly nervous, so use long pauses only at the most powerful moments within your message. One final type of pause is the "spontaneity pause," which is a planned pause that appears unplanned from the perspective of the audience. Using such pauses, you stop for a moment to consider the right word or way to phrase a point, only to miraculously come up with the perfect word at the last moment.

Movement and Use of Space

Most novice speakers, quite frankly, forget that they possess bodies, complete with working limbs, particularly legs. They become so heavily focused on delivering the message that they neglect to utilize the space they have at the front of the room. Still others choose to remain glued to the podium, because the podium provides a feeling of "cover" in such a hazardous situation as public speaking in front of a crowd. Movement, however, as mentioned earlier, provides us with a way to dispel much of our nervous energy. It does not take much in the way of movement to burn off excess adrenaline that pools in our muscle cells, resulting in involuntary trembling and twitching, so it is wise to start walking around to help move past the initial wave of anxiety. Additionally, an animated speaker becomes more engaging and easy to follow than one who never moves from the same spot. However, movement should be intentional and can be used to supplement a speaker's points.

Movement from one side of the room to another can be used while transitioning from one point to the next, providing the audience with a physical transition into new material. State your transitions as you begin walking to the other side of your speaking space. To emphasize an important point, consider moving toward the audience. As we close the physical gap between us, as speakers, and the audience, you generate more *immediacy* (a sense of urgency to listen or interact) among your audience members. Moving away from the audience can signal an impending conclusion, almost as though you are moving away from the message. Above all, avoid pacing, like an animal trapped in a cage. While pacing may make you feel better (almost as though you become a moving target and thus, harder to hit), excessive, uncontrolled movement actually creates a distraction for your audience.

Advanced Delivery Tips

As you incorporate all of the above into your delivery planning, at some point, you may choose to take your speaking to the next level, so here are some additional tips to continue to refine your delivery and add power to your messages.

Pronoun Consideration

Martin Luther King, Jr. was well known for his frequent use of inclusive pronouns instead of singular pronouns: we, us, and our, vs. I, you, your, me, or mine. He understood that, to invite an audience into his message, he needed to rearrange the language to make it subtly more inviting to them. Take a look at the following examples:

1. *Today, I will show you what I mean by inclusive pronouns being inviting.*
2. *Today, we will look at how inclusive pronouns help us become more inviting.*

Although each sentence essentially states the same core message, the second one has the tendency to draw us into it, while the first one almost creates a sort of psychological divide, between speaker and audience members. Strive to use inclusive pronouns when possible.

Balance

Strive for balance in all aspects of your speech delivery. If your material is serious and heavy, for example, seek to balance it out with lighter, more positive material. Take, for instance, the topic of the atrocities of the Holocaust. Such a serious topic needs to be treated seriously, but at the same time, this topic can be emotionally draining for an audience, so how might we balance it out? One idea might be to spend the majority of the time speaking to the atrocities, but near the end of the speech, share an uplifting story of perseverance and survival, despite the odds. Similarly, if your speech topic is humorous and lighthearted, seek to include research-based information that has serious value to it.

Regarding your personal delivery attributes, if you tend to speak softly, look for ways to increase your intensity during important points. Likewise, if you tend to have a booming voice that projects well, see how you can soften it a bit for more variety and impact. If you have a tendency to stand still, challenge your comfort zone to get out from behind the podium and use the space, but if you tend to be a mover and pace a lot, then see how you can balance your movement out by standing still more often.

WOW Factor

Every speech, at some point within the delivery, should have what some refer to as a "wow factor." Think of this as a moment of highly memorable and profound brilliance that captivates your audience and potentially makes the hairs on their arm stand straight up. A wow factor could be any one of the following or a combination thereof:

- A powerfully gripping story, well told, that builds suspense and pays off with a satisfying ending. Such a story could begin in the intro, continue part way through the body, and conclude with an epic finish in the conclusion.
- A memorable and striking visual aid that perfectly encapsulates the main ideas of your message and drives it home within the audience's minds.
- Your personal appearance could potentially provide a wow factor, such as a speaker dressed in full zombie latex special effects, speaking in character as a zombie, to talk to the audience about the importance of preparing for disasters.
- A startling fact that resonates with audience members could be a wow factor, especially if it is powerful enough for them to want to share the fact with others, outside of the context of your speaking engagement.
- A practical demonstration that shows people the content of your message, rather than merely telling them, such as a black belt in karate demonstrating a flying roundhouse kick.
- The general tone of your delivery could also provide a wow factor. A comedian named Anthony Griffith has a speech on YouTube, delivered for The Moth, a storytelling project, where he talks about the year he lost his young daughter to cancer,

and his delivery covers a wide range of extreme emotions, using varied levels of intensity from soft-spoken to all-out rage, leaving audience members in tears by the end—and it is only nine minutes long.

Momentum vs. Accuracy

There are times in our speeches when we may forget important points. There are other times when we might forget entire sections! However, as you continue through your message, if you get to the recap point in your conclusion and suddenly realize that you may have forgotten something back in your first main point, it is generally best to cut your losses and go ahead with the conclusion. If, instead, you back up, share the information, all while placing your conclusion on hold while you do so, then you sacrifice your momentum or your "flow" for the sake of being accurate. The problem with this approach is that it does little for audience information retention. The audience, unless they have a copy of your outline, will not know that you accidentally left out information, so it is best to save it for another time. In fact, there are times when you can sneak the missing information into the Q&A portion of the speech, if you do so via answering an audience member's question.

Using "Bits" for Practice

In public speaking terminology, a "bit" is a smaller section of interrelated material from a larger speech, such as a main point, an introduction, or a conclusion. Professional speakers do not memorize their talks, but instead, practice their speeches using the concept of bits. They break up their speeches into these bits and then spend time practicing each bit, often out of order. The advantage to practicing in this manner is that it more closely plays to our brains' strengths, as we already have a tendency to compartmentalize information when we process it. For example, memorizing a 7-digit number may seem daunting at first, but we do it all the time when remembering someone's phone number, and we do this by separating the 7 digits into two bits: a three-digit bit and a four-digit bit. We also do the same for Social Security numbers, addresses, and many more important unforgettable items.

Learning a speech in this way helps speakers rapidly and efficiently get away from their notes so as to maintain their full attention on the potential audience. In doing so, the speaker's credibility automatically rises, since the audience gains the impression of the speaker as a person who knows the material so well that notes become unnecessary. Learning bits to get away from notes also has other benefits, like freeing the speaker from the podium, so that you are able to move around the room without carrying anything, placing yourself closer to your audience, which we already know increases the tendency to create rapport. Learning bits also tends to make us speak more naturally and conversationally (less scripted and memorized), increases our confidence as we get to know the material more intimately, and makes our practice times shorter and more efficient by helping us practice 3–5 minutes at a time, rather than running through the entire speech all at once.

Mental Preparation Before the Speech

On the day of your speech, there are certain steps to take that can help put you in the right frame of mind. If your speech topic is exciting and upbeat, consider listening to music that is exciting and upbeat, such as music you might listen to when exercising. The faster rhythms tend to put us into the right mood for such an occasion. Similarly, if your speech is more somber and requires more seriousness, consider listening to music of the same emotional feeling, likely slower and more downbeat. Some people choose to develop their passion and vocal power through listening to speeches from famous or powerful orators, such as those found on TED.com or even historical heavyweights such as Martin Luther King, Jr., Malcolm X, John F. Kennedy, or Eleanor Roosevelt, all of whom can be found via www.americanrhetoric.com.

Expressing Emotion

When speaking about potentially emotionally heavy topics, a speaker must be prepared for an emotional flood. As adrenaline hits our bloodstream, it alters the way we experience our emotions by magnifying their effects. Someone experiencing an adrenaline rush due to the fight-or-flight response that comes with the territory in public speaking will be more prone to emotions becoming overwhelming than the same person in a normal state of rest. Therefore, if your speech topic, for example, will reference a close and well-loved family member who recently died, be prepared to cope with the inevitable emotional reaction that could bubble up to the surface. Even when such a speech is practiced at home without any emotional side effects, it is highly likely that the same speech, when given in front of an audience, will result in tears that well up, seemingly out of nowhere. If this happens, let it. One of the worst things you can do is to fight the tears if and when they arise, because that will only hinder your ability to continue speaking. As the emotion arises and overwhelms you, if you persevere through the emotion regardless, your audience will sympathize with you and respect your decision to continue. Audiences are remarkably empathetic and supportive in such situations. Don't allow yourself to end the speech prematurely because your emotions bring you to tears. Be prepared for such situations by having a tissue handy, just in case, and consider what your response will be in advance.

Question and Answer Period

While first impressions are incredibly important—and it is your job to maintain these impressions throughout your speech via effective delivery methods—it is also vitally important that you maintain a positive final impression as well, and this is done through effective moderation of your Q&A period. As your conclusion wraps up and you state your final clincher, be prepared for the audience to applaud. One of the hardest things for many speakers is to stand up front, often awkwardly, and absorb the applause, but don't rush the audience by interrupting their ovation; after all, you've earned it!

As soon as the applause dies down a bit and before you leave the podium to tear down your visual aids setup, announce that you have time for questions. As for how much time, as a general rule, try not to allow your Q&A to run any longer than about 25% of the total time you've been allowed. For an hour-long presentation, allow up to 15 minutes for questions. For a 10-minute speech, allow up to two minutes. After announcing the Q&A, you may get lucky enough to have generated immediate questions, at which point, it becomes a matter of calling on people in the order they raised their hands. However, with some topics, it may take the audience a while to think of questions, but be patient.

If nobody raises a hand, don't take this as an indicator that your speech did poorly; it could be due to the audience simply needing a moment to digest the information. Wait for at least 10 seconds before deciding to end without a single question.

As you field the questions, answer fully, yet briefly. This is not the time to dive headfirst into a whole different speech topic. Maintain eye contact with the question-asker while the question is being asked, but when answering, return your eye contact to the entire audience. If you do not know the answer to a question, the worst thing you can do is make up an answer or try to bluff. If you do not know the answer, simply say so, and then offer to find out the information for that person (more importantly, actually follow up with the answer later to increase your credibility with that audience). Speakers who try to bluff their way through a Q&A run the risk of having an audience member who knows the right answer, in which case, their hands will be the very next to go up!

If someone asks a "gotcha question" designed to entrap you or directly points out misinformation from your speech, avoid getting defensive with that audience member. Instead, acknowledge the possibility, be humble, and promise to look further into the matter later. If certain questions end up too far off-topic, it is perfectly acceptable for you to decline to answer. Consider offering to meet with that audience member afterward to discuss your responses.

As your time comes to a close, you will need to end the Q&A session. Even if hands are still going up with further questions, you need to be respectful of your audience's time, as well as other speakers, if there are more, so politely announce the end of the Q&A and thank the audience for their time and attention.

Chapter Summary

Memorably connecting your message to your audience is done through careful planning, practice, and strategy regarding how you will deliver that message. Practice and preparation must be undertaken early and often. Start with a minimum of three separate practice sessions. The first session tests the amount of time your speech will take to deliver. The second session transfers your information from the outline to your note cards. The third session is when you get to know your notes and develop your style. Any and all sessions of practice after that are merely to refine your delivery and potentially add many of the advanced tips offered in this chapter.

As George Washington Carver once stated, "There is no shortcut to achievement. Life requires thorough preparation." Public speaking and communication in general are learned skills that require dedication and commitment to refine and perfect!

Chapter 9

Listening Skills and Critical Evaluation

> *"We have two ears and one mouth so that we may listen twice as much as we speak."*
>
> *—Epictetus, Greek philosopher, 55–135 AD*

Listening effectively is a challenging task. It is essentially one-half of the communication process, and often, the more neglected half that we fail to both teach and put into practice. The purpose of this chapter is to examine listening as a learned skill, much in the same way that we are examining public speaking, and to learn how critical listening in the context of public speaking involves complex processes that can be perfected through practice.

Hearing vs. Listening

How many times have most of us been sitting in an audience, "listening" to a speaker, only to realize moments later that we have basically heard nothing that the speaker said because we were too distracted? In fact, because we are currently living in a day and age that actually promotes methods of distraction by way of technology, our attention spans have become fragile and easily manipulated.

This highlights the difference between hearing and listening. Hearing is a passive process. Changes in air pressure (sound waves) enter the ear, pass through the ear canal, and vibrate the structures within the ear, creating nerve impulses that are sent to the brain and processed as sound. We do not need to do anything active for this process to take place; as long as our ears are working, and there are no barriers such as headphones or earplugs, the sound will register. That is hearing. Listening, on the other hand, requires us to take hearing a step further and process or interpret what we are hearing. To listen is to add an active cognitive component to the hearing process.

Preparing to Listen

As mentioned in Chapter 1, we listen with a set of preconceptions or filters through which we interpret what we experience. For example, a fanatical devotee to the world of science fiction will likely process everything he or she hears through a science fiction lens. Likewise, a political junkie will view various experiences through a politically charged viewpoint. To truly listen, we must be willing and able to set aside these preconceptions, at least initially, so that we are able to take in what we are experiencing nonjudgmentally. Only after we have received the entire message, should we analyze it through our personal frame of reference.

We must also clear our minds of distractions, both external and internal. Training ourselves to focus when there is a loud air conditioner in the room, a train passing by outside, or noisy next-door neighbors can be difficult, but it is necessary to be able to take in the whole of the message. Similarly, any internal interference, such as worries about a test coming up, a job interview, a fight with a loved one, etc., must be set aside for the time being, or else we will find ourselves distracted and unable to listen.

In addition to setting aside filters and distractions, we must be aware of our nonverbal signals that we are sending the speaker. While you might be tired or have a sore neck, and your hand and forearm offer you a handy kickstand to rest your head upon, remember how the speaker might view your resting pose: "I must be boring the audience!" Or, you might feel perfectly comfortable tying up your loose appendages (arms) in a knot to keep them from dangling about, but to a nervous speaker, your pose may appear defensive. Lastly, if you are nervous about an upcoming interview or somewhere urgent you have to be after the speech, and you keep glancing up at the clock, to the speaker, it may appear as though you cannot wait for the speech to end. Be aware of how your posture, gestures, or facial expressions could possibly be interpreted by the speaker, and do your best to remain supportive and attentive.

Vladimir Gjorgiev/Shutterstock.com

Recognize that listening is an active process that requires energy. When we listen, our brains are actually working and burning calories. The harder we listen and the more effort we expend, the more draining the process can become. This stands in stark contrast to binge-watching your favorite television series on a weekend at home, where you are acting more passively and simply absorbing what you experience. Critical listening requires you to remain alert, undistracted, attentive, and focused. For any of us, there are times when our attention may drift, so try to make yourself aware of these tendencies, and do your best to break these habits through self-awareness and empathy, or the ability to place yourself into another speaker's position.

Activity

Go to www.TED.com, and find the 2011 TED Talk, "5 Ways to Listen Better," by well-known speaker and sound expert Julian Treasure, who discusses the idea that we are, in fact, losing our ability to listen. In a world where we are bombarded by sound and visual stimuli, our ability to listen well continues to dwindle. One strategy Treasure suggests to begin improving our listening is to sit in silence for only three minutes a day, removing all distractions. In a world of constant social media updates and checking our phones, this may be more challenging than we might think. These few minutes of silence help us refocus, retrain our ears, and as Treasure called it, "recalibrate" so that we can appreciate the sounds around us.

Strategies for Listening Well

As speaking begins, focus on individual portions of the message, rather than examining the overall message itself. Identify main ideas and supporting points. Listen for oral citations (sources being verbally cited, such as "According to..."), and evaluate their credibility. Listen analytically as you piece together all of the components of the speech individually. Consider paraphrasing the speaker in your mind. The average person may speak conversationally at a rate of about 150 words per minute, but the average listener is capable of thinking at a much faster rate, at amounts around 400–500 words per minute. Taking this into consideration, we can use "down time" in between words and sentences to paraphrase speakers' points into our own words, adding to our ability to retain and understand them.

If you are a kinesthetic/tactile learner, and taking notes is a valuable retention tool for you, then consider taking notes on the speaker's points. For people with this learning type, they often take notes on speakers or lecturers, only to never refer back to those notes again. The physical action of writing the notes is how their brains register and record the information being consumed. However, perhaps you are more of a visual learner who needs to see the speaker during the presentation; in that case, taking notes could be detrimental to your ability to listen.

One of the hardest things to do while listening involves resisting distractions. There could be auditory distractions, such as a loud fan or buzzing noise, people talking loudly in the hallway, or someone sitting nearby with a cold and the sniffles. There could be visual distractions, such as a compelling visual aid left up by the previous speaker, someone with a visually striking outfit or item of clothing seated nearby, or a speaker who is wearing clothing with a distracting message emblazoned across the front. Physical distractions include stomach growls, leg cramps, a headache, sinus pressure, or temperature that is either too hot or too cold, not to mention the worst distractions of all: a vibrating cell phone! Lastly, there could be mental or internal distractions, as mentioned previously. To resist these distractions requires self-discipline and careful preparation before the speech begins. Turn off the phone. Be sure you have gotten enough to eat. Set aside distracting thoughts. Collect yourself in the single focus of paying attention, on purpose, in the moment.

Be sure to give each and every speaker the benefit of the doubt. Some speakers may come out with "guns blazing," so to speak, and deliver their message bluntly, almost as though they are trying to get a rise out of the audience. If you tune out these speakers initially, you may not be present enough for when they take an unexpected turn or twist. Likewise, if a speaker takes a while to warm up into the speech and you tune out due to boredom, you may miss out on incredibly valuable information that simply was not delivered as good as it could have been delivered.

Keep your emotions in check. It is highly likely that a speaker will say something at some point that will evoke a question, and you could easily be tempted to dwell on that question, allowing it to *ruminate*, or circle round and round in your mind. If this happens, consider writing the point or question down to save it for later. Some speakers skillfully evoke questions that they end up answering later in the speech. This technique requires a lot of practice to perform successfully, but effectively keeps audiences listening closely for the answers.

Being a Respectful Listener

The Golden Rule suggests that we treat others how we would expect to be treated, and in public speaking, this rule holds especially true. Ask yourself, how would you feel if someone leaned over and started talking to a neighbor during your speech? In such a moment of high anxiety, you would likely assume these two people were making fun of you, resulting in a pretty serious distraction. However, the person could have just as likely leaned over to remark on what a great speaker you are, but when we are experiencing high levels of self-doubt, that is the last thing that runs through our minds. Would you want someone texting under the table as you talked, or would that come across as rude and disrespectful? What if someone yawned or fell asleep during your speech? What might that do for your self-esteem? As you listen as a member of a public speaking audience, remember how these various situations would feel if it was reversed, and you were the speaker.

Electronic Distraction

During speeches, avoid phone, tablet, or laptop use, unless previously arranged with the speaker in advance due to a special and documented accommodation need. The first reason for this is, if you have your laptop open, it is almost impossible not to check email or briefly surf the internet, even if you did not mean to or have told yourself that you will not do so. Most of us have the same impulse if we have our laptops open in a meeting. The problem is, that studies indicate that this kind of multitasking impairs learning (Murphy Paul, 2013); once we are on email or the web, we are no longer paying attention to what is happening in the room.

One could argue that it is your choice about whether you want to use your time as an audience member to engage actively with the material at hand, or whether you would like to multitask. After all, you think you are not bothering anyone (one could argue) as you quietly do your email or check social media, but there is a flaw with that theory. From what we can tell, you are actually damaging the learning environment for others, even if you're being quiet about it. A recent study (Sana, Weston, & Cepeda, 2013) found that, not only did the multitasking student in a classroom do worse on a post-class test on the material, so did the peers who could see the computer. In other words, the off-task laptop use distracted not only the laptop user, but also the group of students surrounding the laptop user.

In addition, the speaker can find multitasking on a laptop a bit distracting because sometimes, the audience member is not typing at the right times. Even when the speaker is not saying anything noteworthy, and the supposed listener is engrossed in typing, this suggests that they are doing something other than being fully engaged and listening. That thought alone serves to distract the speaker's attention.

There is also the issue of the speaking environment. If you are on a laptop, the speaker and your peers are often looking at the back of your computer screen and the top of your head, rather than everyone making eye contact with each other. Learning in communication happens best when everyone is actively engaged with one another in the exchange of information. This can mean looking up from your notes to listen, which means you may need to make strategic decisions about what to write down. Note taking is designed to support the learning and retention of material; note taking itself is not learning.

Another study (Mueller & Oppenheimer, 2014) that got a lot of attention in mainstream press suggests that taking notes by hand rather than typing them on a laptop improves comprehension of the material. While students taking notes on a laptop (and only taking notes—they were not allowed to multitask) wrote down more of the material covered in class, they were often typing what the instructor said verbatim, which seems to have led to less processing of the material. The students taking notes by hand had to do more synthesizing and condensing as they wrote because they could not get everything down. As a result, they learned and retained the material better. There is also something to the ease with which one can create visual connections on a handwritten page through arrows, flowcharts, etc.

It is good for all of us to break addictive patterns with regard to email, texting, social media, etc. When we step back, it seems a bit silly that we cannot go for an hour without checking our phones or other devices. We have developed the habit of checking, and we can see practice as a listener as a chance to create or reinforce a habit of not checking as well.

Provide Encouragement

In continuing to follow the Golden Rule of listening—treating speakers as you would like to be treated when you are speaking—one of the best ways to support a speaker is to provide solid nonverbal encouragement and be mindful of the nonverbal messages you send. First, start with eye contact. Full, consistent, and prolonged eye contact tells speakers they have your attention. Also, sit up straight or lean forward, as this posture also suggests a higher sense of immediacy, or intention to be involved in the communication taking place. If the speaker mentions something you like or agree with, smile in approval and be free and generous with your head nods, though not to an extreme, where it appears fake or forced.

Speakers (as well as any other performer, such as a singer, an athlete, or a dancer, etc.) derive their energy from supportive crowds, and when crowds lack energy, it tends to have the opposite effect. The more encouragement you provide to one another, the more confident you will find yourself feeling. In return, as the speaker's performance improves with your added encouragement, your return on investment is larger as well, since you are then an audience to a much higher caliber of speech.

Peer Evaluations

While you will undoubtedly perform graded peer evaluations within your speech class, learning to evaluate a speaker is a valuable skill to have and should be practiced even beyond your public speaking class. Evaluation employs the skills involved with critical thinking to listen to, dissect, analyze, and critique a message, so that you may discover both what worked well in the speech, as well as what could be improved upon in the future.

Essentially, a peer evaluation is a formal critique based on a set of pre-established criteria that you perform on one of your classmates as she or he is speaking. To complete this task requires practice of all that has been laid out within this chapter, including setting aside all distraction, focusing on individual portions of the speech objectively, and maintaining a laser-sharp focus.

Good evaluators are good coaches, and a good coach encourages good behaviors. In a quest for excellence, good coaches also point out areas that need improvement. When good coaches can express their opinions accurately with good interpersonal skills, the participants can excel and feel good about that important teaching moment. When evaluating a speech, be that good coach. Encourage good behaviors, and help the speaker become even better in the future. Here are some points to keep in mind:

1. Be prepared to evaluate. Bring peer evaluation forms (provided by your instructor) to class on speech days, even if your instructor requires them to be submitted online. These forms are invaluable for helping you follow along with the various components of the basic speech organizational pattern at first, until you obtain more experience and commit those components to memory.

2. Learn how to evaluate correctly early on in the semester. During speeches, your evaluations will count toward your grade. Bottom line: learning how to do a proper peer evaluation will not only help your grade, but will also help *you* become a better speaker!

3. Know the "criteria" for evaluating speeches. The criteria are the standards by which you will judge the speech. Look over the assignment objectives and the appropriate evaluation forms for criteria.

4. You will need to write while the speaker is speaking. This may seem rude at first, especially if you are not accustomed to note taking, and it will also be difficult initially, but you will soon feel that it comes naturally as you learn to listen for and provide constructive feedback. Most students don't take long to become efficient and effective at doing the evaluations.

5. Read over and study the samples at the end of this chapter. These were taken from actual student evaluations. Use them as a model for your own evaluations.

6. A great place to start for learning how to perform peer evaluations is to use the "3-2-1" method of evaluation:

    a. Begin by listing three positive aspects of the speech, or three things you think the speaker did very well. Be sure to support these with specific examples. It is not enough to say, "Good speech," or "I really liked it." Take it further and articulate not only which details were effective, but why.

    b. Follow this up by discussing two areas of improvement. What could the speaker have done better, and then support your assertions with clear and specific details. How might the speaker improve upon these areas or learn from them for the next speech? For example, if the speaker's opening statement is lackluster, provide a suggestion or strategy for how to improve it, such as, "In future speeches consider opening with something such as a quote or staggering statistic for improved impact." This last component is essential to growth; the speaker must not only know what needs to be improved but also *how* to improve it. This is where you need to become a good coach.

    c. Lastly, include your overall impression. If this was an informative speech, how well informed did you feel afterward? How unique and innovative was the speaker's treatment of the topic? How well did the speaker relate the topic to you, as an audience member? Again, support this impression with details from the speech itself.

Above all, remember that the peer evaluation process is designed to help others learn from their experiences to become better communicators, so all feedback provided during this process should pursue that purpose. Positive feedback should encourage speakers to capitalize on those strengths. Constructive criticism should not break a speaker down, but instead, point to areas where further development and refinement are required to communicate more effectively.

Chapter Summary

One of the most important concepts to remember regarding listening is that it is an active process that requires preparation, effort, and commitment—the same as required for public speaking. Listening is vastly different than the passive process of simply hearing, so we must prepare ourselves in advance by taking steps to resist or eliminate common distractions, and set aside our prejudices. This alone takes practice to develop, refine, and eventually perfect, but through a process of trial and error, we can increase our self-awareness to the point of becoming sharp, focused listeners.

Also, remember the Golden Rule: treat other speakers the same way you want them to treat you when speaking. Avoid disrespectful behaviors such as side-talking, failing to silence your phone, texting, or falling asleep, but also avoid behaviors that could be taken the wrong way, such as an unintentional nonverbal signals like folding your arms or resting your head on your hands. Be mindful of how you might appear to a nervous speaker, and instead, be supportive.

Lastly, the process of critical speech evaluation is a valuable one that you will inevitably practice in class, but it also provides you with a skill you can use in many other situations throughout life. Learning to recognize the strengths of a speaker can help you by showing you what you can do in your speeches, while learning to recognize and critique opportunities for improvement will help you recognize those behaviors and tendencies in your speaking as well.

Completing In-Class Peer Evaluations

Good evaluators are good coaches, and a good coach encourages good behaviors. But in a quest for excellence, good coaches point out areas that need improvement. When good coaches can express their opinions accurately with good interpersonal skills, the participants can excel and feel good about that important teaching moment. When evaluating a speech, be that good coach. Encourage good behaviors, and help the speaker become even better in the future. The previous chapter provides good guidelines, and here are some points to keep in mind as you listen critically:

- Be prepared to evaluate. If your instructor provides you with forms similar to the examples at the end of this chapter, bring them to class on speaking days (even if your instructor requires them to be submitted online).
- Learn how to evaluate correctly early in the semester. During speeches, evaluations will likely count toward your grade. Bottom line: learning how to do proper peer evaluation will not only help your grade, but through the practice of listening, it will also help you become a better speaker!
- Know the "criteria" for evaluating speeches. The criteria are the yardstick upon which you will judge the speech. Look over the assignment objectives and the appropriate evaluation forms for criteria.
- You will need to write while the speaker is speaking. This may seem rude and it will be difficult at first, but you will soon get the hang of it. Most students quickly become efficient and effective at doing the evaluations.
- Read over and study the samples that follow. Use them as guides.

At a minimum, write five comments: three positive comments and two areas for improvement. Address only one criterion per comment.

- Use a "+" or "–" sign in front of each of your comments to help identify them easily. Address one criterion per statement.
- Start with a positive comment. Always begin by commenting on a strength.
- Use "you," not "he" or "she." You will be addressing the speaker personally.
    - What is good? Describe what you noticed using specific examples.
    - Why is the behavior positive? Explain.
- Although we stress good aspects of a speech so the person will continue to do what works well, your job will also be to point out two weaknesses/areas of improvement so the person can improve. While pointing out areas of weakness of a speech can help the speaker improve in the future, accompany each comment with a constructive alternative. Be sure to word your comment demonstrating interpersonal skills.
    - What was not so good? Describe the behavior using specific examples.
    - Why was the behavior considered an area of needed improvement?
    - How can the speaker improve that behavior? Give a helpful coaching suggestion.
- Be specific. Study the differences between the two samples when it comes to specificity. Describe the behaviors you observe. Why is something effective or not effective?

Sample 1: Good Peer Evaluation—Speech to Inform

<table>
<tr><td colspan="2">Speaker: Zeke</td><td>Section: 2</td></tr>
<tr><td colspan="2">Evaluator: Zelda</td><td></td></tr>
<tr><td>CRITERIA TO WATCH FOR</td><td colspan="2">COMMENTS</td></tr>
<tr><td>ORGANIZATION</td><td colspan="2"></td></tr>
<tr><td>Introduction</td><td colspan="2" rowspan="24">+ When you previewed your main points, I liked how you repeated the phrase, “Alternative schools are…” and then added the point. That is what the text talks about to keep your audience focused. Good job!

+ Your visual aids were well done and followed the guidelines outlined in the book. They added to your speech rather than becoming a speech by themselves.

– You use the phrase “and stuff” like some use the filler “uh.” Such fillers become noise interference. You may begin to eliminate that by just becoming aware of it.

– I don’t believe you had a real attention getter. In fact, I think you began with a purpose statement, “Today I’m going to talk about…” The text says avoid such starts! Starting with the purpose statement doesn’t really pull me into your speech. You’ve had so many experiences with troubled kids, you could have started with a story—one that connects with us.

+ I really liked the way you followed the speech recipe. When I listened to you, I could follow you easily, especially when you made your transitions clear. You made me think you really wanted us to understand your message.</td></tr>
<tr><td>Gain attention</td></tr>
<tr><td>Give audience incentive to listen</td></tr>
<tr><td>Establish credibility</td></tr>
<tr><td>Introduce subject; central idea</td></tr>
<tr><td>Preview main points</td></tr>
<tr><td>Transition to body</td></tr>
<tr><td>Body</td></tr>
<tr><td>Clear, well-developed organization</td></tr>
<tr><td>Sufficient support material</td></tr>
<tr><td>Related topic to audience</td></tr>
<tr><td>Oral footnotes</td></tr>
<tr><td>Transitions between main points</td></tr>
<tr><td>Conclusion</td></tr>
<tr><td>Signal the end</td></tr>
<tr><td>Recap main points</td></tr>
<tr><td>Clincher</td></tr>
<tr><td>Delivery</td></tr>
<tr><td>Eye Contact: Looked at everyone in audience and held eye contact</td></tr>
<tr><td>Notes: Used to jog memory; did not read from notes</td></tr>
<tr><td>Vocal/Verbal: Volume, rate, fluency</td></tr>
<tr><td>Appearance: Appropriate attire, posture</td></tr>
<tr><td></td></tr>
<tr><td></td></tr>
<tr><td colspan="3">After listening to this speech, the degree to which I feel informed: 1 Not at all 2 3 Somewhat 4 (5) Very

What was the central idea of this speech? I’m not 100% sure, but I think the C.I. was “Alternative schools have several unique benefits over traditional schools.”</td></tr>
</table>

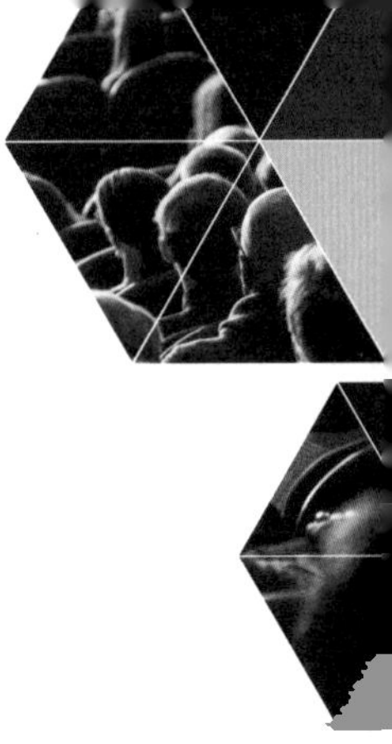

Sample 2: Poor Peer Evaluation—Speech to Inform

Speaker: Hilda	**Section:** 10
Evaluator: Mildred	

CRITERIA TO WATCH FOR	COMMENTS
ORGANIZATION	Yes
Introduction	Was OK but could have been better
Gain attention	
Give audience incentive to listen	
Establish credibility	yes
Introduce subject; central idea	Yes
Preview main points	
Transition to body	
Body	OK—I followed it pretty good
Clear, well-developed organization	yes
Sufficient support material	
Related topic to audience	OK
Oral footnotes	- kind of awkward
Transitions between main points	
Conclusion	?
Signal the end	Needs work!!
Recap main points	Not sure
Clincher	OK
Delivery	good
Eye Contact: Looked at everyone in audience and held eye contact	
Notes: Used to jog memory; did not read from notes	
Vocal/Verbal: Volume, rate, fluency	
Appearance: Appropriate attire, posture	

After listening to this speech, the degree to which I feel informed:	1 Not at all	2	(3) Somewhat	4	5 Very

What was the central idea of this speech? Alternative schools

Chapter 10

Designing and Using Effective Visual Aids

> *"Create your own visual style...Let it be unique for yourself and yet identifiable for others."*
>
> *—Orson Welles*

Even the most well-written and carefully crafted speech has the potential to tax an audience's collective attention span. We live in a media-rich society, in which images tell stories and help us retain information more effectively than mere words alone. In creative writing, an old saying—*Show, don't tell*—suggests that it is far more important in engaging an audience to help an audience *see* whatever we are trying to convey, and that is where visual aids become a critical component of public speaking.

First, however, we need to understand the definition of the term, visual aid:

- *Visual: Of, or pertaining to, the sense of sight*
- *Aid: To help, add support, or give relief*

When we combine these two terms together, our new term—visual aid—suggests that the primary purpose of such a presentation tool is to give visual support to a speaker. All too often, novice or unprepared speakers treat visual aids as though they were the speech itself. Think back to a time when you witnessed "PowerPoint karaoke"—when a speaker lost your interest because she or he turned away from the audience and instead, read everything off the screen to you. Not only does this tend to lose attention spans, but in the worst cases, it can insult the audience's intelligence. When this happens, the visuals overtake the speaker as the central focus in the room, meaning that they are no longer adding aid, help, support, or relief, but have become the speech itself. The main idea behind a visual aid is to create something engaging for your audience that will hold their attention and add tremendous value to the main idea behind your message. Keep this in mind as you design your visuals.

A well-designed set of visual aids has many advantages over mere words alone. Visual aids enhance:

- **Clarity:** Think about how difficult it would be to explain how to tie a shoe without a visual aid!
- **Interest:** It would be one thing to discuss the after-effects of an oil spill, but another entirely to show images of catastrophic environmental damage.
- **Credibility:** Well-designed visual aids dramatically increase how audiences perceive the credibility (or believability) of a speaker; however, this can also backfire on a

speaker if the visuals are designed poorly, as an audience may perceive the speaker as having far less credibility in that case.

- **Information retention:** Audiences presented with visual representations of information being spoken are considerably more likely to remember that information.
- **Brevity:** Using visual aids can cut down on the amount of time required to explain difficult concepts.
- **Appeal to a broader array of learning styles:** You are well aware that some people prefer to learn visually, some through sound, and others through their sense of touch. Using visual aids with your speech provides an added dimension for your audience by providing elements that will enhance their ability to retain the information you present.

Types of Visual Media

Before you begin designing visual aids for your speech, it is important to think about the best type of medium to communicate your message. Some media may work better than others, depending upon the point you wish to make or the type of information being presented. Ultimately, visual aids can be divided into two major types: **active** and **passive** visual aids. An active visual aid is one that the speaker uses and interacts with actively throughout the presentation of information, such as a speaker discussing how a car's engine works while utilizing the actual engine as a visual aid. A passive visual aid is one that, for the most part, remains in the background during the presentation, but its presence in the room still adds value to the information, such as an image of a person being displayed on a screen while the speaker talks about that person. Generally, you want to utilize more active visuals than passive, but the ratio of active to passive visuals will depend upon the topic being discussed.

Poster Boards, Flip Charts, and Tri-Folds

Remember back in grade school, around third grade or so, when you may have made a colorful collage on dinosaurs that you were so proud of, then you brought it home, and your parents were so proud of it, they hung it on the refrigerator for the world to see? Poster boards have their time, place, and purpose, but once we become adults and try to establish more credibility among our listeners, we need to think more critically about the impressions we create.

A poster board made at home with markers and cut-outs from a magazine simply will not do the job; a professionally printed poster is a better choice. However, such posters are fairly expensive in comparison with other visual options, so a poster board or tri-fold should be left as a last resort, or used only when no other option will suffice. An example of a situation in which a poster would be the best choice might be at a convention or trade show, which would allow passers-by to stop and review your information for themselves, up close. Another option could be in a smaller meeting, where electronic media may not be available and everyone in the meeting could easily view your poster. For larger audiences and rooms, however, posters simply will not work.

IrenD/Shutterstock.com

Figure 10.1. Sample of a Professionally Made Poster Board

Static Displays

A static display is a visual accompaniment to the information being presented, and is mostly a passive visual aid. For example, if a speaker was doing a biographical speech on Stephen King, that speaker could set up a static display of some of King's most popular books on a table near the center of the room. This adds value to the presentation because it adds listener interest and reinforces the information being presented.

PremiumVector/Shutterstock.com

Figure 10.2. Sample Book Display

Maps

Any time you are discussing a location that may be unfamiliar to members of your audience, consider using a map to show the location. For example, if a speaker was discussing how to take a family road trip with an audience, then to use a map as an active visual aid to explain the process of designing a route would be an effective method of presenting that information. Maps could be used for anything from explaining historical trade routes to how to get to a scenic hiking path. When incorporating a map, be sure to avoid overcomplicating your visual, as you do not want your listeners straining to read captions and determine where something is located.

Graphs/Charts

Graphs and charts present a highly effective method for showing an audience how statistics and figures affect them. As with maps, remember to keep them simple and clear, allowing your listeners to digest all the information at once.

A **pie chart** is a circle that has been broken up to show proportions of numbers relating to one another. Use this type of graph to show how elements relate to one another, giving your audience an idea of size and relationship.

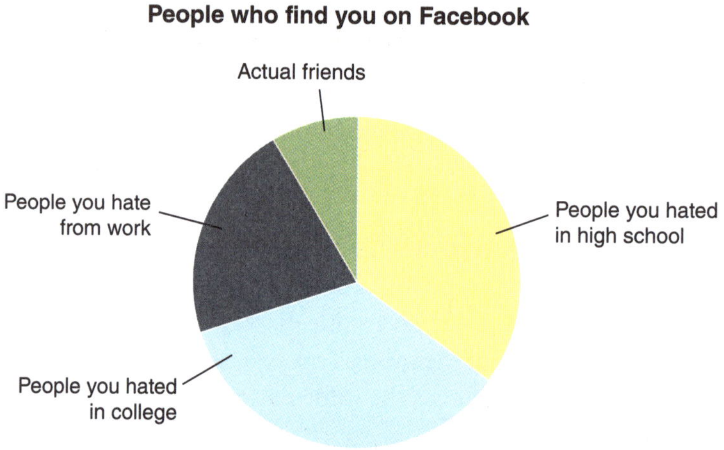

Figure 10.3. Sample Pie Chart

A **line graph** is a type of visual aid one might use to show trends over time. An effective line graph should be simple, have a clearly labeled x- and y-axis, along with data labels showing how the numbers change over time.

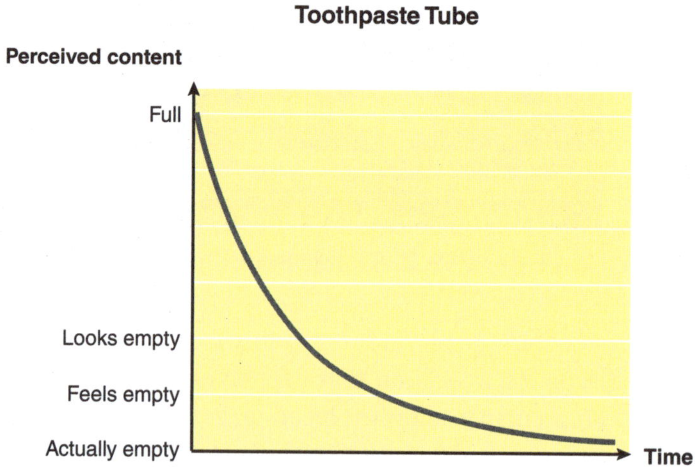

Figure 10.4. Sample Line Graph

A **bar graph** is effective for demonstrating quantity relationships between items (as with pie charts) and often over time (as with a line graph). Bar graphs present a method for potentially detailing a large and complex amount of information using a single image.

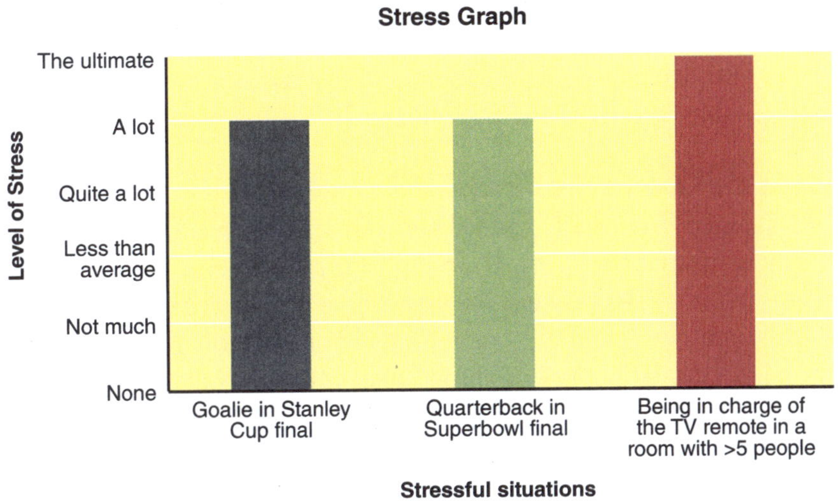

Figure 10.5. Sample Bar Graph

Physical Objects

An object, whether large or small, can bring an element of presence to the visual presentation of your information. It is one thing to view a picture of what you are trying to represent visually, on a two-dimensional screen, but it is another to physically see the object in question.

For example, in a speech on breast cancer and early detection, a student utilized a set of marbles of varying sizes to show the audience what real-life tumor sizes are like when discussing breast cancer detection. The student walked the samples around the room as she talked, allowing listeners to see in front of them what she was discussing, before returning to the front of the room, where she displayed the very same marbles using a picture on the screen. Had this student only used the visual on the screen, it could have been difficult for the audience to get a sense of proportion when discussing the size of the items in question, and since size was the most important characteristic of the visual aid, this student thought critically about how best to present it.

An important consideration to keep in mind when using objects as visual aids is this: Avoid passing around physical objects during your speech unless absolutely necessary to make your point. When most listeners receive an object, their attention span is broken momentarily, causing them to miss out on potentially important information. Instead, as in the example above, you could walk around with your objects, still allowing everyone to see the object, but maintaining focus on yourself as the speaker.

Video/Audio

Regardless of how well we explain something using the most visual language we can possibly muster, there are times when words fail. If the old saying, "A picture is worth 1,000 words" is to be believed, then a brief video clip can be worth 100,000 words! For example, if delivering a speech about the importance of supporting a specific charity, look into the charity to determine if they have a brief promotional video or commercial to supplement the points you are making within your presentation.

Pro Tip
When using video or audio clips, try to keep your clip length to less than 10% of the total amount of time you are allowed for the speech. If you have 10 minutes, keep the total time of your clip(s) to one minute or less. If you have an hour, keep them to less than 10 minutes total.

When using a clip, it is best to preface the clip with some sort of introduction, pointing your listeners in the right direction and priming them to watch for or listen for specific information. Also, avoid talking over the sound in a clip, as competing for your audience's attention during such a viewing could be difficult at best.

Handouts or Leave-Behinds

A handout is something, usually printed material, that you want to give your audience to remind them of what they learned during your presentation. Sometimes, these are called "leave-behinds." For example, in a speech on the science behind chocolate chip cookies, you might want to hand out a copy of your favorite recipes. Or, if you are speaking on blood donation, you might write up a summary of the steps involved and where audience members can go to donate blood. Regardless of the leave-behind, be sure that, as with physical objects, you do not pass these out during your speech, as they can create an unneeded distraction.

Yourself

When can you become the visual aid? Consider a speech on wildland firefighting. Such a student could show up in full protective gear, and although it would likely be pretty hot for that student to deliver the full speech in uniform, it would provide for a powerful visual aid. Similarly, a student doing a speech on yoga may choose to demonstrate certain poses and may want to dress appropriately to do so.

In addition to yourself, there may be times when you need a volunteer's help, such as in demonstrations of martial arts techniques or, as one student courageously attempted, a blood draw, to demonstrate phlebotomy. Be cautious in using other people (or animals), as they could become problematic or unpredictable. Always have a backup plan, just in case, and be sure to prearrange any volunteer activities to ensure smooth operation and as little time used as possible.

PowerPoint/Prezi

Presentation software, such as PowerPoint or Prezi (www.prezi.com), allows relative newcomers to presentation design to create powerful and engaging visual aids of all types. While PowerPoint is a Microsoft Office product, tools such as Prezi often offer free access for educational purposes and can offer a fresh, unique take on the classic presentation slides. However, it can come with a much steeper learning curve, so be prepared. If you are not comfortable with the complexity of designing your own Prezi from scratch, be sure to look up the pre-made templates available for use. There are also several free open-source presentation software options available, such as Google Slides and OpenOffice. Many of these are simplified and provide video tutorials on getting started. It's merely a matter of your willingness to explore the possibilities and tackle something new.

PowerPoint/Prezi Tips

Whatever you are using in a slide, make it large enough to be seen by anyone in the room. This is what we call "aiming for back row comprehension." Be sure your font choices are easy to read and are large enough to read without squinting. In general, choose fonts for screen projection that do not have serifs, such as Arial, Verdana, or Tahoma. You can accent with exotic fonts or word art, but don't overdo it.

Bimbim/Shutterstock.com

Figure 10.6.

- Make it simple. Too many novice speakers try to do too much with their visual aids when something simple would have done the job just as well. Do more with less.
- Make it clear. Try not to assume your listeners will "get" what you are trying to say. Be sure to fill in the blanks with missing information and leave nothing open to random interpretations.
- Make it consistent. Avoid changing up your slide design, background, animations, or font styles halfway through your speech.
- Think critically about the colors you choose. A bright white background with plain black text may be simple, but for listeners up front, it may be hard on their eyes. Similarly, a black background with red text may be easier on the eyes, but without sufficient contrast, could be difficult to see.
- Use images wherever possible, instead of text. A picture is worth 1,000 bulleted points!
- Images are not for decoration. All images chosen should support your information (active vs. passive), and should represent an authentic connection to you and your topic.
- Avoid using disturbing or offensive photos that might evoke a strong emotional reaction from your audience. If it is necessary to use graphic images, first, warn your audience before showing them. This helps them overcome the shock factor and pay attention instead to the message being displayed. Second, do not display

them for any longer than necessary to make the impact you are looking for and then move on. Once you gross someone out or overly shock them, you have lost their attention for the remainder of your speech. There is a fine line between shock *value* and shock *overload*. Ask someone to look over your images to give you outside perspective and help determine whether a photo adds value to your speech or whether it becomes a distraction.

- Keep to a single message per slide. Make sure that the slide matches whatever you are talking about, or else your visual aids will be working against you.
- Use the 5 × 7 (or 5 × 5 or 6 × 6, all depending upon your specific instructor's advice) rule: What these rules refer to is avoiding having excessive lines of text (5–6 lines total), with each line avoiding excessive wordiness (5–7 words across for each line). This general rule will guide you and prevent slides from becoming too wordy.
- Use black slides in between points as filler slides. This can help prevent the light from the projector beam blinding you as you talk.
- Don't allow your slides to take your place as the speaker. If the audience becomes too focused on your visual aids, and you fade into the background, then your visuals are no longer "aiding" you, but stealing the spotlight.
- Use only high-resolution images for your slides (to avoid pixelation), and fill the space on the slide with your image.

- Do not talk to the screen. There is a natural human tendency for us to look in the same direction as others in our vicinity, so when our audience looks up at the screen behind us, we automatically want to turn toward the screen as well. However, maintain eye contact with the audience as you explain your visual, or at least as much as possible. If you must look, try not to turn your whole body away from the audience and look only briefly, for about 1–2 seconds. Helpful tip: Plant your foot that is closest to your visual aid solidly. When you look back at your visual, leave your foot planted, and you will naturally spring back toward the audience.

- Use **progressive revelation** if you have multiple lines of text. This is when you reveal only one point at a time on the same slide. For example, if you have seven lines of text all relating to the same main point, as you click forward through the slideshow, only one of those subpoints is revealed at a time, helping to build suspense and maintain attention.

When/Where to Use Visuals

Visual aids should always be used at key, critical, or confusing points in your message. Consider using a powerful visual as you gain attention in the beginning. Or, you could use visuals in your transitions. Think of these as mini attention getters to keep the audience engaged in your material. You can also use visuals to clarify difficult, complex, or potentially confusing information, as well as to reinforce main ideas.

Be mindful of how well the audience can see your visuals. It may become necessary to move furniture or objects (or yourself) around to ensure every audience member can easily see your visuals. After all, if they cannot see them, they are not truly visual!

Plan Everything

Even the greatest speakers make mistakes, but the hallmark of a great speaker is in how well she or he adapts when those mistakes occur. For example, if the battery to a presentation remote fails mid-speech, a great speaker has already thought of the "what ifs" and adapts accordingly, walking calmly over to the computer keyboard and using the space bar to advance the slides instead, without skipping a beat. Or, in the worst of situations, let's say that a projector light bulb burns out and a speaker has only brought a PowerPoint presentation. A great speaker will have a backup plan in place, having brought printed copies of the slides to hand out in such a situation. While handouts are certainly not ideal and break the rule of handing things out during your speech, they are still better than the alternative of having no visuals at all. Additionally, as the audience sees this level of preparation and foresight, it automatically increases the perceived level of credibility.

It is also important to test your technology *before* the presentation. Often, what works on your computer at home may not work on the computer available in the presentation venue. Differences in operating systems (Mac vs. Windows), versions of presentation software, or even different browsers (Firefox vs. Chrome vs. Internet Explorer) can cause drastic differences in the way a presentation appears (or even whether or not it will function). It is best to not only test everything before you get up to speak, but preset your system volume, ensure all links to outside media work, and have a backup plan ready in case of failure.

Chapter Summary

Remember that a visual aid's primary purpose is to assist you, as the speaker, in delivering the core meaning of a message. It should supplement your message, working with you, rather than against you. Too many speakers try to make visual aids (especially PowerPoint) overly complex in an attempt to wow their audiences, but end up missing the mark because audiences are often overwhelmed by flashy visual aids. It is important to start with a well-written speech and design visual aids around the core of the message, focusing your efforts on designing visuals that will clarify your message, add credibility to your presentation, and provide the audience with a memorable visual experience. Above all, as you insert a visual aid into your presentation, ask yourself if you really need it. Will it help further your specific purpose and reinforce your central idea? If the answer is no, throw it out. As mentioned several times before, do more with less.

Additional Resources

- Prezi—http://www.prezi.com
- PowerPoint Ninja—http://www.powerpointninja.com
- Presentation Zen—http://www.presentationzen.com
- Six Minutes Blog—http://sixminutes.dlugan.com/contrast-repetition-alignment-proximity

Part II
Speaking to Persuade

Chapter 11

Persuasion Theories

> *"They may forget what you said, but they will never forget how you made them feel."*
>
> *—Maya Angelou*

During the first 10 chapters of this book, we have covered strategies and techniques for preparing to speak informatively with our audiences, but we must now turn our attention toward speaking to persuade. Whereas an informational speech seeks to impart new, unique, and innovative messages to an audience, persuasive speaking takes it a step further by attempting to influence audience members' ways of thinking or motivate them to action. In this respect, persuasion is an art form that requires careful planning and strategic composition, as well as delivery, to succeed. In this chapter, we will look at why some strategies work and why others fail, as well as cover tips for a refined version of audience analysis.

First, however, what is persuasion? **Persuasion** is the act of influencing another person's values, beliefs, attitudes, or behaviors. When learning to persuade, it is important to understand the difference between *influence* and *power.* An instructor may threaten to fail you if you do not complete an important assignment, but if you choose not to do it anyway, then, despite the instructor attempting to exercise her power, she has not necessarily persuaded you. Influence is often divorced from power. Instead of being direct, influence can be subtle, often so subtle as to barely be noticed by those being influenced. The same instructor could choose not to employ power tactics to convince you to complete the paper, but instead, share with you the benefits of the paper on your education, as well as the consequences tied to not completing the assignment, and the decision is left to you. In that case, the information being presented may be compelling enough to influence your decision to act in the way the instructor wanted you to act. Persuading others is truly an art form, which, when wielded properly and ethically, wields a unique power of its own—the power of communication that can change the world, even if changing one person at a time.

Specific Purposes and Persuasion

Before we dive too deeply into persuasion theory (which is regularly offered as a full semester-long college course in communication studies), we need to examine the different types of specific purposes available to choose from within the domain of persuasion.

Speech to influence belief or attitude: In this type of speech, the speaker attempts to win over audience members to a certain way of thinking, attitude, or belief. For example, if a speaker felt passionately about climate change, she or he could present facts, figures, and examples, before working toward a conclusion trying to persuade the audience that climate change is a serious problem. Keep in mind that deeply held beliefs are extremely difficult to change, especially in a 10-minute speech.

Speech to influence behavior: This type of speech uses the elements of persuasive speaking, as outlined previously, to gain audience action or participation as a result of successful persuasion. Using the prior example, if the speaker wanted to convince the audience that, not only is climate change a real phenomenon, but that they should begin carpooling to help curb carbon emissions, then the speaker has spoken to influence behavior. This type of speech is often referred to as a speech to motivate to action.

Regardless of the specific purpose you choose for your speech, the most important step of all when preparing a persuasive presentation is to get to know your audience. As we mentioned earlier in the book, without knowing your audience, you may as well be speaking to yourself in a mirror. With persuasion, this is even more critically important, for an audience will not be moved to change their minds, take action, or be inspired if you do not know what their existing attitudes, opinions, values, and beliefs are. To begin, an audience analysis is in order, as mentioned in Chapter 4, but this time, your focus is going to be on attitudes, opinions, values, and beliefs with respect to the topic you have chosen to cover. Once you know those, you can begin to determine your strategy. For example, if you have an audience that is strongly opposed to the information you will be presenting them, then you know you have an uphill battle in front of you, so it is best to consider the most realistic strategy possible.

Persuasive Strategy

The following is an example of a **semantic differential scale**, which is the primary tool for a persuasive speaker:

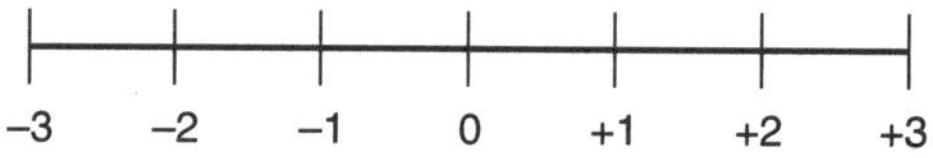

You may have seen something like this before, most likely on a survey instrument of some sort, but what the numbers represent are levels of agreement, with *strongly disagree* (−3) at one end, *neutral* (0) in the middle, and *strongly agree* (+3) at the opposite end. As you design your audience analysis questions, be sure to utilize something similar to this to determine what your audience's attitude is regarding your topic. An example question may look like this:

Climate change is a scientific certainty (circle one):

Strongly Disagree	Disagree	Somewhat Disagree	Neutral	Somewhat Agree	Agree	Strongly Agree
−3	−2	−1	0	+1	+2	+3

After collecting your audience surveys, simply add up the total responses for each segment along the scale (e.g., 3 strongly disagreed, 4 disagreed, 2 were undecided, 7 agreed, and 7 strongly agreed). Then, divide each result by the total participants in your survey to find out the percentages for each one. From there, you can use this information to determine the best strategy to present your message.

Strongly Opposed (–3)

For an audience that (unfortunately) registers toward the strongly opposed side of the semantic differential scale, your sole purpose is going to be to create uncertainty in their minds. At this point, you will have to accept that, no matter how effectively you deliver your message, they may be too firmly entrenched in their beliefs to convince them to act upon something related to your topic. It is best for you to realistically only attempt to create an element of uncertainty. This is like planting a seed for the future that may one day grow into a full-fledged idea. Provide the audience with information that will sway them to your side. To imagine how this would work in a real-world situation, consider a young child going to his mother to ask for a substantial raise in his allowance. To create uncertainty in a topic he knows his mom is strongly opposed to, his approach might be as follows: *"I know you haven't given me an allowance before, and I know I haven't done much to earn one, but that could all change. I'm not opposed to working to earn an allowance, so maybe this is something we could discuss."*

Moderately Opposed (–2)

For audiences not entirely opposed to your ideas, you might first seek to create uncertainty in their opposition, as above, but then follow that up with attempts to reduce resistance to what you are proposing. Consider spending your energy on refuting objections. In a way, this is like our sample child going to his mother and saying, *"Perhaps you think I am not responsible enough to complete my chores, but I've already made my bed and fed the dog. Or, maybe you don't think you have enough money to pay me allowance; however, you will actually save money. I know I'm not going to convince you to give me an allowance of $20 a week right now, but perhaps you could consider meeting me in the middle at $10 a week."*

Neutral or Weak Opinions (–1, 0, +1)

If your topic is relatively unknown, then your audience will be somewhere along the midpoint of the semantic differential scale, having either neutral/no opinions, or they may slightly lean to one side or the other. In such cases, we can ignore the previous two strategies and begin striving for actual changes in attitude and behavior. Simply put, if our audience has no opinion, it is up to us to provide them with information leading to opinion shift resulting in behavioral or attitude change. Spend your energy on explaining the problem. Consider our child again, this time, approaching his mother, who has never before considered an allowance request: *"You know, Mom, I was just thinking the other day about the possibility of earning an allowance. Right now, any time I want to buy something, you have to buy it for me. If I had an allowance, I wouldn't have to bug you for money."*

Moderately Favorable (+2)

On the positive end of the scale, this is where we find that the fun begins. When an audience is already moderately favorable toward what we are presenting, then all we need to do is amplify their attitudes. Spend your energy on showing your audience why your solution is the most desirable. This is the point along the scale where inspiration takes place. Again, with our child example, perhaps he has been volunteering to work around the house without being asked (as part of his master plan, of course), and one day, he strategically opens a conversation as follows: *"I've really been enjoying helping out around the house lately, Mom. I always feel so accomplished whenever I finish a chore, but, as I was thinking about it, I remembered that there was this sort of expensive toy I really wanted to start saving for, so what are the chances I might be able to earn some money for the chores I've been doing?"*

Highly Favorable (+3)

Once we reach the opposite end of the scale, we have arrived at the proverbial "pep rally" stage of persuasion. At this point, our audience is ready to commit to action on our behalf, so it is merely a matter of capitalizing on those attitudes to gain behavior or action. As with the previous step, we want to begin by amplifying attitudes before connecting those attitudes to the action we desire to obtain. For our young (and oddly well-spoken and persuasive) child, his approach might look like this: *"Remember when you mentioned the other day how proud of me you were for all the work I've been doing around the house lately, Mom? Also, remember when you were mentioning to Dad how you would like to teach me how to save money? Well, do I have a suggestion for you..."*

Knowing these strategies in advance can help you approach an audience wherever its current beliefs may be. If you approach a strongly opposed audience overconfidently seeking to get them to commit to action, your message is doomed from the beginning. Likewise, if you approach a strongly favorable audience sheepishly and only seek to reduce their resistance, you will quickly lose their attention. Always be sure to match your level of persuasive approach to the level of audience agreement.

Table 11.1. Persuasive Strategies

Level of Audience Agreement	Persuasive Strategy
Strongly opposed	Plant the seed. Provide information.
Moderately opposed	Refute objections.
Neutral or uninformed	Explain the issue.
Moderately favorable	Show why your solution is most desirable.
Highly favorable	Get the audience to take action.

Rhetorical Triangle

Over 2,300 years ago, the Greek philosopher Aristotle developed a three-pronged strategy for persuading others. He suggested that a careful balance of all three vertices of his **rhetorical triangle** is required for effective and successful persuasion. The three elements of that triangle are: *ethos, pathos,* and *logos,* which you have probably encountered before in a writing class at some point. For the sake of seeing exactly how they all fit together with respect to persuasion in oral communication, let's break them down individually.

Ethos

As the popular movie *My Big Fat Greek Wedding* suggested, we borrow many of our words in the English language from the Greek language, and this word forms the basis for several words, including ethics, ethology, and ethnicity. Literally translated from the Greek, ethos means "spirit" or "character" and forms the basis of a speaker's credibility or persona. A speaker's ethos is essentially **personal appeal**, how an audience views a speaker or the speaker's image that she or he portrays outwardly. Think of ethos as our first impression of a speaker, and there are several questions a speaker must ask of herself or himself to help think critically about how to establish a solid ethos:

- How will you generate respect from your audience?
- How will you create a connection or rapport with your audience?
- How will you build trust with your audience?

To begin, let's take a look at the first question above, regarding respect. One way to gain the respect of an audience is to establish expertise, a reputation, or a closeness with respect to your topic. If you are speaking about biological pathogens, and you happen to be a biology major, establish that in the beginning. If you have extensive experience working on cars, and your speech is about how to change your oil, be sure to explain that early in the speech. Regarding closeness, if you happen to be speaking about the dangers of drunk driving, and you have unfortunately lost a close family member to drunk driving, then that closeness becomes your ticket to earning audience respect.

Secondly, with respect to generating rapport with your audience, seek out similarities between yourself and the audience. If you are a student and so are they, be sure to find a way to use that to your advantage. Also, be sure to adapt your "style" to the audience, similar to the way a chameleon adapts color to its environment. This means that you adapt the style of your visual aids, the language you use, your clothes and appearance, and even your mannerisms to reflect the audience. Essentially, the more similarities your audience notices between you and them, the easier it will be to establish rapport.

The third question addresses trust, one of the most difficult items regarding ethos to build and maintain. Begin your quest for trust with first impressions set even before you take the stage, so to speak. Show up early. Dress for the occasion. The way you look will make a strong first impression. Be prepared, and when it is your turn to speak, demonstrate that readiness in advance. Stand tall and confidently (even if you feel a little nervous—see Chapter 2). Establish your credibility early in the speech (third step in the introduction) and do so sincerely. As you continue speaking, use easily identifiable stories to illustrate your points, and even better, share your own personal stories to help the audience get to know you better. Use familiar language and avoid overpowering the audience with your impressive vocabulary. Using "big words" can often turn an audience away. Reference the people in the audience, such as referring to an earlier speech, as you highlight similarities or parallels between your topics, or reference your audience survey, if you have completed one. Above all, speak with conviction, for if you don't believe yourself, why would your audience? Trust is built one step at a time, but as you put all of these seemingly minor details together, they fit with one another to build a trustworthy and inherently believable sense of ethos.

Pathos

Pathos, like ethos, provides us with a significant number of words in the English language, such as pathogen, pathetic, pathological, sympathy, empathy, apathy, and many more, but its root meaning from the Greek is "suffering" or "experience." What pathos refers to in the context of the rhetorical triangle is **emotional appeal**. Human beings are highly emotive animals, and our decisions are primarily based on our emotions. In fact, almost all decision making takes place in the limbic brain, which is responsible for those "gut feelings" and yet, has no capacity for language. What this means for you as a public speaker is that, if you can tap into your audience's emotions, you can persuade them to take just about any action you desire. However, that also means pathos is often the most easily manipulated of the three.

To begin thinking about how you will utilize emotional appeals in your persuasive speech, you must first consider how your central idea ties to specific emotions, as well as how your individual main points evoke emotion. For example, if you wanted to persuade people to work on their public speaking delivery, you would not name the speech, "How to speak in public better" when naming it "How to conquer your fears of public speaking" evokes a much stronger emotional response. Always try to find the emotional tie-in with the material you plan on presenting by asking yourself, "How do I want my audience to *feel* about this?"

The next step, as you are writing the speech, is to think about the emotions evoked by the language you use, for certain words have stronger emotional connotations, such as the difference between "injured veteran" and "wounded warrior." Your language can potentially frame your message in such a way as to encourage development of certain emotions in your audience. Consider the use of rich analogies and/or metaphors here as well, such as stating, "Terrified, you suddenly feel like you're stuck in quicksand," versus saying, "When fear strikes, you feel as though you cannot move."

As with establishing ethos using stories to connect and create rapport, stories can also build an emotional connection to your message. Consider the difference between two speeches on cancer, where one covered nothing but facts and statistics to demonstrate cancer research, while the other one told deeply rich and emotionally heavy stories about people who had survived cancer, thanks to research breakthroughs. Which one would potentially be more moving to convince you to donate money to research? Odds are, it is the one you *feel* more connected to, and that will most often be the one with the compelling story.

Not only can that connection be made through stories, but also through the visuals we choose to display. Imagine telling the story of a cancer survivor and seeing images of that person going through treatment, only to come out the other side of that treatment, looking happy, healthy, and surrounded by loved ones. When we can *see* our emotions being played out in front of us instead of simply having information *told* to us, we naturally feel a significantly greater connection.

Above all, with pathos, you must be genuine and authentic, not forced. If you find yourself being moved by the power of what you are presenting, allow those emotions to come through in your delivery. Also, be sure your tone matches the level of emotion you want to convey. If you are going for a heavier, serious, somber tone, slow down your rate, and be deliberate about how serious you sound. On the other end of the spectrum, if you intend to be more upbeat, positive, and happy, you might want to avoid sounding as monotone as the high school teacher in the classic 1980s movie, *Ferris Bueller's Day Off*—"Anyone? Anyone? Anyone?"

Lastly, when it comes to intentionally deciding which emotions to evoke, consider this: Your message and its point of view should be associated with positive emotions (happiness, satisfaction, contentment, love, belonging, etc.), while your competing perspectives that you are attempting to refute should end up associated with more negative emotions (guilt, fear, obligation, jealousy, sadness, disappointment, etc.).

Logos

Logos, as with the previous two Greek words, gives us several words in the English language as well, with the most obvious word being *logic*. Literally translated, logos means "word" or "to reason," and it is the portion of our speaking where we invoke logical, rational argument to make an **appeal to reason**. The most important element to logos is whether or not our argument makes sense or adds up. Establishing strong logos involves using credible facts, statistics, and evidence supporting our various claims.

You may have been subjected to a persuasive argument that did not make much sense, leaving you wondering why you were being persuaded at all. Perhaps it was a salesperson trying to solicit you to purchase a product that you would never likely use, leaving you wondering how the salesperson arrived at the conclusion that it would be a good fit for you. This is what it feels like to experience arguments based in poorly constructed logos.

Types of Reasoning

To construct well-reasoned logos, understand the two types of reasoning you may use to develop your arguments: *inductive reasoning* and *deductive reasoning.* Inductive reasoning is, according to the Internet Encyclopedia of Philosophy:

> ...an argument that is intended by the arguer merely to establish or increase the probability of its conclusion. In an inductive argument, the premises are intended only to be so strong that, if they were true, then it would be *unlikely* that the conclusion is false.

For example:

- Two witnesses claimed Eric committed the murder.
- Eric's fingerprints are the only ones on the murder weapon.
- Eric confessed to the crime.
- So, Eric committed the murder.

Deductive reasoning, on the other hand, tends to be more grounded and possible to prove true. According to the Internet Encyclopedia of Philosophy, a deductive argument is:

> ...an argument that is intended by the arguer to be (deductively) valid, that is, to provide a guarantee of the truth of the conclusion provided that the argument's

premises (assumptions) are true. This point can be expressed also by saying that, in a deductive argument, the premises are intended to provide such strong support for the conclusion that, if the premises are true, then it would be *impossible* for the conclusion to be false.

For example:

- Sarah is sick today.
- If someone is sick, then she will not be able to attend our meeting today.
- Therefore, Sarah will not be able to attend our meeting today.

Deductive reasoning, therefore, is a more concrete way of arriving at logical conclusions, whereas inductive reasoning is often what audiences will do in response to a deductive argument when they create objections to your reasoning.

To explain this using a real-life scenario, let's say that you are trying to convince your audience to try a new weight loss program or diet:

- This new diet will reduce your hunger. (Premise A)
- This reduction in hunger will reduce the amount you eat. (Premise B)
- Reducing the amount you eat will result in weight loss. (Premise C)
- This new diet will, as a result, cause weight loss. (This is a sound, deductive conclusion that *must* be true if premises A, B, and C are true.)

While you are using your sound, concrete deductive reasoning, what could your audience be thinking?

- "Every time I have tried something like this in the past, I failed miserably." (Premise D)
- "This new program is just like those failed diets." (Premise E)
- "This new diet will fail miserably." (This is a reasonable inductive conclusion drawn from premises D and E.)

Because the audience's conclusion is based on strongly ingrained emotional experience, and because the experience of failure is an emotional one, it presents a high degree of pathos and probably outweighs the strength of your deductive conclusion. If your audience has to resolve conflicting emotional conclusions, then they will look for flaws amid your arguments, often resulting in imaginary flaws that are not even there. Although your deductive conclusion is sound, they will doubt your premises:

- "But I'm always hungry when I am on a diet!" (Counters premise A)
- "But if I reduce how much I eat, I won't have enough energy to exercise, and I'll gain weight anyway!" (Counters premise C)

How could you remain persuasive in this challenging scenario? Remember, that in persuasion, your success depends greatly on your ability to make your argument stronger while, at the same time, make opposing arguments weaker. For example:

- Boost your argument by providing supporting facts, research, or even your personal success story with the new diet program.
- *Show* why this new program is unlike past failures. If successful, you would be casting a shadow of doubt on premise E, and therefore, their entire inductive argument.

Addressing Objections

This example of types of reasoning highlights the necessity of addressing potential objections, rather than allowing them to take root in the audience's minds, creating barriers to our persuasive message. The longer you allow an objection to sit and ruminate (or swim about inside an audience member's head), the greater the chance that objection will prevent that listener from being persuaded.

The best way to determine which objections need to be addressed is to constantly ask yourself the following question: Why would any member of my audience *not* want to take this action or adopt this position? For example, if you are trying to convince your audience to take additional courses in communication studies to improve their skills in interaction with others and build a stronger resume, you would need to consider all of the possible reasons why someone would not want to take these classes, which may include:

- "I'm terrified of public speaking."
- "There's not enough room in my schedule with all other degree requirements."
- "I'm not a communication major."

Each of these objections could be discovered fairly easily with the right audience analysis (see Chapter 4), and once known, you can compose refutations to these objections to include in your speech as a way of heading off objections before they can take root, as follows:

- "Not all communication classes focus on public speaking. In fact, most courses, outside the public speaking course, focus on in-class discussions, writing papers, and performing fascinating activities outside of class."
- "Communication courses can be used to fulfill a wide variety of degree requirements, including social sciences, arts and humanities, and of course, oral communication."
- "You don't need to be a communication major to refine your communication skills, seeing as how, regardless of industry, all employers consistently rank communication skills as their #1 most desired soft skill in a potential employee."

Syllogisms

Syllogisms and fallacies relate very differently to public speaking versus writing an argumentative essay. A **syllogism** is typically defined as a deductive argument with two premises and one conclusion. It is the most basic kernel/nugget of deduction. It's a very intuitive reasoning structure that we all use quite often without even realizing it. For example, "All dogs are mammals. Fido is a dog. Ergo, Fido is a mammal." A syllogism can be thought of as a sort of mathematical formula for analyzing persuasive speaking points. A syllogism is essentially reasoning used to arrive at a conclusion based on two or more propositions (premises) that may or may not necessarily be true. For example, "All ordinary men are mortal. Bruce Wayne is no ordinary man. Therefore, Bruce

Wayne is immortal." With respect to public speaking, for a syllogism to work effectively, it need only be *perceived* as true and accurate, so this is where the connection between logos and ethos meets. A speaker who has established a strong ethos (rapport with the audience, credibility, believability, and/or likeability) has a significantly higher chance of a syllogism being accepted as true, regardless of its accuracy.

Such syllogisms could be full of fallacies, so it is important for us, as critical listeners, to understand what fallacies are and how they are used. A **fallacy**, simply defined, is faulty reasoning, or a hole in one's attempt at a rational argument. Common fallacies include the following:

- **Ad hominem:** Derived from the Latin for "to the person," this type of fallacy is one in which criticism is directed at the person, rather than at the position being argued. Example: "Why would anyone believe someone like him, when he has such shifty eyes?"
- **Ad populum:** Derived from the Latin for "appeal to the people," this fallacy can be thought of as the bandwagon effect; do it because everyone else is doing it. Example: "Everybody knows the Earth is flat, so why do you persist in your crazy claims?"
- **Hasty generalization:** This type of fallacy involves making an inductive argument without sufficient evidence for the conclusion, or using a single instance to generalize a much larger group of people. Example: "My grandmother smoked a pack of cigarettes a day and lived to be 95, so I don't think smoking is really hazardous."
- **Red herring:** This fallacy involves misdirection, or distracting someone from the argument at hand with something completely unrelated. Example: "While we understand your frustration with not getting a raise in the last five years, we do work hard to provide great customer service."
- **Straw man:** This fallacy involves substituting an actual position or argument with a distorted, exaggerated, or misrepresented version of the position of the argument, so as to make it easy to refute. Example: "After John said we should spend more on health and education, Dave responded by saying he was shocked that John hates our country so much that he wants to leave it vulnerable to attack by cutting military spending."
- **Post hoc:** This fallacy is short for the Latin phrase, *post hoc ergo propter hoc*. When translated from Latin, it means "after therefore because of." Also called the "false cause" fallacy, this is where someone assumes that correlation automatically means causation. Example: "Incidents of shark attacks correlate directly to increases in ice cream sales; therefore, we should reduce our ice cream intake before swimming in the ocean." In this example, no cause-effect connection exists between the rates of ice cream sales and shark attacks. The cause of these two effects was most likely the fact that summer was in full swing.
- **Slippery slope:** This fallacy (also called the domino fallacy) occurs when someone claims that A will lead to B, which will lead to C, and so on, all the way to F, without providing good reasons for predicting all the cause-effect connections between A and F. Example: "If we let our teenage son leave the house, the next thing we know, he will be running with the wrong crowd, drinking, and doing drugs!"

- **Weak analogy:** Similar to the hasty generalization in a specific context, the weak analogy attempts to connect two items based on a thin or irrelevant thread of similarity. Example: "Guns and hammers are both made of metal and can kill people, so if you want to regulate guns, then you might as well regulate hammers, too." Analogies are a good way to help an audience understand your information. However, when you use an analogy to support a conclusion, the similarities need to be both strong and relevant.
- **Appeal to authority:** Just because someone famous or credible said it, then it must be true. Example: "Abraham Lincoln once warned us that we should not believe everything we read just because we see it on the internet." Far too many quotes are attributed to figures such as Einstein, when in reality, he may have never weighed in on the topic. Advertisers have keyed into this fallacy when they select celebrities to endorse their products, such as the Proactiv commercials that feature famous singers.
- **Burden of proof**: This fallacy occurs when the person putting forth the argument suggests that the burden of proof lies with someone else to disprove the argument. Example: "There is currently a truck orbiting Venus, but because you cannot disprove it, then it must be true."
- **False dichotomy:** When someone suggests that there are two—and only two—possibilities, they are setting up a false dichotomy, which is also called the black-or-white or either-or fallacy. Example: "You're either with us or you're against us!" or "My way or the highway—there's no in between!" FYI: There is no fallacy if only two options truly exist. It's only a fallacy when two are offered but more than two actually exist.
- **Genetic fallacy:** Related to the old saying, "Don't throw the baby out with the bathwater," this fallacy occurs when someone doubts the validity of a claim simply on the basis of who said it. Example: "The president suggested that this year has 365 days, but we all know how much of a liar he is."
- **No true Scotsman:** Often used as a last resort out of desperation, this fallacy proposes an appeal to purity, as if to suggest criticism is invalid if certain "pure" conditions aren't met. Example: "No real man would drink his coffee with a pink straw" or "They must be from California; a true Idahoan would not do that."

Fallacies might be highly persuasive to the untrained eye or ear; however, an ethical speaker would never knowingly use fallacies to persuade an audience. A speaker might unintentionally or accidentally use fallacious reasoning, but the speaker who knowingly tricks an audience with poor reasoning is an unethical speaker.

Blending Ethos-Pathos-Logos Together

Think about what a speech would look like if a speaker focused solely on one of these three elements. A speech employing pure ethos, but no pathos or logos, would be charismatic and enjoyable, but as you considered the message further, you would find that it is empty, vapid, and devoid of substance, and in the end, would lack an emotional connection or logical argument to support claims. A speech using pure pathos, but little ethos or logos, would come across as emotionally manipulative. A speech utilizing pure logos without ethos or pathos would be dry, boring, and full of factual information, but no emotional or personal connection to relate those claims to the audience.

This illustrates effectively why Aristotle was so adamant about the need for balanced arguments. We can think of ethos as setting the stage for engaging our audiences, earning their trust and respect, and maintaining their attention, while pathos is used in conjunction with ethos to nurture the emotional connection necessary to generate action based on our persuasive messages. Logos effectively balances out pathos by providing substance to those emotional connections and makes good on promises made by the use of ethos. Using all three elements in careful consideration with one another provides not only a more balanced persuasive message, but a more effective one as well.

Communication-Specific Persuasion Theories

While there are many theories surrounding effective persuasion, several of them are specific to the field of communication studies. Two of those theories we have chosen to showcase here, and those include the Elaboration Likelihood Model (Petty & Cacioppo, 1986) and Social Judgment Theory (Sherif, 1963).

Elaboration Likelihood Model

This theory, abbreviated ELM, attempts to describe why certain methods of persuasion work, even though mysterious, and why others fail. Known as a dual-process model, ELM describes a *central route* to persuasion and a *peripheral route* to persuasion. According to communication theory expert, Em Griffin (2014):

> Message elaboration is the central route of persuasion that produces major positive attitude change. It occurs when unbiased listeners are motivated and able to scrutinize arguments that they consider strong. Message-irrelevant factors hold sway on the peripheral path, a more common route that produces fragile shifts in attitude.

In the central route, the persuader practices many of the techniques described in this chapter. For someone to utilize the central route, ELM suggests that motivation must be present. In other words, the person you are attempting to persuade must commit to the mental energy required to listen to the persuasion process. ELM also suggests that, at the beginning of a persuasive interaction, listeners decide almost immediately if they are going to continue listening or not, which is why your initial communication when persuading is of critical importance. While the central route is cumbersome and difficult, as it requires mental effort, use of logic and rational support, and most often, more time than the peripheral route, use of the central route results in significantly longer attitude or behavior change.

In the peripheral route, the message recipient has little to no interest in the subject being presented, and as such, has no desire to commit the mental energy to go through the central processing route. If the listener takes the peripheral route, she or he will look for information that "feels right" and often make decisions solely based upon first impressions. In the peripheral route, listeners are swayed more by irrational appeal to emotion than logical and balanced messages. Advertisers frequently rely on the peripheral route, as most commercials last only 30–60 seconds. Use of a celebrity endorsement or unrelated humor in commercials are both examples of the peripheral route to persuasion. Consumers making purchases based on a celebrity endorsement or simply because an ad made them laugh means that the persuasive message was effective, but these effects are often short-lived and vulnerable to outside influence, unlike the central route.

Social Judgment Theory

This theory, developed by Muzafer Sherif, attempts to explain how we evaluate and rationalize various ideas and positions. According to SJT, every new idea we hear from a persuasive message is weighted and evaluated against our current points of view before being placed on an attitude scale. SJT explains how we subconsciously sort out ideas as they occur at the instant we perceive them. Em Griffin (2014) explains SJT as follows:

> The larger the discrepancy between a speaker's position and a listener's point of view, the greater the change in attitude—as long as the message is within the hearer's latitude of acceptance. High ego-involvement usually indicates a wide latitude of rejection. Messages that fall there may have a boomerang effect.

As we assess ideas, we place those ideas within one of three zones, or latitudes:

- The latitude of acceptance (agreement with the idea)
- The latitude of noncommitment (no opinion)
- The latitude of rejection (opposition to the idea)

When we have a high level of interest or involvement with the idea, our scale, with these three zones present, reduces to two, as the latitude of noncommitment shrinks with more rigidly held opinions. If the idea falls within our latitude of acceptance, we will adjust our attitude or behavior to match the idea, but if the idea falls inside our latitude of rejection, we will adjust ourselves away from the idea.

Em Griffin (2014) suggested that, to achieve the greatest level of influence, choose a message on the edge of your audience's latitude of acceptance or noncommitment. In other words, if your audience has a high level of interest, find out what minimum acceptable connections you can make between their current attitudes regarding your topic and the action you want them to take, and then tailor your message along that idea. Griffin also noted that persuasion is a slow and gradual process that most often consists of small movements.

Chapter Summary

Persuasion is truly an art form, one that often takes years of trial and error to develop into a natural habit. However, we can actively learn this art and practice it by first considering our specific purpose: Are we persuading, motivating, or inspiring? Then, we must focus on getting to know our audiences and what motivates them based on their attitudes, opinions, values, and beliefs. Without this critically important information about our audiences, even the best and most carefully worded persuasive message has the potential to fail miserably. A poorly worded persuasive message that is mindfully tailored to the audience for which it is intended will be more effective than a well-polished message that does not take the audience into consideration.

Once the audience is known, compose your persuasive message by considering how to balance ethos, pathos, and logos. How will you connect with your audience, by tapping into your mutual similarities, establishing rapport, and earning their respect and trust as a speaker? What emotions will you need to tap into for your message to resonate emotionally with your listeners? And, what facts, statistics, figures, and evidence will you need to bring to your message to add substance and ensure your arguments are sound and well reasoned? Answering these questions carefully and methodically can set you up to become a powerful and dynamic, yet ethical and authentic, persuader.

Additional Resources

- Thou Shalt Not Commit Logical Fallacies—http://www.yourlogicalfallacyis.com
- Internet Encyclopedia of Philosophy—http://www.iep.utm.edu/ded-ind

Chapter 12

Motivating Others to Act

> *"Motivation is the art of getting people to do what you want them to do because they want to do it."*
>
> *—President Dwight D. Eisenhower*

In the middle of the 1930s, a Purdue University communication professor by the name of Alan H. Monroe began noticing that successful persuasive messages all had a strangely common pattern about them. These messages were successful in the sense that, using the art of persuasion, the composers of such messages were able to motivate listeners to take action, even in situations where it would seem that the listeners were opposed to the core of the message itself. Monroe examined the psychological principles of these successful messages and, from analysis of these messages, he derived a five-step speaking process, which today, is affectionately named, **Monroe's Motivated Sequence**. This sequence can be found just about everywhere we look today, from stationary ads like billboards or magazine advertisements, to more active marketing such as television or internet advertising. This five-step pattern is not entirely different from the earlier pattern of speaking we explored for the purpose of speaking to inform, which has an introduction, three main points, and a conclusion. Monroe's Motivated Sequence also contains an introduction, three main points, and a conclusion, but in using this specific method, each of these steps provides more direction and structure regarding what you should be talking about in each step. As a result, Monroe relabeled the five-step process as follows:

- **Gain Attention:** This first step is essentially the same as the introduction discussed earlier in Chapter 6, but in a speech to motivate others to act, this step is even more critical. If you fail to grab the audience's attention up front, then it limits the effectiveness of all subsequent steps.
- **Present the Need:** Also referred to as the "problem" step, this is your first main point of the speech, immediately following the introduction. In this step, you present a need that must be satisfied or a problem that must be solved. You must show the audience that this need is important and that it affects each and every member of the audience.
- **Satisfy the Need:** In your second main point, you will satisfy the need or present a solution to the problem framed in your first main point. You are responsible for showing the audience not only how to apply the solution being presented in a concrete, step-by-step fashion, but you must also show them that what you are suggesting will adequately satisfy the need or solve the problem.
- **Visualization:** In your third main point, you will verbally paint a picture of the benefits of using your proposed solution to satisfy the need. Conversely, you may

also present the consequences of not applying your solution, should the audience ignore your proposal.

- **Call to Action:** This is essentially structured the same as in the speech to inform from Chapter 6, but with a slight twist. You signal the end and recap each of your main points, but instead of a conclusion or "clincher" that reinforces the central idea, you will end with a final call to action, where you directly call on your audience to act upon whatever solution you presented.

Planning the Topic

At this point, it is helpful to examine each of these steps more closely, using a sample speech topic, so that we can look at how the persuasion theory from Chapter 11 is applied to Monroe's Motivated Sequence as outlined above. For the purpose of our example, we will take a look at a speech to persuade audience members not to text and drive. Once topic selection has been completed, the next step is to address a number of questions that will help you better plan your persuasive strategy, as well as compose the speech. Answering these questions can potentially head off a number of creative roadblocks later in the speechwriting process.

1. **What is the action you want your audience to take?** Answering this question saves many a headache. By definition, a speech to motivate others to act necessitates the inclusion of an action, and if you are not 100% clear on what that action will be, then you will run into major difficulties later on. For example, you may be passionate about speaking out against the death penalty and may want to persuade your audience that it is wrong, but what action are they supposed to take? As is, that would be a speech to influence others' thinking. If you had a petition for them to sign as a way to send a message to lawmakers, then it would be a speech to motivate others to act. *Example answer: I want my audience to stop texting and driving.*

2. **Why do you want to deliver this speech?** By answering this question, you discover your motivation from the beginning. By understanding your motivation to deliver the speech, you can better understand what motivations you may want to use to tap into your audience's motivation. Answering this question also prepares you to establish your credibility within the Gain Attention (introduction) step. *Example answer: I was struck by a driver who was texting while driving, which resulted in my hospitalization and a six-month rehabilitation before I could walk again.*

3. **Why does your audience need to take the action you are proposing?** Be careful with answering this question. Many novice speakers approach this question by describing the benefits to their proposed actions, but that only answers the "what" of the speech, not the "why" motivating it. Benefits are a result of an action, not the driving force behind it; you need to understand the *need* behind your action. Often, this is stated as the problem you will be attempting to solve through the action you are proposing. *Example answer: Texting and driving, an all too common occurrence on roads today, drastically reduces driver attentiveness and creates life-altering hazardous driving conditions.*

4. **How will your audience satisfy this need?** Answer this question with your concrete, step-by-step set of solutions to the problem you established as a need. State not only

your solution, but also specifically how the audience will enact this solution. Be detailed and clear. *Example answer: To stop texting and driving, my listeners will need to shut off their phones whenever they start their cars, put them away in the trunk or glove compartment, or pair their phone with a compatible Bluetooth hands-free system before putting it out of sight.*

5. **If your action satisfies the need we currently have for taking it, then why is your audience not doing it already?** Answering this question often points you in the direction you need to be guided in order to research your proposed solution(s). Answering this question may require audience analysis through surveys, because if your audience is already doing what you are proposing, then you may need to refine your topic. *Example answer: Using mobile technology to stay socially connected to others is remarkably addictive, and even the most moral person can find him or herself succumbing to the temptation of glancing down at a recently received notification.*

6. **What obstacles are likely to prevent your audience from doing what you are proposing and what are your counterarguments against those objections?** As mentioned in question 5 above, audience members likely have reasons for not enacting your proposed solution earlier, so be ready for those arguments. As mentioned in Chapter 11, you must not allow potential objections to take root in your audience's minds, so you need to refute these objections early. *Example answer: "Checking a text only takes a second, and I'm a good driver." Refutation: "According to a recent study, the average person glances at their phone for 5 seconds to check a message, and the average crash happens within 3 seconds of driver distraction."*

7. **What are the benefits of doing what you are asking?** Identify the benefits early, before you even write the speech. This may require some research and even a little creativity, but your task is to identify the most tantalizing benefits possible for your audience. Also, consider what benefits may matter most to your specific audience members. Think critically about where their priorities are and what motivates them. *Example answer: The benefits of putting your phone away while driving go beyond staying safe, as you will be able to feel free from distraction and worry. You won't need to worry about your phone dinging every few seconds and feeling pressured to respond immediately. You will feel responsible and alert.*

8. **What are the consequences of your audience not acting on your proposed solution?** Sometimes the benefits of a solution are not as persuasive as covering the consequences. Depending on the topic, there may be very few benefits involved, such as with our sample topic. Covering the negative aspects of the consequences one must face when not doing what you are calling on the audience to do may end up being far more persuasive. *Example answer: Text messaging while driving puts you at a 23% higher risk of getting into a serious crash. Nearly two million auto accidents a year are caused by texting and driving. According to the Virginia Tech Transportation Institute, texting while driving is six times more likely to cause an auto crash than driving when intoxicated.*

By identifying all eight of these responses, you have already completed nearly half or more of the work involved in composing a motivational speech. You can now confidently compose your specific purpose, such as, "My specific purpose is to motivate my audience to stop texting while driving," as well as your central idea, such as, "Texting and driving is dangerous, not only to yourself, but to all other drivers sharing the road with you." From here it is only a matter of filling in the blanks and working on the details within each of the five steps: Gain Attention; Need; Satisfaction; Visualization; and Call to Action. Let's take our sample topic through each of these steps in more detail.

Gain Attention

While the attention step was important in an informational speech (see Chapter 6), as it was used to set the tone and provide your audience with a reason to listen, it is even more critical in the speech to motivate others to act. As mentioned earlier in the chapter, without your audience's attention, subsequent steps will not have the psychological effect needed to make your message persuasive. As with the introduction outlined in Chapter 6, the subcomponents of the Gain Attention step are all the same:

- Grab attention
- Relate topic to audience
- Relate topic to self (establish credibility)
- State central idea and specific purpose
- Preview main points

Let's take a look at how our sample topic might look using this formula:

- **Grab attention:** *On February 19, 2011, a young girl named Ashley Jones-Davis was killed in a gruesome automobile accident. She was texting and driving when she swerved out of the center lane and drove head-on into a box truck. Ashley died on the scene. Since that time, her family has dedicated countess hours and emotional energy telling Ashley's story, because they don't want other families to go through the trauma and sense of loss they experienced.*
    - ***Notes:*** This speech begins with a story that many can relate to, whether audience members are parents, students, female, or simply drivers who have texted while driving before. While brief, the story sets the stage for subsequent information by putting a personal connection to the topic. This speaker could also show Ashley's photo, juxtaposed with a photo from the crash for added appeal to emotion.
- **Relate topic to audience:** *According to my audience survey, nearly 100% of you stated that you have read and/or answered a text while driving before. Though many of you stated that you try to save phone use for stoplights, statistics show that you are not alone. According to the National Highway Traffic Safety Administration, more than 11% of drivers on the road at any given time are distracted by phone use.*
    - ***Notes:*** By appealing to the audience survey, this speaker connects directly to the people in the room, but then broadens out the appeal by relating statistics from a credible national organization.
- **Relate topic to self (establish credibility):** *Two years ago, I saw my light turn green, and as I started to drive through the intersection, I was struck from the side by a*

driver who ran a red light because he was texting while driving. This accident not only totaled my car, but also resulted in extended hospitalization and a six-month rehabilitation before I could walk again.

- ***Notes:*** Copy and pasted from prep question 2 (Why do you want to deliver this speech?), this speaker clearly has a vested interest in sharing a story that motivates others to avoid texting and driving, but more than that, it also relates to the initial story and the statistics shared in the previous step, carefully weaving the three steps together with a common thread, adding to the flow of the message.

- **State central idea and specific purpose:** *Texting and driving is dangerous, not only to yourself, but to all other drivers sharing the road with you. Today, I would like to motivate you all to stop texting while driving before stories like mine and Ashley's become the norm, rather than the exception.*
  - ***Notes:*** The central idea and specific purpose from earlier (after answering the eight questions) are simply copied and pasted into this point, before being edited for clarity and conversational flow. Not only do these encapsulate the core of the speech's message, but they also tie together all threads present within the introduction so far.

- **Preview main points:** *I will show you how big of a problem texting and driving has become today (point #1, Need step), what you can do to stop it (point #2, Satisfaction step), and how you can personally benefit from doing so (point #3, Visualization step).*
  - ***Notes:*** Notice how brief this stage is. Without revealing too much information too soon, this speaker has effectively shared with the audience what they can expect to hear in the next few minutes or so, providing them with a roadmap on where the conversation is heading.

Need Step

The first main point of this five-step speaking pattern is called the **Need step**, and for good reason, because you will be framing a need for your audience so that you can follow it up with a satisfying solution, which is the action you are essentially proposing. Also referred to as the "problem step," this main point involves explaining the *why* behind your proposed action.

In September of 2009, Simon Sinek, an author and speaker in business and leadership studies, gave a TEDx talk in the Seattle area, where he presented the idea of what he dubbed, *The Golden Circle*. To explain this, Sinek used the following diagram:

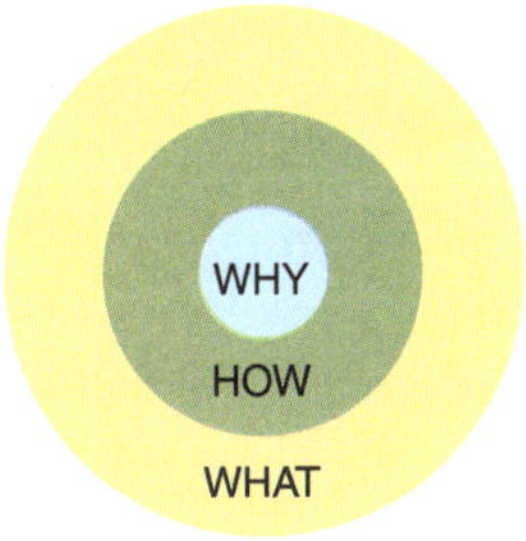

Using this model, Sinek explained that the majority of persuasive messages that we see, read, or hear on a regular basis work from the outside in. They start with the *what*, or the result, and then explain the *how*, which is their method or product, but stop there, expecting us to buy into their idea, their services, or their products. The examples Sinek used in his speech included: "Here's our newest model of SUV (what). It has dual airbags, great gas mileage, and looks sharp (how)." Sinek went on to explain that these messages fail because they are uninspiring. They do not tap into our decision-making center of the brain—the limbic system—because they fail to inspire us or engage us by explaining *why* we need to buy this product.

Sinek then went on to describe the model used by Apple, which is a highly successful persuasive model because it works from the inside out. As a company, Apple's messages clearly begin with an explanation of *why* they are in business by communicating with the world that, in everything they do, they believe in challenging the status quo and thinking differently. Only after the *why* is explained does Apple go on to state that they achieve this goal by creating products that are beautifully designed, easy to operate, and challenge the limits of technology (*how*). Apple's message then ends with the *what*, by showing its audiences the products they can expect to benefit their lives by adhering to this philosophy.

In motivating an audience to act, we, as speakers, must be able to tap into our audience's *why* by explaining to them that a genuine and relatable need exists. We can complete this task by addressing the Need step in four components:

- Show your audience that a need or a problem exists and that it can and will affect each and every member of the audience in some way.
- Explain to the audience why it exists by providing context and history behind the need or problem. In other words, explain where the need arose and perhaps why nothing has been done about it until now.
- Demonstrate to the audience that this problem needs to be solved or this need must be addressed immediately—that it will not simply disappear on its own if left alone.
- Overcome potential objections—why might the audience not believe that this need or problem affects them personally?

Returning to our example speech from earlier, let's take a look at how this step could look:

Need Step

A. *Texting and driving is an all too common occurrence on our roads today.*

   1. *Using mobile technology to stay socially connected to others is remarkably addictive, according to a study performed by Dr. David Greenfield, founder of the Center for Internet and Technology Addiction, when cell phone users compulsively check their devices it is in an effort to stimulate the brain's pleasure centers.*

   2. *In this way, cell phone use can be compared to gambling or gaming addictions, making even the most moral person succumb to the temptation of glancing down at a recently received notification.*

Note: This half of the Need step provides the audience with context and background, effectively setting up the problem being presented. Additionally, it shows the audience that the problem is not going away.

B. *Texting and driving drastically reduces driver attentiveness and creates life-altering hazardous driving conditions.*

   1. *According to a recent study, the average person glances at their phone for 5 seconds to check a message, while the average texting-related crash occurs within only 3 seconds of driver distraction.*

   2. *According to the Virginia Tech Transportation Institute, texting while driving is six times more likely to cause an auto crash than driving when intoxicated.*

Note: This half of the Need step relates the problem to the audience, while also demonstrating a severe and life-threatening need to address the problem immediately.

Satisfaction Step

The second main point within the body of the motivational speech designed to elicit audience action is called the **Satisfaction step**, which is where you satisfy the need presented in the previous step or solve the problem that has been framed. For every aspect of the problem or need that you have presented up to this point, you must demonstrate that your solution fully and adequately addresses that need or problem.

For example, if you presented a need to cut down on fossil fuel usage because you painted a bleak picture of the Earth in 50 years being a toxic wasteland, then in this step, you must clearly and explicitly show how the audience's specific actions will avert such a scenario. It would not be enough to simply suggest the audience carpool or drive hybrid electric vehicles. If that were your suggestion, you would need to include credible research to show that this solution is connected to averting the problem you presented previously. In other words, avoid presenting a problem or a need that is larger than the solution you have in mind. Ensure that the Need step and the Satisfaction step complement one another perfectly.

One of the most important aspects to this step is to address potential objections. As with the eight preparation questions discussed at the beginning of this chapter, think of all the hurdles or barriers that might prevent audience members from adopting your proposed solution to the problem being presented. Then, consider how you will address and refute those objections *before* they have a chance to take root in your audience's minds.

Another way to look at objections is to look at the number of steps involved in enacting the solution. Think of your solution as a transaction, and find ways to make that transaction as easy and straightforward as possible. For example, if you wanted your audience to write letters to their senators and representatives, think of how you could reduce the number of steps involved. To write such a letter, one must: 1) find the time to sit down and write; 2) compose the letter; 3) print the letter; 4) look up the address; 5) find an envelope; 6) address the envelope; 7) locate a stamp; 8) seal the envelope; and 9) drop it in the mailbox. Regardless of how passionate your speech, at any of these nine steps, a distraction could come along and derail your wonderful solution. To reduce these specific steps, you could prewrite the letters for them, place them in preaddressed, stamped envelopes, hand them out to each audience member, and then instruct them to sign them and drop the envelopes in the mailbox after the speech. At that point, you have effectively taken advantage of the fact that you have a captive audience, and you have gotten them to take some form of action before they even leave the room!

Let's take a look back at our sample speech, and see how the Satisfaction step plays out:

Satisfaction Step

A. *The first step in reducing and eliminating texting and driving is to increase your awareness of how much your phone's notification system controls you, and not the other way around.*

   1. *One way to do this is to instruct a partner to ride with you as a passenger and record the number of times you give in to the temptation of glancing at your phone.*

   2. *Another method involves the psychological technique of Cognitive Behavioral Therapy (CBT), where you shut off your phone completely when you get into the car, and as you drive, regularly assess your anxiety levels out loud. For example, every mile or so, talk your way through the anxiety or discomfort you experience as you wonder what you might be missing.*

Note: This half of the Satisfaction step directly addresses the first half of the Need step, employing highly specific and guided actions to address the problem that was established.

B. *To stop texting and driving, we need to cut it off at the source, which involves shutting off our phones whenever we start our cars.*

   1. *In addition to shutting them off, I recommend putting them away in the trunk or glove compartment so that they are completely out of sight.*

   2. *If you have the option available to you, you could pair your phone with a compatible Bluetooth hands-free system before putting it out of sight.*

   3. *Being out of sight significantly reduces the temptation to use a phone while driving, as you will not be able to physically get to it.*

   4. *If you find yourself feeling the effects of "nomophobia" (the fear of being without your phone), simply remind yourself that anything anyone has to say to you can wait, as it is not worth your life, your safety, or the well-being of others around you.*

Note: This half of the Satisfaction step addresses the second half of the Need step by providing a concrete solution to the dangers presented earlier, but additionally, it acknowledges and addresses the potential objections (barriers) that were identified in the eight preparation questions at the beginning of the chapter.

Visualization Step

The third main point within the body of the speech to motivate others to act on a specific issue is appropriately named the **Visualization step**, as its purpose is to help your audience "see" the amazing benefits they can expect to enjoy if they apply your solution to the problem or your satisfaction to the need. This does not need to be positive and rosy, however, as some topics will require a negative approach, or the presentation of negative consequences arising as the result of ignoring your proposed solutions. The best persuaders understand that negative emotional appeals here are fast-acting, meaning that people are easily scared into immediate action, but are short-lived, while positive emotional appeal is slower to act, but tends to last considerably longer. Think critically about what you will use for your topic. Will you focus solely on benefits, solely on negative consequences, or a mixture of both? If you choose a mixture, will you start with the bad news and end on a positive note, or the other way around? These decisions will affect the flow and style of your delivery here, so be critical.

In this step, you need to use colorful, rich, descriptive language. You may also consider saving some of your most prominent visual aids to use here as well. The Visualization step becomes most persuasive when the benefits are so tantalizing, your audience simply cannot imagine life without them. Conversely, this step could be persuasive if the consequences being presented are terrifying or off-putting enough to make your audience realize that your proposed solution is a requirement, not an option. Think of this step of the speech as the "What's in it for me?" stage. By this point in the speech, you have successfully presented a stark need and demonstrated to your audience how to satisfy that need, so now, it is time to show them what they can expect to happen once they enact your solutions, or what can happen if they continue allowing the need or problem to persist and worsen. Consider using a lot of vivid imagery, as well as "what ifs" in this step. Engage the audience's imagination and help them picture themselves applying your solutions.

Let's take a look at this final main point using our sample speech topic:

Visualization Step

A. *The benefits of putting your phone away while driving go beyond staying safe, as you will be able to feel free from distraction and worry.*

   1. *You won't need to worry about your phone dinging every few seconds and feeling pressured to respond immediately.*

   2. *You will feel responsible and alert, as a properly defensive driver should feel.*

B. *If you choose not to put your phone away, however, understand that nearly two million auto accidents a year are caused by texting and driving. Text messaging while driving puts you at a 23% higher risk of getting into a serious crash.*

Call to Action

As with your previous speeches to inform, the speech to motivate others to act on an important issue requires a conclusion, and in Monroe's Motivated Sequence, the whole conclusion is called the **Call to Action**. Begin this conclusion as before, by signaling the end of the speech, followed by a brief recap of your three main points. *Why* do we need to take action again? *How* do you propose we solve this problem? *What* is in it for us? Also, recall that, in a conclusion, you should not bring in any new information. This is merely a recap, not your chance to insert one more shocking fact that you hope will drive your central idea home. Bringing in new information at this point would only confuse the audience as to your speech organization. Once your recap is complete, the last thing you say will be a clincher that makes your final call to action. This clincher should clearly reinforce your central idea from the beginning of the speech, while explicitly reminding your audience in a simpler fashion what action you want them to take. Be direct and be firm. Avoid being vague or wishy-washy with this step.

A great acronym for assessing your final Call to Action is C.A.S.T., or concise, achievable, specific, and tangible. A call to action should be concise, meaning that it doesn't take long to explain. It should be achievable by every single person in the room, and furthermore, they should be able to achieve your goal in a relatively short amount of time. It should be specific, and finally, it should also be tangible, meaning that there is a concrete action for your audience members to take.

Let's take a look at our sample topic as we conclude:

Call to Action Step

Signal End: *As you all leave here today, you will undoubtedly check your phones to see if there are any new notifications. It is likely that even I will do this as well.*

Recap Main Points: *However, remember what we talked about today. I showed you how addictive checking our phones can be, even while driving. I also showed you the dangers of giving in to those temptations while operating a motor vehicle, before I showed you some possible solutions, including shutting your phone off when you get into your cars or using a Bluetooth hands-free system. Lastly, I shared with you not only the benefits of doing so, by becoming a safer, more responsible, and more alert driver, but I explained how, if we all continue to do this, the problem can only get worse.*

Clincher (Call to Action): *Texting and driving is dangerous, not only to yourself, but to all other drivers sharing the road with you. Don't allow this (show picture of screen capture from text messages) to lead to this (show picture of my surgery scars while in a wheelchair). Turn off your phones while driving, and keep your eyes on the road where they belong.*

Chapter Summary

Monroe's Motivated Sequence can be found just about everywhere we look if we analyze the various persuasive messages we see. Billboards along the highway grab our attention visually (step 1), present a need that we can identify with (step 2), provide that organization's solution to that need (step 3), suggest benefits to their product or service (step 4), and have a call to action, such as "Buy our product now" (step 5). Commercial advertisements, whether on television or in a forced viewing before a YouTube video, follow a highly similar format. It is estimated that the modern human living in an urban society is subjected to anywhere from a conservative estimate of 300 up to a more realistic estimate of 1,000 persuasive messages every single day (Gass & Seiter, 2015).

The most successful persuaders using Monroe's Motivated Sequence are those who start with explaining the *why* behind their message. This is why the eight preparation questions are so important to be able to answer before composing your persuasive strategy. Knowing beforehand why you are choosing to present the topic you want to present can help you develop the *why* behind it. Helping your audience members identify and relate with your *why* naturally leads them to seek out the *how*, which is the solution you are proposing.

If you cannot motivate your audience to understand the *why*, though, the subsequent steps are more likely to fall flat, so concentrate on presenting a need so pressing (but do so realistically) that the audience begins desiring satisfaction for that need or a solution to the problem. Then, ensure that the satisfaction or solution is presented clearly, explicitly, and concretely, with plenty of step-by-step detail. Make your solution as easy as possible for your audience to enact. Lastly, drive your persuasive message home by showing (not telling) your audience what they can expect once they have adopted your wonderful solutions. Tantalize them with rich imagery, but again, do so realistically—don't advertise falsely.

Lastly, follow through with a firm, direct, and clear call to action, reminding your listeners why they need to take action, how to do it, and what they can expect from doing so. Balance your approach, ensuring that each step builds upon one another. Make sure that your need step is adequately tailored for your audience, before ensuring that your solution adequately addresses each aspect of the problem. In doing so, you are communicating directly to your audience's decision-making centers of their brains, activating their limbic systems with balanced emotional appeals, supported by logic and personal credibility.

At the end of this chapter, you will find sample outlines to see how other students from the past have approached Monroe's Motivated Sequence. Be sure to utilize these as your models when creating outlines for your chosen topics.

Sample 3A: Speech to Motivate Action

Name: Kristopher Arnold

Audience Analysis

Answer in complete sentences and use examples from your audience analysis questions.

A. If what you are asking the audience to do is such a good idea, think about those in the audience who might object to your idea. How will you address possible objections in your speech? **I am planning to hit head-on any varying objections within my speech, to refute the refuted. Some people think buying products made in other countries means they can have more stuff. I will show them how short-sighted this is.**

B. How much interest did the audience have in your topic? How will you make the topic interesting to them? **The audience didn't have a lot of interest in my topic since they like to buy "lots of cheap stuff." I will show them that by supporting American-made goods that their chances of high-paying jobs will increase when they graduate from college. That should get their interest.**

C. How will the audience demographics (not what you learned on your Audience Analysis) impact the development of your speech? **Being mostly students, it impacts my speech greatly. Most college-aged individuals do not have plenty of money floating around, nor are they usually working full-time, so they have good and feasible reasons to want to purchase cheap foreign products.**

Title: *Made in Chimericakorpan*

General Purpose: To motivate to act

Specific Purpose: To motivate my audience to purchase American-made products

I. **ATTENTION Step**

   A. **Grab Attention:** My neighbor Pete is currently unemployed but is a hard-working American. He goes to bed at 11 pm and wakes up to his alarm clock (made in Japan). He turns on his coffee pot (made in China), stands on tile floor in the bathroom (made in Italy) while he shaves with a razor (made in Hong Kong). He puts on his dress shirt (made in Sri Lanka), designer jeans (made in Singapore), and tennis shoes (made in Korea), jumps into his car (made in Japan), turns on the radio (made in India), checks his watch (made in Switzerland), grabs his briefcase (made in Japan). And, Pete wonders why he cannot find a good paying job.

   B. **Relate to Audience:** Actually, you all need to be thinking about this. This scenario likely hits close to home with most of you and you don't even know it (or don't really want to admit it). Most lower-priced items which so many of you are purchasing are not made in America. I would even go as far as to say that most of the possessions you have here with you today are not made in America.

C. **Relate to Self (Establish Credibility):** In the past I have simply not known what the consequences of purchasing foreign products does on a mass scale, but I will have you know that over the past several years I have changed my ways and have personally made a point to buy local and buy American-made. All of my automobiles and recreational vehicles are made in the good ol' U.S.A., and I now regularly make an effort to keep my money in America and so should you.

D. **Central Idea:** You should buy American-made products whenever possible.

E. **Specific Purpose:** Today, I would like to invite you to consider this option.

F. **Preview Main Points:** I will go over...

II. **Need:** Why we all need to buy American-made products.

III. **Satisfaction:** How you can implement this behavior into your life.

IV. **Visualization:** How your lives will be better after implementing this solution.

Transition to #II: Let's begin exploration of this topic by taking a good look at the problem.

II. **NEED Step**

A. Buying products from China affects employment in the U.S.

1. Mr. Robert Scott indicates that it's a fact that buying products that are made in China decreases jobs in the U.S. (Economic Policy Institute)

2. Something you all know but probably wouldn't want to admit is that buying products made in China also supports the abuse of exploited workers. (*Businessweek.com*)

B. China has become the world capital of contaminated goods.

1. One million toys were recalled recently in China because lead paint was used on the toys, and chewing on these toys can lead to behavioral problems and sometimes death in children. (*USA Today*)

2. Chemicals that are used to make antifreeze are being found in toothpaste from China. (*MSNBC.com*)

Transition to #III: Now that you can see what you support when you buy foreign products, let's look at solutions.

III. **SATISFACTION Step**

A. With a little common sense, it's easy to find American-made products.

1. Look at the packaging for the "made in" sticker.

2. Visit *MadeInUSA.org* for a list of American manufacturers and a list of items that are 100% made in the U.S.

B. Even though it is impossible to get around buying foreign products, we shouldn't use that as an excuse to avoid buying American-made products when possible.

Transition to #IV: Solving this foreign products issue for the United States will take focus on my part (as well as each of you), but the rewards are worth it.

IV. **VISUALIZATION Step**

A. Imagine what it could be like searching for a job and actually finding many good-paying jobs to choose from.

B. You will feel good knowing that the toys your children and grandchildren play with are safer than before.

C. You will have the satisfaction of knowing you do not support the abuse of other human beings.

Signal End: If you have been listening, you now better understand the benefits of spending your money a little more wisely, so I will conclude now.

V. **ACTION Step**

A. **Restate Central Idea:** Buying products made in America leads to a better future for you.

B. **Recap Main Points:** Today, I told you why we need to purchase American-made products, how easy it is to do, and what benefits you'll experience as a result.

C. **Call to Action (Clincher):** I want to ask for a show of hands. I am going to ask each of you to raise your hand showing that you will just try...just try to pay closer attention to the things you are buying. Let's raise our hands for the future of our children and grandchildren. Let's fight this fight from our own soil and spread the word. Will you raise your hand for America today? Thanks. Please go from here today and purchase wisely, and you remember Pete, my neighbor? For Pete's sake, let's buy American.

Works Cited

"FDA to check toothpaste imports from China." *MSNBC.com*. 24 May 2007. Web. 30 Apr. 2019.

Kerr, Jennifer C. *USA Today.com*. 05 June 2018. Web. 25 Apr. 2019.

MadeInUSA.org. 09 July 2018. Web. 25 Apr. 2019.

Roberts, Dexter, and Aaron Bernstein. *Businessweek.com*. 02 Oct. 2016. Web. 28 Apr. 2019.

Scott, Robert E. "Costly trade with China." *Economic Policy Institute*. 01 May 2017. Web. 02 May 2019.

Sample 3B: Speech to Motivate Action

Name: Justine Bunch

Audience Analysis

Answer in complete sentences and use examples from your audience analysis questions.

A. If what you are asking the audience to do is such a good idea, think about those in the audience who might object to your idea. How will you address possible objections in your speech? **Some might object to that planning is yet another task to complete, but I will argue that good planning actually frees up time for the planner.**

B. How much interest did the audience have in your topic? How will you make the topic interesting to them? **They were somewhat interested, but they've had people telling them how important time management is for most of their lives. I'll try to use some current statistical data/research to approach the topic from some unique angles to give them a new perspective on it.**

C. How will the audience demographics (not what you learned on your Audience Analysis) impact the development of your speech? **Since my audience consists of college students, my planning strategies will focus around the main items that college students must plan for.**

Title: *Time Management*

General Purpose: To motivate to act

Specific Purpose: To motivate my audience members to manage their time better

I. **ATTENTION Step**

A. **Grab Attention:** How well do you plan? I consider myself a generally good planner, but whenever I find myself writing a paper at midnight, I must pause to consider the effectiveness of my time management. Let us complete a short quiz from the Dartmouth College Academic Skills Center to determine your individual planning effectiveness before continuing on….

B. **Relate to Audience:** As college students, each of us has procrastinated, prioritized poorly, and generally failed at planning. Even if you feel comfortable with your time-management abilities, it always helps to reassess your effectiveness and to find new strategies to plan well.

C. **Relate to Self (Establish Credibility):** Being a person who struggles with procrastination as well as over-extensive planning, I went on a quest to find the most effective time-management strategies.

D. **Central Idea:** You should improve your time-management strategies.

E. **Specific Purpose:** Today, I would like to motivate you all to manage your time more effectively.

F. **Preview Main Points:** Today I will cover...

I. **Need:** The reasons why it is necessary to be an effective time manager for the community college student

II. **Satisfaction:** The means by which each of us can make better use of our time

III. **Visualization:** And the future benefits to our time-management choices now

Transition to #II: First, why must we manage our time better?

II. **NEED Step**

A. When we forsake effective time management, our present decisions do not serve to fulfill future goals.

1. "Planning is about the future impact of present decisions." (Warnick)

2. Planning frees us up to focus on the important rather than the urgent.

3. Planning allows us to focus on people, not tasks.

B. Not planning leads to anxiety.

1. "Anxiety is the warning light on our spiritual dashboard." (Warnick)

2. If your daily routine is not going to complete your goals, there is a problem with your daily priorities.

3. Planning allows us to complete necessary tasks without stress.

Transition to #III: Now that we have assessed the reasons to plan, let us determine the methods by which to plan.

III. **SATISFACTION Step**

A. Plan around your short-term and long-term goals.

1. Plan tasks that follow the "Smart Tips" strategy.

2. Write a paragraph to determine your individual mission statement, and make sure your schedule is serving to follow your set of values.

B. Create a master/weekly schedule. (Dartmouth College)

1. Write everything down.

2. Create margin within your schedule. (Leave time for things you don't expect.)

Transition to #IV: In the end, what does it look like after you've improved your time-management strategies?

IV. **VISUALIZATION Step**

A. When good planning occurs in your life, you have time to do the things that are most important.

1. Good planning allows you to have worry-free rest.

2. When short-term goals are fulfilled, it is refreshing and fulfilling.

B. When things are orderly in your daily life, you can pursue excellence in a carefree manner.

1. If you're living to fulfill a long-term calling, the end goal is what will motivate you in your daily life.

2. When your vision is for the long-term, the worries of the short-term are only temporary.

Signal End: Let us review what we have learned and decide what to do about it.

V. **ACTION Step**

A. **Restate Central Idea:** After listening to my speech, I expect that you will have taken away effective tools for better managing your time.

B. **Recap Main Points:** After discussing the reasons to plan, the means by which to plan, and what it really looks like to lead a time-managed lifestyle, I hope you will go out and add some more freedom through structure to your daily schedule.

C. **Call to Action (Clincher):** Do not think of planning as yet another commitment, but as something that will free up time to do the things you want to do. "You do what you have to do so you can do what you want to do"—*The Great Debaters.*

Works Cited

Ellis, D. *Becoming a Master Student.* Boston: Houghton Mifflin. 2014. Print.

"Managing Your Time." *Dartmouth.* Trustees of Dartmouth College. 10 Oct. 2018. Web. 2 May 2019.

"Smart Tips." *The University of Chicago.* The University of Chicago. 2018. Web. 2 May 2019.

Warnick, David. *Self Leadership.* New Life Interns. New Life Community Church, Rathdrum, ID. 21 Sep. 2018. Lecture.

References

Chapter 1

Blair, A. (2010, Nov. 28). Information overload, then and now. *The Chronicle of Higher Education*. Retrieved from http://chronicle.com/article/Information-Overload-Then-and/125479.

Davenport, T. H. & Beck, J.C. (2001). *The attention economy: Understanding the new currency of business.* Cambridge, MA: Harvard Business Press.

Harper, D. (2015). Online Etymology Dictionary. Retrieved December 3, 2015, from http://www.etymonline.com/index.php?term=communication.

McCornack, S. (2010). *Reflect and relate: An introduction to interpersonal communication.* Boston, MA: Bedford/St. Martin's.

Rieland, R. (2012, May 7). Big data or too much information? *Smithsonian*. Retrieved from http://www.smithsonianmag.com/innovation/big-data-or-too-much-information-82491666.

Simon, H. A. (1971), Designing Organizations for an Information-Rich World. In M. Greenberger (Ed.), *Computers, Communication, and the Public Interest* (40–41). Baltimore, MD: The Johns Hopkins Press.

Wurman, R. S. (1989). *Information anxiety.* New York, NY: Doubleday.

Chapter 2

Schlegel, A., Kohler, P. J., Fogelson, S. V., Alexander, P., Konuthula, D., & Ulric Tse, P. (2013). Network structure and dynamics of the mental workspace. *Proceedings of the National Academy of Sciences of the United States of America, 110*(40). 16277–16282.

Chapter 3

Williams, J. R. (1998). Guidelines for the use of multimedia in instruction. *Proceedings of the Human Factors and Ergonomics Society 42nd Annual Meeting*, 1447–1451.

Chapter 5

Burton, N. (2012). Is suicide more common at Christmas time? *Psychology Today.* Retrieved from https://www.psychologytoday.com/blog/hide-and-seek/201212/is-suicide-more-common-christmas-time.

Chapman, C. (2011). A brief history of blogging. *Webdesignerdepot.com*. Retrieved from http://www.webdesignerdepot.com/2011/03/a-brief-history-of-blogging.

Giles, J. (2005). Internet encyclopedias go head to head: Jimmy Wales' Wikipedia comes close to Britannica in terms of the accuracy of its science entries. *Nature, 438*(7070). 900–1.

Knoblauch, M. (2014). A brief history of the domain name. *Mashable.com.* Retrieved from http://mashable.com/2014/03/10/domain-names-history/#Wxnv32uQSqqt.

Chapter 6

Dukette, D., & Cornish, D. (2009). *The essential 20: Twenty components of an excellent health care team*. New York, NY: RoseDog Books.

McCroskey, J. C., & Teven, J. J. (1999). Goodwill: A reexamination of the construct and its measurement. *Communication Monographs, 66*, 90–103.

Chapter 7

Loftus, E. F., & Palmer, J. C. (1974). Reconstruction of auto-mobile destruction: An example of the interaction between language and memory. *Journal of Verbal Learning and Verbal Behavior, 13*, 585–589. https://webfiles.uci.edu/eloftus/LoftusPalmer74.pdf.

Chapter 8

Andersen, P. (2007). *Nonverbal communication: Forms and functions* (2nd ed.). New York, NY: Waveland Press.

Rapport [Def.1]. (2016). *Google definitions*. Retrieved from https://www.google.com/search?q=define%3Arapportandie=utf-8andoe=utf-8.

Chapter 9

Mueller, P. A., & Oppenheimer, D. M. (2014). The pen is mightier than the keyboard: Advantages of longhand over laptop note taking. *Psychological Science, 25*, 1159–1168.

Murphy Paul, A. (2013). You'll never learn! Students can't resist multitasking and it's impairing their memory. *Slate.com*. Retrieved from http://www.slate.com/articles/health_and_science/science/2013/05/multitasking_while_studying_divided_attention_and_technological_gadgets.html.

Sana, F., Weston, T., & Cepeda, N. J. (2013). Laptop multitasking hinders classroom learning for both users and nearby peers. *Computers and Education, 62*, 24–31.

Chapter 11

Griffin, E. (2014). Theory resources. *A first look at communication theory*. Retrieved from http://www.afirstlook.com/theory_resources/by_type/overview.

Petty, R. E., & Cacioppo, J. T. (1986). The elaboration likelihood model of persuasion. *Advances in experimental social psychology, 19*, 123–192.

Sherif, C. W. (1963). Social categorization as a function of latitude of acceptance and series range. *Journal of Abnormal and Social Psychology, 67*, 148–56.

Chapter 12

Gass, R. H., & Seiter, J. S. (2014). *Persuasion: Social influence and compliance gaining*. New York, NY: Routledge.

Sinek, S. (2009, September). Simon Sinek: How great leaders inspire action [Video file]. Retrieved from http://www.ted.com/talks/simon_sinek_how_great_leaders_inspire_action.

Appendix A: Sample Grading Rubrics

Instructor Evaluation Speech 1: Speech to Inform

Student:				Section #:
Speech Format (35)				**Comments**
Introduction (10)				
Gain attention		2		
Give audience incentive to listen		2		
Establish speaker credibility		2		
Assert Central Idea		1		
Preview Main Points		2		
Transition to Body		1		
Body (20)				
Clear, well-developed organization		5		
Sufficient support material		5		
Related main points to audience		4		
Oral Footnotes	#1	2		
	#2	2		
Transitions between main points		2		
Conclusion (5)				
Signal ending		1		
Restate Central Idea; Recap Main Points		2		
Clincher		2		
Delivery (15)				
Eye Contact: Looked at everyone in audience and held eye contact		6		
Notes: Used to jog memory; did not read from notes		4		
Vocal/Verbal: Volume, rate, fluency		3		
Appearance: Appropriate attire, posture		2		
		Subtotal		
Speech Time:		**Time Penalty**		
		TOTAL POINTS (out of 50)		

Instructor Evaluation Speech 2: Speech to Inform with Visuals

Student:				**Section #:**
Speech Format (55)				**Comments**
Introduction (10)				
Gain attention		2		
Give audience incentive to listen		2		
Establish speaker credibility		2		
Assert Central Idea		1		
Preview Main Points		2		
Transition to Body		1		
Body (40)				
Clear, well-developed organization		7		
Sufficient support material		7		
Related main points to audience		5		
Transitions between main points		6		
Oral Footnotes	#1	5		
	#2	5		
	#3	5		
Conclusion (5)				
Signal ending		1		
Restate Central Idea; Recap Main Points		2		
Clincher		2		
Delivery (25)				
Eye Contact: Looked at everyone in audience and held eye contact		10		
Notes: Used to jog memory; did not read from notes		6		
Vocal/Verbal: Volume, rate, fluency		5		
Gestures: Natural, appropriate		2		
Appearance: Appropriate attire, posture		2		
Visual Aids (15)				
Professional design		6		
Purposeful		6		
Set up; used appropriately		3		
Question and Answer Period (5)		5		
		Subtotal		
Speech Time:		**Time Penalty**		
		TOTAL POINTS (out of 100)		

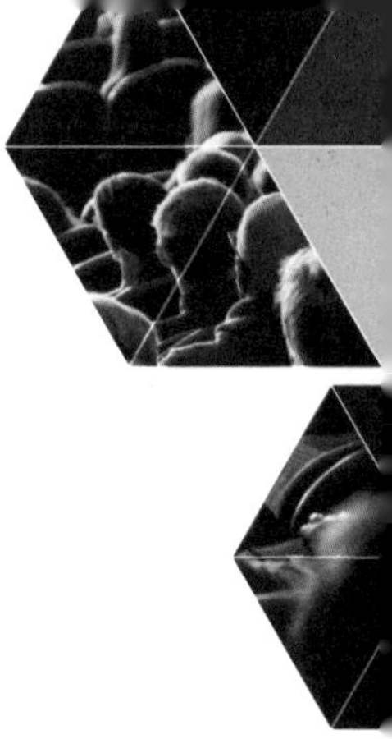

Instructor Evaluation Speech 3: Speech to Motivate Action

Student:			Section #:
Speech Format (80)			**Comments**
I. Attention (15)			
Gain attention	3		
Relate to Audience	3		
Relate to Self	3		
Assert Central Idea	3		
Preview Main Points	2		
Transition to Need Step	1		
II. Need (20)			
Clear problem established/supported	10		
Related problem to this audience	8		
Transition to Satisfaction Step	2		
III. Satisfaction (15)			
Audience-centered plan/solution offered	5		
Plan meets this audience's needs	5		
Satisfy possible objections	3		
Transition to Visualization Step	2		
Oral Citations (15)			
Oral Footnotes #1	5		
Oral Footnotes #2	5		
Oral Footnotes #3	5		
IV. Visualization (10)			
Relate benefits to audience	5		
Vivid mental image of aud. involvement	5		
V. Call to Action (5)			
Signal Ending	1		
Restate Central Idea; Recap main points	2		
Call to action/clincher	2		
Delivery (50)			
Eye Contact: Looked at everyone in audience & held eye contact	15		
Notes: Used to jog memory; did not read from notes	10		
Vocal/Verbal: Volume, rate, fluency	10		
Language: Adapted to audience/context	5		
Nonverbal: Movement/gestures, posture, appearance	10		
Visual Aids (18)			
Design	6		
Purposeful	6		
Implementation	6		
Question and Answer Period (2)	2		
Subtotal			
Speech Time: **Time Penalty**			
TOTAL POINTS (out of 150)			

Appendix B: Communication Academic Certificate

Fact Sheet

Communication skills, both verbal and nonverbal, are essential to success, sustainability, and upward progression in the workplace. Beyond the workplace, competence in communication is an integral component of relationships as well as positive local and global community citizenship. Good communication skills are unfailingly ranked as one of the most important attributes sought after by the business community.

This program offers students an opportunity to develop and refine communication skills in a variety of professional and personal contexts which are critical to success in the job market. The flexibility of the communication certificate, as well as the range of classes offered, will allow students to hone their communication abilities in areas specific to their needs and desired career path. Few assets are more valuable to career or community than a basic understanding of the dynamics of communication.

This program applies toward the requirements for an associate degree in communication.

Up to six transfer credits from an accredited institution may be applied toward this academic certificate. Students must earn a C– or better in the 12 credits to qualify for the Communication Certificate. Students must apply through the Registrar's office after they have earned a C– or better in the 12 credits.

Program Requirements

Choose twelve (12) credits from the following:

COMM-101	Introduction to Speech Communication *(3 credits)* GEM 2
COMM-103	Oral Interpretation *(3 credits)*
COMM-111	Interview Techniques *(2 credits)*
COMM-207	Dynamics of Social Media (3 credits)
COMM-209	Argumentation *(3 credits)*
COMM-212	Nonverbal Communication *(3 credits)*
COMM-220	Introduction to Intercultural Communication *(3 credits)* GEM 5
COMM-233	Interpersonal Communication *(3 credits)* GEM 6
COMM-236	Small Group Communication *(3 credits)*
COMM-252	Introduction to Public Relations *(3 credits)*
COMJ-140	Mass Media in a Free Society *(3 credits)*

Questions? Email the Communication Department at *commdept@nic.edu.*

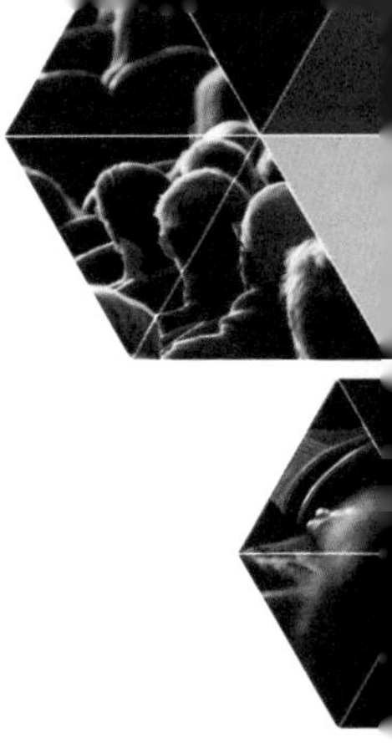

Appendix C: NIC Communication Course Offerings

Communication courses are ***much more*** than public speaking! Remember, one of the most important skills considered when hiring a person, is one's ability to communicate effectively. Good communication skills add competence to any career choice or relationship, and since all students must round out their studies at NIC with electives, why not receive some additional communication training that could pay off for you the rest of your life by adding an additional appropriate communication course to your class schedule! Here's a brief description of other courses we offer:

Interviewing Techniques (COMM-111) 2 credits
You cannot go through life without having to face interviews. In fact, your entire future career may depend on how you conduct yourself in an interview situation. Will you leave that to chance? In this class, the entire interview process is analyzed and practiced. This is an excellent course for those pursuing careers in journalism, communication, law enforcement, psychology, counseling, law—in fact, anyone who will ever need a job!

Oral Interpretation (COMM-103) 3 credits
This course makes literature come alive through effective reading and interpreting is the goal of this course. Students will learn to select, analyze, and perform literary pieces including stories, plays, poems, and famous orations.

Dynamics of Social Media (COMM-207) 3 credits
This course explores emerging and established social media communication platforms and their impact on human interaction. Topics discussed and explored include social media history, structure, and functions; virality; and persuasion and marketing via new media.

Argumentation (COMM-209) 3 credits
Arguments are all around us. Learning how to use and refute arguments will be beneficial to anyone's career and personal life. This class will equip you with critical thinking skills which will help you create and evaluate arguments. While argumentation involves debate, this class is much more, as it is an exercise in deciphering and delivering arguments in spoken, written, and visual form.

Nonverbal Communication (COMM-212) 3 credits
75% or more of all communication messages are nonverbal! So, what you don't know about what you are *not* saying could hurt you! This course introduces you to the basic concepts of body language, symbols, and various means of communicating without using the spoken language.

Introduction to Intercultural Communication (COMM-220) 3 credits
We live in a shrinking world, and our contact with other cultures is inevitable. This may be the only course you can take in college that addresses the crucial issues of communicating successfully with other cultures. *(GEM 5 course)*

Interpersonal Communication (COMM-233) 3 credits
This course deals primarily with understanding one's own communication in relationships, and how to improve relationships through better communication. It is an excellent course for developing skills necessary in everyday life and living where relationships must be developed and maintained. It is impossible not to personally benefit from this course! *(GEM 6 course)*

Small Group Communication (COMM-236) 3 credits
This is an interactive and practical course that teaches you how to become a more effective and productive member of a small group/career team. As more organizations use small groups to solve problems and conduct business, acquiring team leadership skills can be an asset on any resume. This course includes service-learning projects in our community.

Introduction to Public Relations (COMM-252) 3 credits
This course examines issues, tasks, and responsibilities of public relations practitioners in a variety of professional settings. Public relations is a strategic communication process that builds mutually beneficial relationships between organizations and their publics. This course will cover the theories and foundations of public relations and provide an overview of the principles, strategies, and practices of the profession. Legal and ethical issues facing public relations professionals will also be addressed. Multiple writing assignments address basic requirements of public relations professionals.

Mass Media in a Free Society (COMJ-140) 3 credits
This course examines the development, successes, and failures of today's American media. Students will learn to become media-literate consumers of books, magazines, newspapers, film, television, the internet, and other modern formats. Media theories, public relations, and advertising will also be discussed. (*GEM 6 course*)

Appendix D: Sample Demographic Analysis

Please—no names!

___ Full-time
___ Part-time

Type: ___ Transfer/General Studies
___ Professional-Technical
___ Dual Credit/High School

Major: ___ General Studies
___ Business
___ Education
___ Pre-Medical-Related
___ Psychology
___ Communication
___ Other: ____________________

Directions: Circle the appropriate answers.

1. **Age:**
   a. 19 and younger
   b. 20–24
   c. 25–39
   d. 40 and older

2. **Sex:**
   a. Female
   b. Male

3. **Marital status:**
   a. single
   b. committed relationship
   c. married
   d. separated
   e. divorced
   f. widowed

4. **I have:**
   a. no children
   b. one child
   c. more than one child

5. **Religious preference:**
   a. Atheist/Agnostic
   b. Christian
   c. Jewish
   d. Muslim
   e. Buddhist
   f. Other: ________________

6. **I identify myself as:**
   a. Democrat
   b. Republican
   c. Independent
   d. Supporter of a third party (Libertarian, Green, Socialist, etc.)
   e. Non-Political

7. **My personal/family income is:**
   a. $10,000 or below
   b. $10,001–15,000
   c. $15,001–30,000
   d. $30,001–60,000
   e. over $60,000

8. **I am from:**
   a. the country
   b. a small town
   c. medium-sized town
   d. a city
   e. a big city

9. **My financial support mainly comes from:** (mark as many as apply)
   a. parents, spouse, or other family member
   b. full-time job
   c. part-time or summer job
   d. savings
   e. scholarships/grants/loans

10. **I currently live:**
   a. at home with parents/family
   b. in a rental room/apartment/house
   c. in the residence hall
   d. in a home I own
   e. Other: __________________

Appendix E: Sample Audience Analysis—Informative Speech

Name: Sally Student

Topic: Developments of the personal computer

3 Main Points:

I. Origins
II. Current and emerging technology
III. Computers of the future

1. **Rate your interest in learning about the PC.** (circle number)

   1--------------2--------------3--------------4--------------5
   Uninterested   Very interested

2. **How often do you use a computer at home?** (select one)
   A. Never / Seldom
   B. Once or twice a week
   C. 3–5 times a week
   D. Daily

3. **How do you use your computer?** (check all that apply)
   ☐ Browsing
   ☐ Research
   ☐ Email
   ☐ Instant messaging
   ☐ Games
   ☐ Word processing
   ☐ Databases
   ☐ Spreadsheets
   ☐ Other: ______________________________

4. **Have you ever used a tablet computer (e.g., iPad®)?**

   ___ Yes ___ No ___ What's a tablet?

5. **Do you find that user interface (e.g., Start menus in Windows) could be improved in a way that the machine would be easier to use?** ___ Yes ___ No

6. **What feature or function would you most like to have in future computers?**

Appendix F: Sample Audience Analysis—Persuasive Speech

Problem: *Big Box Store* hurts local economies, uses cheap overseas labor and corrupt and discriminatory business practices

1. **What is your position on this problem?** (circle one)

1	2	3	4	5
Unaware	Aware/Opposed	Aware/Neutral		Aware/Agree

2. **How urgent of a problem is this issue in your life?** (circle one)

1	2	3	4	5
Not urgent at all				Very urgent

3. **How frequently do you shop at *Big Box Store*?** (select one)
   A. Never
   B. Once a week
   C. More than once a week
   D. Every day
   Explain why you shop/don't shop at *Big Box Store* with that frequency.

   ____

   ____

4. **Are you aware of the charges of corruption/discrimination that have been brought against *Big Box Store*?** ___ Yes ___ No

5. **Does *Big Box Store* have a union in America?** ___ Yes ___ No

6. **Where are most of *Big Box Store's* labor and products outsourced?** (select one)
   A. Japan
   B. Mexico
   C. China
   D. Other: ____________________

7. **What is the average yearly income of a *Big Box Store* employee?** (select one)
   A. Less than $20,000
   B. $20,000–$30,000
   C. $30,000–$40,000
   D. Less than $40,000
   E. I have no idea

8. ***Big Box Store* employees on tax-funded assistance programs cost taxpayers ________ per year.** (select one)

   A. $50 million
   B. $500 million
   C. $1.5 billion
   D. I have no idea

Appendix G: Speech Topic Ideas

How nuclear power works
Biography of someone you admire
How to make pizza
The history of comic books
How to change your car's oil
The story of how your school was founded
How to pick a bottle of wine
The history of your hometown
How to swing a golf club
Trends in the stock market
How to drive a stick-shift
History of a favorite product brand
How to shoot a basketball
Description of life in another country
How to weave a basket
The three branches of U.S. government
How to read a map
How roads are built
The Seven Wonders of the World
Disneyland
How to knit a scarf
Professional baseball stadiums
Local folklore
Roadside attractions
Chinese food
UFOs
Real-life vampires
Types of cheese
How to play chess
Key phrases in a foreign language
How to plan a wedding
How to tie various knots
Cruise vacations
Crazy laws
How to improve your health
Electric cars
Life in the future
How to throw a good party
Working in the fast food industry
How to play the kazoo
Origins of superstitions
Lesser known presidents
Computer viruses
Types of poetry
Evolution of video games
Raising pet snakes
Serial killers
Foreign TV shows
How to make a website
Civil War generals
Famous diplomats
All about your favorite vacation spot
Famous speeches
How to get good grades
How to write a resume
How to survive a job interview
Types of tropical fish
Dog shows
The newspaper business
All about a favorite radio show
How a computer works
How to organize a closet
U.S. territories
Voodoo
Comparison of different religions
Schools of painting
The latest discoveries in astronomy
Fringe political parties

How to find cheap airline tickets
Competitive horseback riding
How to make fishing lures
Labor Unions
Internet dating
Cults
Dyslexia
Impact of media on society
Branches of the military
Famous advertising campaigns
Nursing homes
How to write a will
The United Nations
How to find your ancestors
Deep sea fishing
A particular period of architecture
How to construct an argument
Saving money on your income taxes
Sports card collecting
The history of the Bible
Book reviews for a particular author
How to avoid boredom
Sales tactics
Comparison of economic systems
Censorship in history
Psychological profiling
Picking a name for your children
America's fastest growing cities
How to improve your manners
How to improve your conversation skills
World War II heroes
The Miss America Pageant
Interesting cultures
How to raise rabbits
Exotic pets
Ballroom dancing
Euthanasia
Identity theft
Evolution of voting laws
Natural disasters
Breeds of dogs
Dream interpretation
Drinking problems
Drug problems
The FBI
Basic economic principles
Advances in education
Spies
Evolution of the English language
National Parks
Young billionaires
Former child stars
Obesity epidemic
How to be more romantic
Types of common plants
How to cook vegetarian
Muscle cars
Antique collecting
Dog training
Model railroading
How to perform a magic trick
The intelligence of dolphins
Multi-Level Marketing
Choosing a digital camera
Funny inventions
Stupid criminals
Code breaking
How to play poker
Child geniuses
Spoon collecting

- Charitable organizations
- Reincarnation
- How to break bad habits
- Weight lifting
- How the circulatory system works
- Origin of holidays
- Interior decorating
- Lie detecting
- The Supreme Court
- Learning styles
- Life in jail
- How to properly brush your teeth
- How to set up an aquarium
- Organized crime
- Street gangs
- How to make soup
- The worst professional sports teams
- How the telephone works
- The U.S. Postal Service
- How to apply makeup
- Investment strategies
- The lottery
- The Industrial Revolution
- Medicines from nature
- Memory loss
- Differences in male and female communication
- Mental illnesses
- The Middle Ages
- How the brain works
- Prohibition
- Drug laws
- Airplane stunts
- The history of your favorite musical group
- Useful websites
- The Great Depression
- Famous riots
- Interesting world records
- Different philosophical perspectives
- The welfare system
- City planning
- Reality TV shows
- Types of birth control
- Choosing the right tires for your car
- Diploma mills
- The most dangerous jobs
- The trucking industry
- Basic first aid
- Coin collecting
- The British Royal Family
- Ice cream making
- How search engines work
- Banned books
- The worst trades in sports history
- How galaxies are formed
- Native American tribes
- Exotic breeds of cats
- How to make a cocktail
- How to turkey-call
- How bottled water is purified
- Sports card collecting
- The U.S. Post Office
- How cellular phones work
- Computers through the decades
- Spring Break destinations
- The rising cost of education
- Early 20th-century film making
- Unique websites
- How to back up your DVDs
- How to make candles

Hand-held PDAs

Famous robberies

Wedding traditions of other cultures

Robots now and in the future

Rock collecting

The career of a favorite musician

How to cure/prevent hangovers

Women in politics

The Great Lakes

Conspiracy theories

Iraq war

Phobias

Immigrants in the USA

Stockholm syndrome

Military benefits

GMOs

Global warming:

- Global warming is happening
- Why we should stop global warming
- What is global warming?
- Global warming vs. climate change

Strategies for healthy eating

E.S.P.

Famous golf courses

Gold rushes outside of California

U.S. immigration patterns through history

Code breaking

Submarines

TV sitcoms

Landfills

Beekeeping

All-terrain vehicles

Satellite radio

Exotic fruits

What to look for in a new car

Firefighting

Canadian football

The sport of "curling"

The insurance industry

Famous comedy duos

Word origins

How chocolate is made

Bio-diesel

New technologies

Ghosts

How the Earth was formed

Overcoming conflict

The longest books ever written

How to ski

How to make beer

Fastest growing careers

Origins of clichés

Schizophrenia

Afghanistan war

Brainwashing

Bartering

Healthcare

Cyber safety

Women in the media

Preventing elder abuse

Civil War history/lore

World Cup

Copyright violations online

Reality of a dream

Importance of vitamins and minerals

The origin of alphabets

The history of tobacco use

Human cadavers—history of, uses of

DNA evidence

Women in the military

Herbs as medicine
The history of greyhound dogs
How to achieve goals
Albert Einstein's contributions to science
Being confident
Believing in yourself
Breaking bad habits
Being optimistic in life
Being a positive talker
Helen Keller's life
How self-motivation works
Handling responsibility
Importance of discipline
Importance of meditation
Life and works of Mahatma Gandhi
Life and works of Mother Teresa
People who changed the world
Powerful communication
Weight issues
What winners do to win
Why travel is beneficial to education
Near death experiences
How to start a good personal inventory
The beauty of wolves
Social networking
Funeral oration
Graduation checklist
Roadside attractions
How to adopt a dog
Allergies
School shootings
Toxic chemicals in food
Brain mapping and paralysis
Hypnosis
The many kinds of tea
The many kinds of coffee
The process of building any given product on the market
Anxiety and its effects
Human facial recognition
Different types of dreams
Resort vacations
World music
Teen pregnancy
Indian culture or Bollywood
What to do on spring break
How to make an income while a student
The basics of financial aid
How to get along with your roommate
Some inexpensive places to take your date
How to get that great internship
Basics of getting a fellowship
What to do when a roommate moves out
How to survive freshman year
How to take the GRE
How get a student job on campus
Great vacation bargains for students
What to do in your senior year
Moving out of the dorm to an apartment off campus
Freebies and discounts for students
How to fill out a FAFSA

Appendix H: The CRAAP Test

The CRAAP Test is a list of questions that help scholars evaluate the quality of the information they gather for use in academic papers, speeches/presentations, and more. Depending on your specific topic area, some questions will be more critical than others.

Evaluation Criteria

Currency: How timely is the information?

- When was the information created?
- Has the information been revised or updated?
- If your topic requires up-to-date information, then will older sources work?

Relevance: How important is the information to your needs?

- Who is your intended audience?
- Is the information presented at an appropriate academic level (i.e., not too basic and not too advanced)?
- Have you examined several sources before deciding that this one is the best?

Authority: Who created the information?

- Who is the author/publisher/sponsor?
- What are the author's credentials or affiliations?
- Is the author qualified to be writing about the topic?
- Is there contact information for the author?

Accuracy: How reliable and verifiable is the information?

- How has the information been collected?
- Is there evidence to support assertions?
- Has the information been reviewed and verified by others?
- Is the language used relatively free of emotion and/or biased language or tone?
- Are there spelling, grammar, or typographical errors?

Purpose: Why does this information exist?

- Is the information presented in more of an informational, persuasive, or entertaining manner?
- Did the author or authors clearly state their purpose?
- Is the information fact, opinion, or propaganda?
- Does the point of view seem impartial and objective?
- Are there political, ideological, cultural, religious, or other biases present?

Subject Index